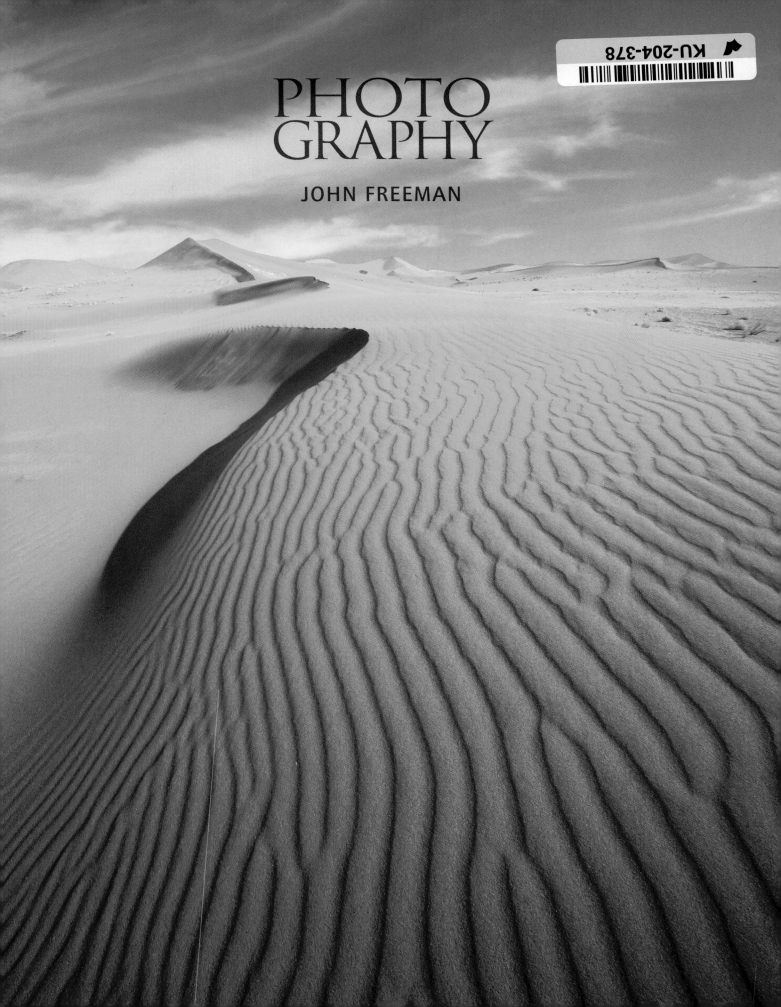

PHOTO GRAPHY

JOHN FREEMAN

PHOTO GRAPHY

THE NEW COMPLETE GUIDE TO TAKING PHOTOGRAPHS

From Basic Composition to the Latest Digital Techniques

JOHN FREEMAN

COLLINS & BROWN

For Allegra
whose life has just begun

First published in the United Kingdom in 2003
This edition first published in 2010 by
Collins & Brown
10 Southcombe Street
London
W14 0RA

An imprint of Anova Books Company Ltd

Distributed in the United States and Canada by Sterling Publishing Co.,
387 Park Avenue South, New York, NY 10016 USA

The right of John Freeman to be identified as the author of this work has
been asserted by him in accordance with the Copyright, Designs and
Patents Act, 1988.

10 9 8 7 6 5 4 3 2 1

British Library Cataloguing-in-Publication Data:
A CIP catalogue record for this book is available from the British Library.

ISBN 9-781-84340-553-5

Reproduction by Rival Colour Ltd, UK
Printed and bound by Craft Print, Singapore

This book can be ordered direct from the publisher at
www.anovabooks.com

Contents

Basic Techniques

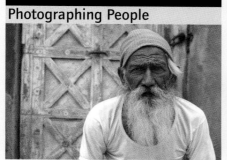

Photographing People

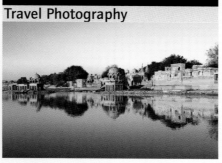

Travel Photography

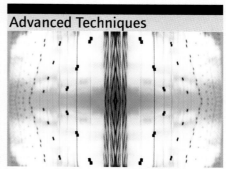

Advanced Techniques

Introduction

Photography is undoubtedly the world's greatest hands-on hobby, to the extent that nowadays people take having a camera for granted. This has never been truer than in today's digital age. After all, who hasn't taken a picture on their cell phone? Although video cameras are extremely popular, the majority of people prefer to look at a still, printed image. Perhaps this is because you can carry such a picture with you in your wallet or handbag, or share it on the internet. It can be framed and hung on a wall or placed on a desk as a constant reminder of an event or person who is meaningful in your life.

Because the image is fixed and can be the subject of close scrutiny – much more so than the fleeting glimpse of a moving image – still photographs have to be so much better in exposure, composition and subject matter. With today's technology, it has never been easier to master technicalities of these key areas, but as with all technology, the camera can be fooled and the result can turn out to be not necessarily what you had in mind.

Digital cameras are now the 'traditional' camera and because they give you the chance to review your images as you work, you can make instant corrections to exposure, composition and framing, so it should be possible to get the perfect picture every time. With

a computer the possibilities increase even further, as you can create your own digital darkroom.

This book will help you to understand the differences in what you see and how the camera sees the same scene. It will help you master the art of exposure when even the most sophisticated metering systems cannot cope. It explains in depth the essential accessories you should purchase that will enable you to take your photography beyond that of the mere snap. But above all, this book will explain fully the art of composition – the one crucial function that, no matter how many devices your camera might have built-in, it will never be able to do automatically.

Whether you are shooting on conventional film or using the latest digital technology, you will find a wealth of techniques explained in an easy-to-follow format, with quick cross-reference guides to other relevant sections. Remember that cameras are only a tool for recording the way we see a subject. In as much as they do not think like we do and need help to interpret our view of the world, this book will help you to get the very best from your equipment and allow you to produce pictures that people will want to look at again and again.

Basic Techniques

Today there are hundreds of different cameras to choose from. These range from mobile phone cameras, some boasting 8MB or more, point and shoot digital compact cameras, simple one-use models, which come complete with film, right through to digital and film SLRs and medium and large format cameras. All of these can be adapted for digital capture – with accessories, this can be a major investment. Besides the camera, accessories such as interchangeable lenses, separate flash guns and close-up attachments, together with the digital darkroom, can all help the serious photographer push back the boundaries of creativity.

One-use and phone cameras

There was a time when the most basic camera you could buy was a disposable model or one-use camera. These cameras came complete with film and after you took the last shot the whole camera was returned for the film to be processed and prints made. Many people may think that these models are a waste of money and not to be taken seriously, but their uses should not be overlooked nor the quality of the photographs that can be achieved dismissed. Many will give just as good results as one of the less expensive point-and-shoot, compact cameras.

Their greatest use is probably for those occasions when you have left your camera at home and realized your mistake too late or when your own camera has broken. Having the option to buy a cheap one-use camera means not all the snaps will be lost and it could open your eyes, albeit accidentally, to a whole new concept in photography. The reason for saying this is that there is a range of these cameras offering features that your normal camera may not have. Such facilities include built-in flash, ultra wide-angle or 'stretch' cameras', and underwater versions that can be used in the sea, swimming pool, bath or the pouring rain – situations that might have disastrous consequences for a more conventional camera. The stretched versions take pictures that, when printed, measure approximately 250 x 90mm. These panoramic views can be very effective, especially for landscape and architectural photography. The waterproof camera is ideal for seaside holidays. Not only are you spared the worry of getting the

◄ **Built-in flash**
Nearly all one-use cameras come with built-in flash. Although this is not as powerful as the type built into regular cameras, it is a useful tool and it is surprising how effective it can be. Here, these neon signs have balanced perfectly with the camera's flash.

▼ **Holiday photography**
A one-use camera makes an ideal seaside holiday camera as you do not have to worry so much about it being damaged by water or sand. The damage to an expensive model could be irreparable.

camera covered in sand (though it is always best to avoid this) or soaking wet, but corrosion is not a problem either. At bath times fun shots can be taken, especially with children, and it gives them the opportunity to take shots of themselves, without the worry of doing irreparable damage to the camera.

Today, however, the 'emergency' camera or, more likely, 'the' camera for many people will be the one built-in to their mobile phone. Once these were very basic and the resolution was extremely low, perhaps just a few kilobytes. The quality of the image, when it came to prints, was far below that of the disposable film camera. Now mobile phone cameras can boast sensors with double digit resolution, built-in flash, auto-focus, zoom lens, anti-red eye and many features that we more readily associate with sophisticated compact cameras. One of the great advantages that mobile phone cameras have over one-use models is that as soon as you have taken your shot you can forward it to another person's phone, or upload it on to the web.

Remember, rather than have no camera at all, the mobile phone or the one-use camera can give you the opportunity to get the all-important shot and save the day!

◀ Underwater photography
It is possible to buy a one-use camera that works underwater and will operate to a depth of about 5m. While the optics are never going to be as good as a proper underwater version, the results can be more than just acceptable.

Pros and cons
FOR
▶ Can carry in pocket
▶ Many different versions available
▶ Some can be used underwater
AGAINST
▶ Poor optics
▶ Fixed focal length
▶ Accessories unavailable

▶ Disposable cameras
One-use cameras come in a variety of different models, pre-loaded with colour or black and white film. The majority have built-in flash and some of them can be used underwater while others take panoramic shots.

◀ Phone cameras
Nearly everyone has a mobile phone and it would be unusual to find a model that did not have a built-in camera. Their advantage is that you can send a picture to another phone or computer almost instantly.

Compact cameras

The camera that has probably been the most popular in recent years is the compact. The range of models that is available is quite staggering, with prices varying according to the features offered. While the popularity of film versions has diminished, the growth of digital models has been phenomenal. The concept behind either of these models is that all the features, or lack of them, are built in so there is no need for you to carry round a sometimes cumbersome bag of accessories and lenses; the camera can simply be slipped into a pocket or handbag.

Film cameras use 35mm size film. This comes in 12, 24 and 36 exposure lengths and is sold in a container called a cassette. When loaded into the camera, the film will usually be advanced automatically. Once the last frame has been shot the film is rewound back into the cassette and can be sent off for processing. The cassette will have all the information about that particular film, such as its ISO (film speed), printed onto it, similar to a bar code. This is known as its DX coding and the camera, when loaded, will be able to read this information and set its auto-exposure system accordingly.

Pros and cons

FOR
▶ Vast range of models available
▶ Good variety of different films
▶ Can be carried in pocket or handbag
AGAINST
▶ Poor optics on cheaper models
▶ Limited range of accessories
▶ Low power of built-in flash

Basic compact film cameras have a fixed focal length lens. This is typically in the range of 35–45mm. This is a slightly wider angle than what is known as a standard lens, which has a focal length of 50mm, and has roughly the same angle of view as the human eye. More sophisticated models come with a zoom lens. These vary from 35–120mm but greater wide-angle and telephoto ratios are available, depending on the manufacturer.

Digital compact cameras, while virtually the same size as their film counterparts, are now the biggest selling cameras worldwide. Because the sensors in these cameras are not the size of 35mm it is difficult to make a direct comparison with regard to the focal length of lenses. For example, the 4.4–22mm lens of the Leica C-LUX 3 is equivalent to 25–125mm in 35mm. Whereas, the Canon Ixus 990IS has a lens 6.6–33mm which is equivalent to 37–185mm in 35mm.

The latest versions of digital compact cameras come packed with features. These might be face detection; image stabilization; various metering programmes; presets for indoor, fireworks, nighttime and underwater; long shutter exposure and many, many more. 12MB or more is now quite common. This means that large prints can be produced with excellent quality.

◀ **The digital compact camera**
The range of digital compact cameras is phenomenal. They are an ideal choice if you want to have a camera with you at all times as they can easily be slipped into a pocket or handbag. The quality is far superior to phone cameras.

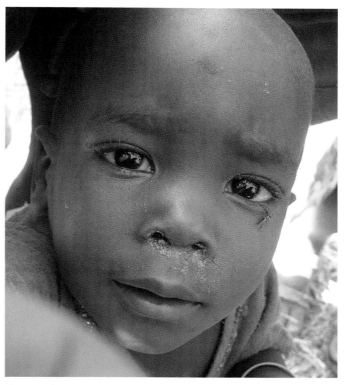

▲ **At the ready**
Digital compact cameras that are higher up the range have less shutter lag. This is the time it takes the camera to take the shot after you have pushed the shutter release. Some subjects won't keep still for long so you need a camera that will respond quickly.

▲ **Zoom lens**
Even the most basic digital compact camera will have a zoom lens. This makes getting in close to your subject easier, as we can see here, while at the same time cropping out unwanted detail that would otherwise ruin your shot.

◄ **Macro lens**
A good quality macro lens lets you get really close to your subject. Make sure that the focusing sensor is on the most important part of the picture. In this case it was the mushroom at the front and I took the shot from almost ground level.

▲ **ISO**
Many compact cameras have the option of allowing you to alter the ISO. This means that in low light, such as this late evening picture, you can increase the ISO rather than use a slow shutter speed, which could result in camera shake.

Rangefinder cameras

Rangefinder cameras, in the medium price bracket, have fallen from popularity in favour of SLRs, compact or digital cameras. However, those that are still made, notably the Leica, are precision cameras and have earned their place not just in camera history but also with many of the photographers who use them. Other models that are available are the Mamiya 7 and the Fujifilm GSW690111. These take 120 roll film and produce negatives or transparencies that are 6 × 7cm and 6 × 9cm respectively.

The camera works by coupling the focusing mount of the lens to a rangefinder mechanism in the camera body. Looking through the viewfinder you will see two images in the centre. These might be the subject that the camera is pointed at or a small circle or square symbol in the middle of the viewfinder. As you turn the focusing ring on the lens, the two images come closer together until only one is visible. It is at that point that the subject is sharp and the picture is ready to take.

This system has the advantage of accurate focusing in low light conditions or against light coloured backgrounds, which some auto-focus cameras have trouble with. Unlike with an SLR where there is always that point where the mirror flips upwards and the viewfinder goes black, you have an uninterrupted view of the subject. This

▲ **Uninterrupted viewing**
Rangefinder cameras are excellent for occasions where you need to remain as inconspicuous as possible. Due to the relatively silent shutter and the uninterrupted view, and because there is no mirror to flip out of the way, they can score over the more popular SLR models, especially in situations like this.

▶ **Sharp accuracy**
In certain situations, such as this hazy church interior, the rangefinder camera scores over auto-focus lenses, which can have difficulty focusing on certain subjects. By aligning the points of focus in the viewfinder, the shot can be focused to pin-sharp accuracy.

is useful when following a moving subject. They are also quiet in operation, which is useful if you want to remain inconspicuous. For this reason they are favoured by many photojournalists. One of the disadvantages is that, unlike an SLR, there is a difference between what the viewfinder 'sees' and what the lens 'sees'. This is called parallax error, and is most noticeable when taking photographs at 1m or less. Most of these cameras have parallax correction marks visible in the viewfinder. These indicate how much compensation is required to allow a correctly composed image to be taken at close range.

In 1924 the Leica was the first 35mm camera on the market. Invented by Oscar Barnack some ten years earlier, it made use of standard commercial cine film. It is this format that is still used today and in amateur photography it is the most popular. Later models used the coupled rangefinder system. The Leica was the forerunner of the modern 35mm SLR in that it was at the heart of a 'system'. The range of interchangeable lenses and other accessories make 'system' cameras incredibly versatile and applicable to any shooting situation.

▲ **Smooth shutter**
This is a situation where quietness of shutter operation is desirable. This baby, born only two hours earlier, was photographed with his sister on a rangefinder camera. The photograph could be taken with the knowledge that the baby would not be woken by a noisy shutter movement.

▶ **Focusing method**
Rangefinder cameras work by aligning two points in the viewfinder until they become one. This is done by either rotating the focusing section of the lens or by turning a knob on the camera body, as can be seen here.

Pros and cons
FOR
▶ Uninterrupted viewfinder
▶ Superb optics
AGAINST
▶ Few models available
▶ Close-up work can be problematic except on digital models
▶ Can be very expensive

Film and DSLR cameras

Although compact cameras are extremely popular with beginners, the camera that most people who are serious about photography aspire to is the digital single lens reflex camera, or DSLR as it is most commonly known. These cameras are now so sophisticated they can tackle almost all aspects of photography. Although film SLRs are still made, their popularity has diminished as has the range of films that go with them.

The term SLR means that there is only one lens and no obvious viewfinder at the front of the camera. This is because when you hold the camera and look through the eyepiece at the rear of the body, the view you are seeing is exactly what the lens sees. The reason for this is that you are actually looking through the lens. When the image passes through the lens it is reflected upside down, at an angle of 45 degrees, by a mirror at the back of the camera. At the top of the camera is a pentaprism, a five-sided glass prism. This receives the reflected image and turns it the right way round and the correct way up, so when you look through the eyepiece the view looks normal. When the shutter is depressed a sequence of events happens in an amazingly short space of time. First, the mirror flips out of the way of the sensor or film plane. The camera sets itself to the desired aperture and the shutter opens for the selected time. The mechanisms then rapidly reverse themselves: the aperture returns to wide open and the mirror returns so you can see your subject in the viewfinder. All you are aware of is a brief interruption,

▲ **White balance**
Digital cameras are great for taking unplanned pictures, such as this shot of the sun setting over an industrial section of river. Ensure the white balance setting on your camera does not neutralize the warm tones of the evening light.

◀ Spontaneous pictures
Being able to show children instantly the shots you have taken of them can make them more receptive to having their picture taken. This shot was taken using the daylight coming through the window behind the young girl's head.

▼ DSLR cameras
DSLR cameras are now the model that all serious photographers aspire to own. Full frame versions are becoming more common, making them easier to compare with their 35mm film counterparts. This is especially true when comparing the focal lengths of lenses.

Pros and cons

FOR
▶ View your pictures instantly
▶ Upload images directly to your computer
▶ Check exposure immediately

AGAINST
▶ Can be expensive to buy
▶ Sensor size can be problematic
▶ You need a computer for best results

▲ Through the lens
Because what you see in the viewfinder of an SLR is through the taking lens, it is possible to place your subject in the frame with complete accuracy. Other film cameras with separate viewfinders can suffer from parallax error at close distances because of the viewfinder's displacement.

▲ Accessories
With the enormous range of lenses available for SLR cameras, there is scarcely a situation that can't be photographed to the most exacting standards. The effect of other accessories, such as filters, can be seen immediately in the viewfinder.

▶ Serious photographers
The range of SLR cameras is truly phenomenal. Models range from quite modest versions through to the highly sophisticated 'system' versions. For everyday use or special occasions, such as holidays, these are the perfect choice for the more serious photographer.

◀ Film SLR
Although not as popular as they once were, 35mm SLR cameras still have a great following. The range of lenses and accessories is as extensive as ever, although the range of different films available has diminished.

the aperture will be at wide open even if it is set at a smaller aperture, f16 for example. This is to give the brightest view possible. However, there is a button on the camera called the depth of field preview. When this is pressed the aperture closes down to your chosen setting. This enables you to see exactly how much is in focus either side of the point that the lens has been focused on. When you release the button the aperture returns to wide open.

Although there is an LCD screen on the back of SLR cameras this is used primarily to review your shot and check other menu functions rather than as a live-view function. However, when set to live view it is particularly applicable to shooting still-life set-ups, as the image can be magnified on the LCD monitor for greater precision when focusing. On some models it is possible to tether the camera to your computer so that a live-view image can be seen on your computer screen.

Another advantage of SLR cameras is the vast array of different lenses and accessories. Like rangefinder cameras, these form the basis of a 'system'. Lenses range from extreme wide-angle such as fisheye, to ultra telephoto such as 800mm, with zoom, macro and shift lenses in between. Close-up facilities such as extension bellows and extension rings enable you to capture minute detail, and dedicated flashguns meter the light through the lens. The recording quality of the image is another feature with both RAW and JPEG options, or both.

Whether you choose the DSLR or film version, this type of camera, its functions and its wealth of lenses and accessories will take your photography to the highest level of professionalism.

as if you had blinked. Of course, the slower the shutter speed, the longer this interruption, and it is because of this that some photographers prefer the rangefinder camera.

Besides the advantages of seeing exactly what the lens sees, focusing is also improved because what is, or isn't, sharp will be seen in the viewfinder. This will help you to choose the best aperture not just for exposure but also for depth of field. The camera metering system will judge the exposure through the lens. This is known as TTL ('through the lens'). The metering will be multi-functional

with options for evaluative, partial, spot and centre-weighted average readings. Some cameras, such as the Canon 1DS MK 3, have multi-spot metering, where you can see the relative exposure levels in different areas of the frame before you set the exposure to obtain the desired result. The metering options will appear in the viewfinder together with the shutter, aperture, ISO, battery level and the frame counter. This gives the advantage of letting you keep your eye to the viewfinder, so allowing you more time to concentrate on the subject. When viewing and framing your subject

Medium format SLR cameras

F or the majority of professional photographers, medium format cameras are the industry standard. Their versatility, both in and out of the studio, is renowned and the variety of models available is extensive. Like DSLRs and 35mm SLRs, medium format cameras are system cameras in the ultimate sense of the term, with a range of accessories and lenses that are the envy of every serious amateur photographer.

Medium format cameras range in film size from 6 x 4.5cm to 6 x 8cm. Some models have interchangeable film backs you can load with 35mm film and instant film backs. The larger the format, the better the quality when enlarging. The 6 x 7cm format, for instance, is over four and a half times bigger than 35mm. Also, the advantage of having a camera with interchangeable film backs is that you can have different film backs loaded with different film. You can shoot just one frame, then change backs. Some camera models let you revolve the back so you can go from portrait to landscape without having to turn the entire camera on its side. An Instant film back can also be fitted to this camera – Fuji still make instant film – so you can set up your shot then take it to check such things as composition, lighting and exposure.

Using a digital back also increases the versatility of these cameras. Digital backs are now available up to full frame 6 x 4.5 and a whopping 60MB. It allows you to shoot directly into a computer via a FireWire or to shoot onto cards inserted into the digital back. The advantage of the card is that the camera is a lot freer, with no trailing wires to trip over.

Different formats

The great advantage that medium format SLR cameras have over 35mm SLRs is the ability to change the film back. This can even be done mid-roll so you can shoot black and white or colour negative, colour transparency or tungsten-balanced colour film, without losing a single frame or wasting a roll of film.

The three most popular sizes are 6 x 4.5cm, 6 x 6cm or 6 x 7cm. With the 6 x 7 camera it is possible to fit the smaller format film size backs to give even greater flexibility. Obviously, with the 6 x 4.5 versions you cannot fit larger format backs. However, they do have the advantage of being only slightly bulkier than 35mm SLR cameras but with a much bigger picture area. If you choose a 6 x 7 model and then find that you use the 6 x 4.5 back most of the time, it will become a cumbersome camera to carry around.

The other point to remember is that the different focal length lenses are not going to relate in the same way from one format to another. For instance, the standard lens on 6 x 6 is 80mm, whereas on 6 x 7 the standard focal length is 110mm. Although these cameras all take the same 120 size roll film, the number of frames per roll varies from 15 with the 6 x 4.5 format, 12 with 6 x 6, and 10 with 6 x 7. This makes the 6 x 4.5 version the more economical to use.

Besides being able to change the backs, you can also change the viewfinder. The standard viewfinder is usually the waist level finder. Others available are prism viewfinders with TTL metering. These have the facility to change between average, centre-weighted or spot metering. Different screens can be inserted in the viewfinder to aid focusing and composition.

All these cameras are supported with an extensive range of lenses. These vary from fisheye through to telephoto. Macro, Shift and tilt and variable soft focus lenses are available as are various tele-converters. Several models have bellows focusing that lets you get in close but extension rings are also available. Motor drives are available if not already fitted as standard and shutter speeds
can range from several seconds up to 1/4000 second. Speed grips give the cameras the hand-held capabilities and feel usually found on 35mm models, but most medium format cameras are better suited to tripod work.

▲ The range of cameras
There are many medium format SLR cameras available, which, together with a huge range of accessories and lenses, makes them the number one choice for the professional and serious amateur photographer. However, this standard of equipment comes at a price.

Pros and cons

FOR
▶ Large picture area
▶ Great range of lenses and accessories
▶ Interchangeable film and digital backs

AGAINST
▶ Can be large and heavy to carry
▶ Not very economical with film
▶ Can be expensive

◀ Large sensor
For many professional photographers this is now the workhorse of their kit. Very much more expensive than a 35mm DSLR, the medium format's large sensor, which could be as much as 60MB, gives an outstanding quality of image.

Large format cameras

Large format cameras, or technical cameras as they are also called, are sometimes mistaken for 'old-fashioned' cameras. Nothing could be further from the truth and these truly professional cameras are often at the heart of an advertising photographer's kit. The reason for this misconception is probably because the photographer has to focus the subject on a ground glass screen at the rear of the camera with all stray light shielded from the screen. He usually places a dark cloth over the camera and his head, which can appear somewhat outdated to the uninitiated. However, the lenses are far superior, and the range of accessories extensive. In fact, advanced digital applications were available for these models long before they were for other types of camera.

What makes these cameras so highly regarded is the range of movements that they afford. As well as being able to shift and tilt the lens, swings are also possible. This is not only applicable to the front standard the lens is mounted to, but also to the rear standard the film is inserted into. These movements give unparalleled control over focusing, perspective and composition, as well as enhanced depth of field without having to stop the aperture down. Probably the most common format is the 5 × 4, using film that measures 5 × 4in (12.5 × 10cm). The other popular format is the 10 × 8 (25 × 20cm), which uses film four times bigger than the former. Sheet film is loaded into film holders, called dark slides. This has to be done in complete

▲ Sheet film
Large format cameras use sheet film, which is loaded into a dark slide. The film has notches in one corner so that when the dark slide is loaded in the dark, the photographer knows that the emulsion side is the right way round.

▲ Camera movements
One of the greatest advantages of a large format camera is the ability to shift, tilt and swing both the front standard (the lens) and the rear standard (the film plane). This provides unrivalled scope for controlling the planes of perspective and the area of sharp focus.

Pros and cons
FOR
▶ Large film area
▶ Good range of lenses and accessories
▶ Big enlargements with fine detail

AGAINST
▶ Bulky to carry
▶ Expensive to buy
▶ Slow in operation

darkness and each dark slide holds only two sheets of film. When the dark slide is inserted into the camera, a slide is pulled out so light from the lens is exposed onto the film when the shutter is released. The slide is then re-inserted and the other side of the dark slide can be exposed in the same way. The film is processed in the same chemistry as 35mm or 120 roll film. Various backs can be attached to the rear of the camera, including roll film panoramic backs and Polaroid backs.

For architectural, food and still life photography, these cameras offer unparalleled versatility, and some of the greatest portraits and landscapes have been taken using these seemingly unwieldy cameras.

▶ Range of accessories

As well as possessing the advantages of a full range of camera movements, large format cameras can be adapted to take an extensive array of accessories such as lenses, film backs, viewing aids, electronic shutters and digital backs.

▲ Large picture area

The large ground glass screen that the image is focused on makes it easier to compose pictures such as still lifes. Each component of the picture can be moved to exactly the right position and the light can be adjusted to the correct intensity and direction with ease.

Additional lenses

A camera that enables you to change lenses increases the versatility of your picture taking enormously. Most people think that any lens, other than the standard one, is a zoom lens. Although not strictly true, zoom lenses are extremely popular and most of the more expensive compact and digital cameras come equipped with them. The term 'zoom lens' means a lens with a variable focal length, say 35mm to 80mm or 80mm to 210mm. With 35mm cameras the standard focal length lens is between 45mm and 50mm. With this lens the angle of view is roughly the same as that of the human eye. Any lens with a lower focal length number, for example, 28mm, will give a wider angle of view. These lenses are called wide-angle. Conversely, a lens with a higher focal length, 210mm, for example, will give a narrower angle of view and bring the subject nearer. These lenses are called telephoto. Remember that because most digital cameras have smaller sensors than full frame 35mm, the focal length of a lens

has to be recalculated for each camera to get a direct comparison.

All lenses are made up of groups of glasses, known as elements. This means if you take a cross section of the standard lens, for example, you would see various groups of concave and convex pieces of glass divided into a series of groups. These groups may vary from six to eight elements depending on the lens and the manufacturer.

Lenses are sometimes put into different categories when describing them. For example, 15mm to 24mm are ultra wide-angle lenses, 28mm to 35mm are wide-angle, 70mm to 120mm are medium telephoto, 135mm to 300mm telephoto and 400mm and upwards ultra telephoto. Although many of these lenses may 'zoom' through a range of focal lengths, others have a fixed focal length. With DSLR cameras the range of fixed and zoom lenses is phenomenal.

One point to watch when buying digital cameras is that they often have what is known as a digital zoom as well

as the more conventional optical zoom. Do not be fooled by this term. All a digital zoom does is enlarge the central portion of the frame, making it appear that you have zoomed into it. However, it will result in a loss of quality because the final image has in effect been enlarged and will then be enlarged again when you come to make a print.

There are also various specialist lenses available. These will only be for use with DSLR cameras but the macro facility is now becoming available on some of the more expensive compact cameras. This facility enables you to get close to your subject without the need for special attachments, such as a close-up lens. Anther specialist lens is the fisheye. This has an ultra wide angle of view, 180 degrees, but its uses are rather limited and the results can look gimmicky and boring if it is not used with care. Shift lenses, or perspective control (PC) lenses as they are sometimes called, are becoming more widely available for DSLR cameras. These are expensive but are essential if you intend to do a lot of architectural photography. How many times, when photographing a tall building, have you had to point the camera upwards to get the whole subject in? This causes the sides of the building to taper towards the top. This is known as converging verticals. By using the PC lens with its shift facility you can photograph the whole building with its sides completely straight and no converging verticals. Shift lenses are also excellent for other applications such as still lifes and for taking shots of highly reflective surfaces such as mirrors.

Choosing lenses

When purchasing any lens, always pay attention to its maximum aperture. One with a maximum aperture of, say, f1.4 or f1.8 on a standard lens will be 'faster' than one with a maximum aperture of f2.8. This means that it will perform better in low light situations with a faster shutter speed and therefore not be as vulnerable to camera shake. However, the faster the lens the more expensive it will be.

Another development to look for, especially in telephoto lenses, is whether the lens is an APO lens. This stands for

apochromatic. However, different manufacturers use different terms such as ED (extra-low dispersion) or UD (ultra-low dispersion). Because light of different colours, or wavelengths, passes through the lens, it does so at different angles and focuses on different points. If this phenomena is not corrected, chromatic aberration can occur and cause both a loss in picture sharpness and colour fringing. To prevent this happening, lens manufacturers use a special glass or coating on the lens.

Range of lenses

Whether you are shooting on a DSLR or a film SLR, the range of lenses available is quite phenomenal. From fisheye to 800mm telephoto, there is a lens for every shooting situation. Many have limited uses so buy wisely. If you are only going to use a particular lens occasionally, it might be better to hire it.

Accessories

Many camera manufacturers lead you to believe that their particular model is so complete that you will get a perfect picture every time you press the shutter release. Although it is true that many cameras come with such features as built-in flash, a zoom lens and auto-exposure, there are many, many more accessories that are available to aid and enhance the photographer's ability.

If your camera was not supplied with a lens hood, it should be the first accessory you buy. Consider how many times, in bright sunlight, we put our hand above our eyes to shield them from glare. Cameras are no different and if you don't shield them from bright light then your finished photographs could be ruined by flare, either directly or from light reflected from a bright surface such as a modern glass building.

A skylight or 1A filter will help to protect the front element of an expensive lens, as well as cut out ultra violet light. There is a whole range of other filters available for colour correction, colour balancing, graduated and special effects.

A tripod is essential for eliminating camera shake, especially at slow shutter speeds. Look for rigidity in a tripod. Some are so light they will have little chance of keeping the camera steady. Choose one with a pan tilt head. This will enable you to pan the camera in a horizontal direction and tilt the camera from side to side in a vertical movement. However, some people find these a nuisance so an alternative might be a monopod, although this has limited uses. When taking shots at slow

▼ Cable release

At slow shutter speeds a cable release is essential. It allows the shutter to be fired without jerking the camera. On some SLR cameras it is possible to get a double cable release that flips the mirror up before firing the shutter.

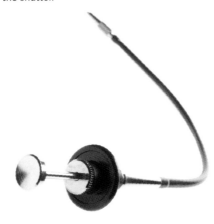

speeds a cable release will also help to keep the camera steady by smoothly operating the shutter.

Although most cameras have built-in exposure metering systems, many professional photographers still like to use hand-held meters. These range from simple but highly effective photoelectric types that don't require batteries to more sophisticated models that can also read flash light. An additional benefit of a hand-held meter is its ability to take incident light readings. This means the amount of light falling on a subject, which is far more accurate, as opposed to the amount of light reflected from it. All cameras with built-in meters take their readings by the reflected light method.

A separate flash gun is far more effective and a lot more powerful than the built-in variety. Mounting the flash gun to the side of the camera will eliminate red eye and that 'full frontal' flash look that so many pictures suffer

▼ Filters

Filters are a useful accessory for the serious photographer. Not only are they useful for creating in-camera effects, but they can also be used for colour balancing and colour correction techniques.

from. Many of these separate flash units are of the dedicated variety and the camera's built-in exposure meter will control the correct amount of flash that is required. As you become more experienced, a ring flash might be another accessory to experiment with.

If your camera has interchangeable lenses, you will be able to use extension rings or bellows. These allow you to photograph subjects in extreme close-ups. There are close-up lenses available that fit onto the front of your camera lenses in a similar way to a filter, but their quality is not as good as your camera lenses used in conjunction with extension rings or bellows.

A bag or case to carry all this kit is a good investment. This could be a solid aluminium case lined with foam that you cut to fit the various pieces of equipment or a foam-lined bag with movable compartments that can be worn like a rucksack.

◀ Tripod

This is such an essential piece of kit and every serious photographer should have one. They will keep the camera rock steady, which is a must for long exposures. If you are going to produce HDR images then they are a prerequisite. They are also perfect for elaborate set-ups where you might have to keep altering the position of your subjects, such as in a still life, while maintaining the camera viewpoint.

▼ Monopod

Sometimes it is inappropriate to carry around a cumbersome tripod. An excellent alternative is the monopod. If you ever have doubts about its usefulness, just look at the professional photographers at, for example, a soccer match.

▼ Exposure meter

Besides the meter built-in to your camera, it is useful to have a separate meter. Many of these double up as flash meters and they can also do incident light readings. This is where you measure the light falling on the subject and not that reflected from it as built-in meters do.

▶ Flash

Although your camera may have built-in flash this will not be as powerful as a separate unit. These either slip into the camera's hot shoe or they are attached by a bracket to the camera's side. Many can be synchronized together for multi-flash techniques.

Digital basics: sensors and processors

When you take a picture with a digital camera it is recorded on a sensor as opposed to film. Many people still equate the size of film, particularly 35mm, with the size of their camera's sensor. However, there are only a few full-frame (36 x 18mm, the size of the 35mm negative) cameras on the market and all of these are at the top end of the professional range.

There are several different types of sensor and these are the CCD (charged coupled device), the CMOS chip (complementary metal oxide sensor) and the Foven X3 sensor. The last sensor is quite different from the first two, which are fundamentally the same but use different technologies.

Whatever the type of sensor, they all collect light in elements called pixels. These pixels are squeezed into the sensor and the more there are the smaller they have to be. While most people think that the more pixels there are the better, there is a downside and that is that smaller pixels can increase noise. This is like the digital version of grain. Each pixel has a micro lens on the top of it that focuses the light accurately within each pixel. Sandwiched between the pixel and the micro lens are filters. These are red, green and blue, or RGB, and it is these that create the colour in your image. The light captured in all the pixels is then converted digitally and transmitted to the camera's processor, or on-board computer.

With Foven sensors the pixels are embedded in the layers of a silicon wafer at different depths. This type of sensor takes advantage of the fact that the components of white light, red, green and blue, can only penetrate the silicon to different and specific depths, so each pixel can record each colour at each pixel location, depending on its depth. This means that no additional colour processing is necessary.

As the camera's processor receives this information from the sensor it analyzes the data and decides how to get the most from the image in the sense of colour and signal processing, image compression, white balance and colour display. Different camera manufacturers often call their processors by a 'brand' name. Canon refer to theirs as DIGIC, which is in its third generation.

Because pixels capture the light that falls on them, it stands to reason that no matter how sophisticated and advanced the sensor is it will only be as good as the quality of the light. Where does the light come from? The lens. Therefore, it follows that a lens with poor optics will produce an inferior image over one with high quality optics, no matter how good the sensor.

▼ **Behind the scenes**
This diagram shows how a Foveon X3 sensor collects the varying colours of light in different depths within the sensor's silicon.

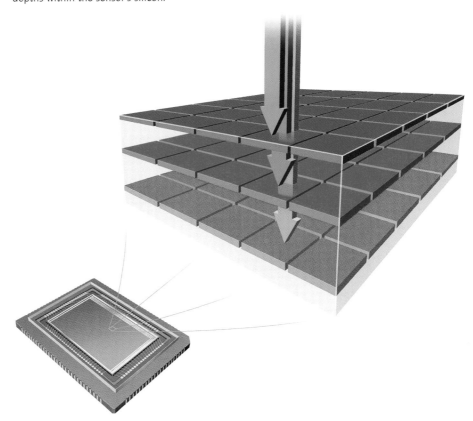

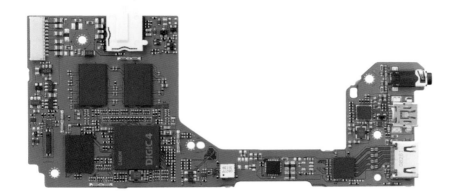

◄ Processor
This is the Canon DIGIC 11 processor.
It is the brains behind the image processing
performance of cameras such as the Canon
EOS 1DS MK3.

▼ Inside the camera
This cutaway illustration of the Canon
500D shows the complexity of modern
DSLR cameras.

▲ Sensor
A CMOS sensor used in the Canon
EOS 1DS MK3.

Equipment care

Having purchased your camera and accessories, it is essential that you take good care of them. It can come as a surprise to many people that a piece of equipment that develops a fault outside the warranty period could cost as much to repair as it did to purchase. If you are going to do any travelling, keep all your equipment in a proper camera bag. This will have padded compartments that can be adjusted to suit your particular kit, both cameras and lenses, films and filters. It will also enable you to see at a glance whether you have everything, which won't be the case if your equipment is scattered throughout your other luggage.

If you are visiting the beach, remember that camera equipment and sand or water, especially salt water, don't mix and however hard you try to prevent it, it is almost inevitable that one or the other will find its way into your camera. A good idea is to keep the camera in a plastic bag fastened with a rubber band or bulldog clip. These can easily be tucked into a pocket when you are shooting, so are not too much of a hindrance if you want to travel light.

Dust on the sensor of digital cameras will be visible in every shot you take until it is cleaned. This can be done by a professional, but is expensive, or you can purchase one of several kits. Do not attempt to use a can of compressed air (as shown in the picture), as this could leave moisture marks on the sensor and permanently damage it.

If you can screw a filter to the front of your lens, it is advisable to buy a skylight or 1A filter when you buy the camera or lens. Apart from cutting out ultra violet light, this will protect the front element of the lens from dust, dirt and grease. If the filter itself gets damaged it will be far cheaper to replace than a lens. If you have several interchangeable lenses, they should all be fitted with this type of filter. Once in place they can remain permanently attached, whatever type of film you are using, whether black and white or colour.

Each lens that you purchase should come with a lens hood. If it doesn't, buy one. It will protect the lens from rain and knocks. However, its main function is to prevent stray and

▼ Small sensor cleaner
A sensor cleaner that is the size of a pen. This type is handy to keep with you at all times.

Cleaning the sensors

1 The first thing to do when cleaning your sensor is to remove dirt and dust particles. This is most effectively done by vacuum cleaning first. The important point is not to touch the sensor but to hover just above it.
2 If the sensor is really dirty after you have vacuumed, wipe it with one of the proprietary wet wipes. These will remove the particles that could not be removed by the vacuum process.
3 After using the wet wipe you can now dry the sensor with the dry wipe. Discard used wipes after each cleaning operation.

1

2

3

unwanted light from reflecting into the lens and, like the filter, it should be attached every time you take a shot.

If the lens or filter does get dirty the first thing to do is to blow away any dust or grit that might be on it. This can be done with a photographic blower brush or a can of compressed air. Use disposable lens tissue to remove grease or finger marks and a proprietary lens cleaning fluid, if really stubborn. Do not use any old cloth, as it might act as an abrasive and cause irreparable damage to the lens surface.

If you are not going to use your equipment for some time, always remove the batteries. This is a precaution against leakage, which could cause extensive corrosion to the camera's electrical circuit. The same applies to flashguns, motordrives and exposure meters.

▶ **Cleaning equipment**
When cleaning photographic equipment care needs to be taken with certain parts of the camera. For instance, you can do irreparable damage to an SLR's mirror if you use a compressed air blower on it. It is far better to use a blower brush.

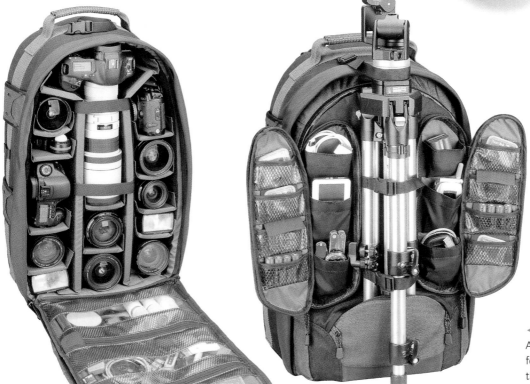

◀ **Backpack**
A good camera bag is essential for holding all your kit. Ones like this are ideal if you are shooting on location and a lot of walking is involved.

Film

With the ever increasing developments in digital technology, film and the cameras that use it, have seen a steady decline over the years. Kodak, for instance, used to have a catalogue many pages thick, which was full of a vast variety of films. These ranged from infrared; high speed surveillance films; medical and aerial films; colour, both negative and reversal; black and white, and so on. Now only a few remain and other manufacturers such as Agfa and Fuji have also decreased the number of films that they produce. Instant film, such as Polaroid, has also disappeared, although Fuji still manufacture an instant film. After all, even with Polaroid you would have to wait a minute for the image to appear, while with digital you can see the image on the camera's LCD screen truly in an instant.

With colour film there are two distinct types: colour negative and colour reversal. The former is what most amateur photographers use, although over the years this type of film has been finding favour with professionals. As its name suggests, this type of film produces a negative from which prints are made. With colour reversal film there is no negative. After the film has been processed you are left with a positive. This is known as a transparency or colour slide. Although you can have prints made from these, it is more usual to project them onto a screen or view them on a light-box. The reason this film is favoured by professionals is that, as the image is a positive, when it is sent off to be printed for use in a book or magazine, the printer

has a direct reference as to what the true colour should be. With colour negative the film, which after processing just looks as if it has an orangey-red cast, is more difficult to judge as to what the printed colour should be.

Where you buy your colour film also makes a difference. Most professional photographers purchase their film from recognized suppliers. The reason for this is that film, especially colour, needs to be stored at a controlled temperature and this usually means in a refrigerated compartment. Film that is stored in direct sunlight or in high temperatures – just think of all those places on holiday – are prone for the colour balance to shift. Quite simply, this means that film kept in these conditions could, for instance, take on a magenta (red) cast and all your finished prints will reflect this. Alternatively, the speed of the film (ISO) could change, which will affect the final exposure.

As well as these two types of film, there are also two different colour balanced films. One is intended for daylight and flash photography and the other is for use in tungsten light. The latter is the type of light you will normally find in the average home but does not include fluorescent light. If you use daylight balanced film in tungsten light, the resulting photographs will have a distinctly orange cast. Conversely, if you use tungsten balanced colour film in daylight it will have a blue cast.

Like colour film, black and white film also comes in a range of different types that vary in contrast and tone and ISO. When choosing a black and white film it

is often fine grain that is paramount to many photographers. Although this is an important consideration, it is not necessarily the reason why a shot will succeed or fail. Grain can be used very effectively to create a particular mood and with today's technological advances aimed at reducing granularity in the emulsion, it can be rather frustrating trying to achieve it.

One of the few specialist films still available is Agfa's Scala film. This is a positive black and white film that has a rich variety of tones, which, produces black and white slides when processed.

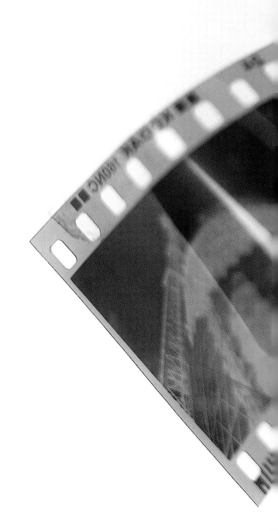

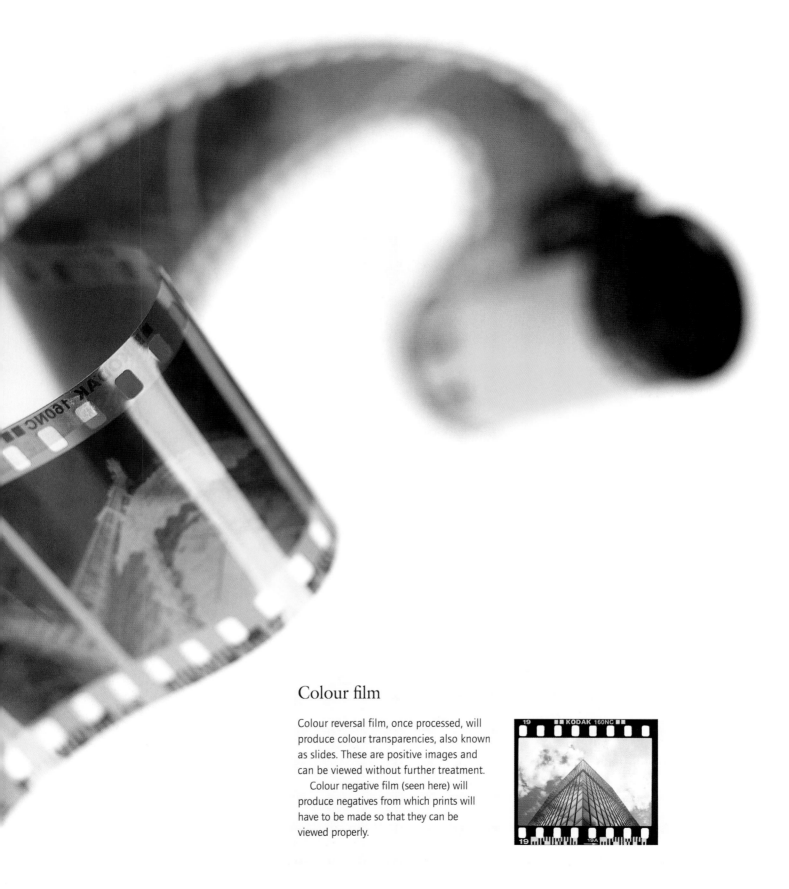

Colour film

Colour reversal film, once processed, will produce colour transparencies, also known as slides. These are positive images and can be viewed without further treatment.

Colour negative film (seen here) will produce negatives from which prints will have to be made so that they can be viewed properly.

Processing film

Once you have taken your photographs you will want to see them as soon as possible. Having your film processed properly is just as important as the care you have taken in purchasing your camera and lenses, and then composing and taking your shots.

With colour film there are two basic processes. For colour negative film the process, or chemistry, used is known as C41 and is undoubtedly the most widely available. There is hardly a high street or holiday destination that doesn't have several of these labs all offering development in one hour. The trouble is that for the discerning photographer these labs do not offer very reliable or consistent quality, whatever they claim. Often the same negative sent back on different occasions, even to the same lab, will be printed with a diverse range of colour variations. This is a situation that a professional photographer could never tolerate. For them, consistency is paramount and most will have established a rapport with a particular lab over a period of time.

For colour reversal film, or slide film, the process is known as E6 and this is still the favoured combination for the majority of professional photographers. Many process their film in a way that most amateurs have never heard of. This is called 'pushing' and 'pulling'. Often when a roll of film of the same subject has been exposed in a consistent way, the photographer will have a 'clip test' done. This means that a small part of the exposed roll will be cut off and processed. Once this has been done the photographer can then judge whether it is correctly exposed. If it isn't then an adjustment can be made in the processing for the remainder of the film or films. If the clip test is slightly under-exposed then the development can be increased. This is known as 'pushing'. If the film is over-exposed then the development can be cut. This is known as 'pulling'. In this way all the remaining film will be correctly processed. With this type of development the adjustments you can make can be quite subtle, with as little as an eighth of a stop in either direction possible.

Just as a professional lab will process film to a higher standard than one of the more common high street labs, the same will be true when it comes to getting our negatives and transparencies printed. With a professional lab you will be able to discuss with the printer exactly how you want the final print to look. Do you want it cropped or full frame? Do you want it slightly angled and if it has a colour cast do you want this corrected? Do you want certain areas of the print that are too dark to be printed up to lighten them or held back if they are too bright? Many of these methods are applicable to black and white and it is easy to see why there can be such a vast difference between the professional and the amateur approach. Of course, you might want to process your film at home. This can be done in something called a 'processing tank'. The only time that you need to be in complete darkness is when you load the film into the tank. The rest of the process can take place in normal lighting conditions. However, when it comes to printing the processed negatives you will need a darkroom or you will have to give them to a lab to print. Chemicals for both black and white and colour are available at all good photographic suppliers.

Viewing prints

After black and white film has been processed it will need printing to produce positive images. The best way to do this is to have a contact sheet made and from this select the shots you wish to have enlarged and made into prints that can be viewed either in an album or framed and displayed.

Scanning film

Although now you might only shoot digitally, the chances are you will have a store of negatives and transparencies. At one time you would have to print these in your darkroom or have them sent off for printing, whereas now you could scan them and output them on your computer's printer, view them as a slide show on your monitor, or put them on the web. In this way you could build a digital archive of analogue photography. The implications of this are quite phenomenal. To begin with, you would not have to search through endless negatives. You can also retouch all damaged transparencies and negatives so that whenever they are printed out they are perfect. They can be manipulated in an image-editing program, such as Photoshop or PaintShop Pro, to produce any of countless special effects.

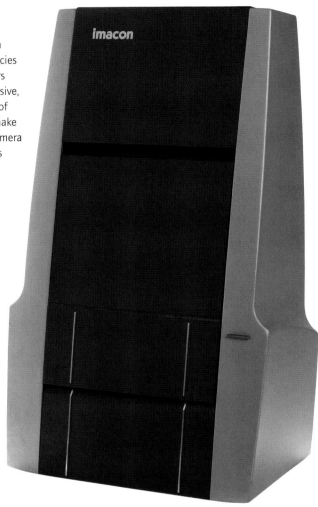

► High-end scanner
This is a top-of-the-range Imacon film scanner and can scan negatives or transparencies up to 5 x 4 (inches). Scanners such as these are very expensive, which unless you have a lot of film scanning to do would make them prohibitive for most camera users. However, the quality is unsurpassed.

▼ Flatbed scanner
Flatbed scanners are ideal for scanning prints and flat artwork. Many have adaptors that enable you to scan film and transparencies. This is the type that most camera users will purchase.

The most common type of scanner is a flatbed scanner. This will copy your old prints and with some models it is possible to fit a film adapter to scan negatives and transparencies. These will give reasonable quality but you might be restricted to 35mm only. If you have lots of negatives and transparencies to scan it will be worth getting a dedicated film scanner. These produce far superior results and work at a faster rate. They will scan 35mm individually or in strips. Some will be able to scan 120 film size, while others at the top end of the range 5 x 4. For the best resolution you should look for the dpi – dots per inch. Some can do batch scanning and even detect automatically individual frames on a strip of negatives. This certainly speeds up your workflow. Although 6,000 dpi is ample, many scanners go higher than this. The other area that you should look out for is colour depth. This is measured in 'bits'. The greater the number of bits the greater is the detail that the scanner can distinguish between colours. Optics is important too. As with digital cameras that might boast huge amounts of pixels, they will be worth little if the lens that the light comes through is of a poor quality; therefore, the optics in a scanner need to be of the highest quality to get the best results. With flatbed scanners the lens moves across the film or print in much the same way as a photocopier. With high-end film scanners the negative or transparency moves across the lens.

Digital capture

With higher-end cameras such as DSLRs you will be able to choose shooting RAW or JPEGS. The difference between these two formats is that JPEGs are processed by the camera's on-board computer and then reduced to a much smaller file size. This means that although you might get more shots on your memory card it will be at the expense of quality. This reduction in information, which could be as much as 25 per cent, will be gone forever even when you have downloaded your card onto your computer. When you shoot in RAW mode all the information is stored. You will then have to process the files with an image processing program, such as Capture One, Adobe Lightroom, Apple's Aperture, once you have downloaded them onto your computer. RAW files are like a digital negative and once processed you will then be able to make a variety of adjustments such as exposure, noise, white balance, fine control of detail, and so on. However,

the original RAW file will remain the same and so you will be able to return to it time and time again without losing any information. Of course, you will get fewer images on your memory card than you would when shooting JPEG, but the quality will mean that should you have a prize-winning shot you can be sure that it will enlarge to exhibition standards without pixelating.

With digital cameras you will also be able to control the ISO (International Standards Organisation). When you purchase film you specify what ISO you want. With digital you can change the ISO in camera. Just like film, the lower the ISO number, the less sensitive the sensor is to light, so in low light 100 ISO will require more exposure than a setting of 400 ISO. What both have in common is the higher the ISO, the greater the increase in grain, or with digital, noise. As a rule of thumb, bright daylight will require an ISO rating of 100–200 ISO, whereas with indoor low

light photography 800–1600 might be necessary.

Another feature with digital is choosing the white balance. Our brain compensates for the different colour temperatures of light entering our eyes but our camera can't unless we have it set to auto white balance (AWB). Light, which we perceive as 'white', is in fact made up of all the colours of the rainbow. These colours are measured on a scale known as degrees Kelvin (K). The lower the K value the warmer, redder the colour, whereas the higher the value the cooler, or bluer, the colour. The trouble with keeping the camera set to AWB is that if you are shooting a sunset, for example, the camera can compensate for the colour temperature, which would be at the warm end of the scale and neutralize the image, therefore making it cooler. The sunset would then come out without that 'warm glow' which is the reason we were attracted to the shot in the first place.

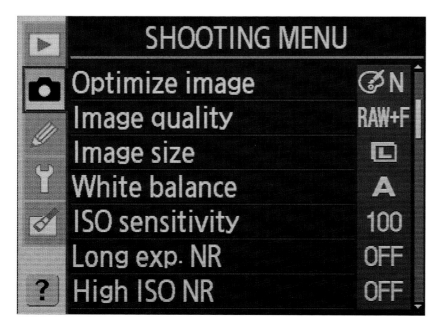

◀ **Menu options**
All digital cameras have menus, such as this one from Nikon, that are displayed on the camera's LCD. These vary from manufacturer to manufacturer. It is important to familiarize yourself with yours by reading the handbook so as to get the most from your camera, especially when setting the camera up for the first time.

▼ **External reader**

Once you have taken your shots you will have to download the pictures that are stored on the camera's memory card onto your computer. This can be done by either connecting your camera directly to your computer or by using an external card reader like this one.

▲ **Memory cards**

Memory cards come in a variety of different sizes. This one has storage for 32GB of pictures. An important point to remember is that it might be convenient to have a card with a large capacity but it also means that you can lose more pictures if something happens to the card.

Printers and calibration

While there are now many methods of displaying and sharing your photographs, prints are still many people's preferred choice. As with all digital equipment, the technology advances at an astonishing rate and the choice of printer is phenomenal. The first consideration when buying a printer is the size of print you will want to produce. At one end of the scale are compact printers, which produce prints roughly 100 x 150mm in size. You can connect them to your camera or mobile phone by USB, Bluetooth, WiFi or infrared. This means that when you are travelling you can produce prints on the move. This can be a real asset if you have photographed a complete stranger and would like to give them a print.

The next stage up are desktop printers that usually produce prints up to A4 but can also make smaller prints should you require them. Normally these printers will be inkjet. Inkjet printers use two different types of inks: dye-based or pigmented. Make sure that you use the correct type for your particular model, otherwise you might damage the printer. Pigment dyes have better archival qualities than dye based but have more of a matt finish. Epson Ultrachrome inks are a combination of the two. Cheaper printers will require four inks: yellow, cyan, magenta and black. In higher-end printers there will be other colours in between these, such as light magenta, light black and even light light black. Altogether, this type of printer will have up to ten separate inks, however these inks are expensive. An alternative to the inkjet is dye-sublimation. These use ribbons with thermal dyes positioned on the specially coated paper. The results are not as sharp as inkjet prints and look more like traditional film-based prints.

Further up the scale are large format printers. These can range from A3 or A3+ up to 64in (162.6cm) wide. The A3+ size is a professional machine and will produce exhibition quality images either on sheet or rolls. Besides colour printing, these machines also print exhibition quality black and white prints, with many using eight inks that include black, light black and light light black. Although you are likely to have made all the corrections and adjustments to your images in a program such as Photoshop prior to printing, you will also be able to fine-tune them in the printer itself.

Whatever printer you buy you will need to calibrate your monitor so that 'what you see is what you get'. At one end of the scale it can be a relatively expensive and complex procedure to accurately calibrate your computer's monitor. However, there are devices available that will get you acceptable results at a reasonable price, such as the Spyder and Eye One calibrators. Having downloaded the accompanying software, you attach the calibrator to your monitor and in a few minutes your screen will be calibrated. This should be done on a regular basis, but at least once a week. If you do not calibrate your equipment it is unlikely you will get consistently high quality prints no matter how good your printer might be.

◄ **Portable printer**
There are many portable printers available, such as this one manufactured by Canon. They are ideal when travelling, as prints can be made on the move. Most will only print from JPEG files, so if you are shooting RAW you will have to duplicate the image to be printed as a JPEG.

▶ Desktop printers

Desktop printers such as this one are capable of producing first rate exhibition quality prints of archival permanence. Considering the quality you can obtain, they are very reasonably priced.

▶ Inks

Most desktop printers use small inks. These tend to be expensive. Larger printers use inks many times the size, which makes printing much more economical. Many large format printers use up to ten different inks, making the accuracy of reproduction superb.

◀ Calibration

To get the best quality prints, no matter what type of printer you are using, it is essential that you calibrate your computer's monitor. This can be done by using a device such as this one called Spyder 3. It attaches to the screen by means of a suction pad.

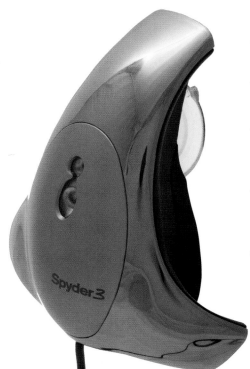

Digital storage and back-up

Once we have taken our shots, edited and downloaded them onto our computer we will need to store and protect them. As a general rule of thumb, a digital image only exists if it is stored in two places at the same time. As file sizes get bigger the more storage you will need, as in a short space of time your computer's hard drive will become full. At present the best way to store and back-up is to have a separate external hard drive. Many models are available, ranging in capacity from 500GB to several TB. However, as these external hard drives are prone to becoming corrupted due to a computer malfunction, or can be erased when someone else uses your computer, you should duplicate your files onto two external hard drives and keep them in different places. This will insure that your images are safe should there be a fire or flood at one of the places your external hard drives are stored.

Another storage device is the portable version. Many will not want the hassle of taking their laptop with them when travelling or on holiday, so this means you can back-up your images onto a less bulky piece of kit. These have less capacity than the external hard drives but should accommodate all of your shots. If you are shooting RAW, your cards will become full quite

◄ **Storage system**
As your archive increases it might be necessary to back-up onto a storage system called a RAID. This one can store over 6 terabytes and has back-up built-in.

quickly so having a device to download your files onto is a distinct advantage. Many of these come with an LCD screen so you will be able to view your images, but some will only show a JPEG image. This means that although the device will show an image it doesn't mean that the RAW data is not corrupted. You will not know this until you have downloaded the files onto your computer. Again, to be completely safe, two of these devices kept in two different places is the professional way of protecting your images.

Another storage method is to upload your images to an online server. This has the advantages of doing away with costly external hard drives. It also means that you can create galleries and folders to organize your images and then share your files online with others. The downside of this method is that no matter how safe your server says the site is, you can never be sure that at best someone isn't looking at your images, or, worse, they are using them without your permission.

► **Portable drive**
When you are travelling, such as on holiday, it might not be possible to keep all your shots on memory cards. By taking a portable back-up drive that can be kept in your pocket you can keep all your shots safe and download them onto a hard drive when you get home.

► **External hard drive**
It is essential that your photographs are stored elsewhere and not just on your computer. As file sizes become bigger this becomes more of a problem. The answer is an external hard drive, or better still two external hard drives. You can keep one to work from and one as a back-up.

Holding the camera

▶ **The correct stance**
Standing with your legs very slightly apart and bracing the body is a good stance to take when steadying yourself to take a picture. If you feel that you are still shaking, try to find something to brace yourself against or to place the camera on.

Many photographs are unsuccessful because not enough care was taken in holding the camera correctly or not supporting it firmly enough.

One of the most common errors with film compact cameras is a stray finger or camera strap across the lens. If this happens then most, if not all, of your photograph will be obscured. Unfortunately, you may be totally unaware of this situation unless you are using a compact digital or SLR camera, in which case you will see the obstruction when you look at the LCD or through the viewfinder.

The first thing to do when you are about to take a shot is to get a good grip of the camera. Do not hold it with your fingertips, as though you are scared of it, but rather so that it feels comfortable in both hands with your right index finger extended over the shutter release. Once you have got it in your hands like this, turn it so you can see the front and the

Getting to grips

Holding the camera properly is the first step in getting a good shot. Here we can see a good grip with none of the important parts such as flash or lens covered up.

Here we can see a common error where one of the fingers holding the camera steady has crept over the flash. A picture taken like this would create under-exposure.

Another common error is holding the camera with one hand. To get a properly composed and framed picture the camera should be held similarly to that shown in the first picture.

lens. Check that your finger or strap are not over the lens or flash, if one is built-in. If you don't your shots might come out incorrectly exposed, blurred or both.

Having checked these points, hold the camera correctly and look at the image on the LCD or through the viewfinder. Decide whether your shot would look better landscape (held horizontally) or portrait (held vertically). If it is to be portrait do not change your grip when turning the camera round. You will find it more comfortable to turn the camera anti-clockwise than clockwise.

▼ **Using a tripod**
Even when there looks to be lots of light, such as in this desert shot, it might still be necessary to use a tripod. This might be because you are using a slow shutter speed or because it is very windy. It could also be because you are using a long telephoto lens, which is almost impossible to keep steady at slow speeds.

When the moment comes to actually take your shot, steady your grip on the camera, not so that your knuckles turn white but so that your subject stays steady in the frame. Depress the shutter release button slowly and steadily. If you fire the shutter quickly or in a jerky manner then the chances are that your photograph will come out blurred.

Often the shutter speed that you have chosen, or that the camera's auto-exposure mechanism has selected, will be slower than it is possible to hold the camera steady without extra support. A good rule to bear in mind is that any speed slower than 1/30th second will be subject to camera shake. Of course, if your camera or lens has IS (image stabilization) then it might be possible to shoot at 1/8th second and still get a sharp shot.

The best way to support the camera at slow shutter speeds is with a tripod. Most cameras have a small threaded recess on the base of the body into which a tripod screws. If you do buy a tripod, make sure it does the job it is intended for. There is no point spending money on a support with legs so flimsy it will blow over in a breeze. An alternative to a tripod is a monopod. Obviously this will not support the camera on its own but will keep it steady, especially when using telephoto lenses. (See page 29.)

Failing either of these methods, try to find a surface you can place the camera on, such as a wall, to keep it steady. Alternatively, try to brace yourself against something such as a lamppost or doorway. With a little thought it is unlikely that you will not be able to improvise a firm support.

How the camera 'sees'

It may seem that if you notice a subject with your eyes, then the way you are 'seeing' it will be the same as when the camera shutter is released. Nothing could be further from the truth and it is this misconception that is probably the basis of more failed photographs than any other cause. Our eyes, or more correctly our brain, are continually evaluating and editing our vision and eliminating any unwanted distractions.

Let's consider for a moment what most of us seem to view more than anything else – the television. It is rare to find a home where the television is against a completely white wall devoid of any ornaments such as plants, shelves or pictures. Even if this was the case, the chances are that there would be a video or DVD recorder nearby and perhaps some sound equipment. When we watch television these items do not disappear but our brain 'pushes' them, so to speak, into the background. If we took a photograph of the television from our normal viewing position, or viewpoint, all the surrounding detail would be just as clear as the television picture when we later viewed the print. The camera would not have made these surrounding details disappear on the film in the same way that our brain would have done. This is because no matter how sophisticated cameras have become, they cannot eliminate unwanted detail if it is on more or less the same plane as the main subject.

Try this simple test. Sit in your normal viewing position while watching television and concentrate on the screen. Although your peripheral vision makes you aware of other objects, nothing distracts from the main area of focus – the television. The only way to 'see' these other objects is to re-focus on them. When you do, the television gets pushed into the background. For the photographer the only way to eliminate these distractions successfully is to move position and find another viewpoint.

Unlike the brain, the camera cannot eliminate unwanted detail by itself, as these pictures show. In the lower shot, not only is the television clear but everything else surrounding it is as well. When watching television our brain concentrates on that alone. Other objects surrounding the television become blurred and the television appears larger than it actually is (top picture).

▲ The camera's advantage

There are times when we want to see more sharp areas in our photographs than it is possible with our eyes. In the picture above left, it is easy to concentrate on the bowl of olives in much the same way that our eyes would see it. But if we change to a wide-angle lens (above), we can see much more than we could with our eyes and the image is sharp all over. Learning to understand what your camera can see is the most important step in improving your photography.

◀ How the camera can improve our vision

Often when we look at a scene, certain sights are too far away for our eyes to focus properly on them (above left). No matter how much we strain, they are not going to become any clearer or nearer. The advantage that cameras have, in this case, is that they can be adapted by using a telephoto lens, to bring distant objects closer so that we can see them in greater detail (left).

The viewfinder and auto-focus

When you look though the viewfinder of an SLR camera or the LCD of a digital model, you can be reasonably sure that what you see is what you are going to get on your film. This is because the view you are seeing is actually coming through the lens. With other types of cameras the viewfinder is slightly displaced from the lens. This means that for general purpose photography, what you see in the viewfinder will give a reasonably accurate guide to what you will get on the film. However, if you get close to your subject, the difference between what the viewfinder and the lens see varies considerably.

For this reason most of these cameras have visible marks in the viewfinder as well as the general outline of the frame. These marks are known as parallax correction marks or guides. When composing your picture, you need to shift the camera slightly to one side so the edge of the frame becomes these marks. It might appear that part of your picture is cropped out of the frame on the opposite side but it is compensating for this disparity in the displacement of the lens from the viewfinder.

Auto-focus gives the photographer the advantage of concentrating on the composition of the picture while the camera takes care of the focusing. Different cameras use different methods to focus lenses. With some models, when you look through the viewfinder, you might see up to five small areas across the centre of the screen. These are focusing points and by turning a dial on the camera you can select which one you want to be the point of sharp

▲ **Parallax compensation**
All cameras (except for SLRs, view cameras and digital cameras with LCD screens) suffer from parallax error when focusing at close distance. Because the viewfinder sees a slightly different view to the taking lens, at close distances your subject will appear to be cut out of your photograph once it has been processed (see above left). This is known as parallax error.

To rectify this problem, the viewfinder contains two or three small marks. At close distances you should use these marks as the edge of your frame. Although in the viewfinder it will appear that your subject is out of the frame on your finished print, they will be perfectly centred (see above right). This is known as parallax compensation.

focus. On other models equipped with auto-focus there is a small area highlighted in the centre of the frame. Wherever you point the camera, with whatever focal length lens, providing it is of the auto-focus type, the camera will automatically focus on this point.

It does this in one of two ways. In one, the camera sends out an infrared beam that is bounced back off the subject to the camera. Having measured the distance this beam has travelled, the camera automatically adjusts the focus. This method is known as 'active auto-focus'. The other way a camera focuses automatically is called 'passive auto-

focus'. This system can be more accurate than the former and works by reading the contrast between an edge of one part of the subject and another. When the shutter release is pressed, small motors either in the lens or camera body focus the lens.

There can be drawbacks to these systems. If you point the camera at a subject with little or no contrast (such as light coloured or misty scenes, night time, low level available indoor light, strong backlit situations, snow, water or shiny surfaces), the auto-focus will have difficulty judging the distance.

To overcome this many cameras have

► **AFL**

Many cameras now have auto-focus lenses as standard. This is a real asset, especially when you need to take shots quickly. However, many of the less sophisticated models only have the focusing sensor in the middle of the frame. This means if you compose your picture with your subject to one side of the frame, in the finished print they may be out of focus. To get round this problem we use what is known as AFL or auto-focus lock.

With the subject positioned in the middle of the frame (1) she is perfectly sharp and the background out of focus. When she is placed to one side of the frame (2), the auto-focus sensor focuses on the background leaving her out of focus. The solution is to point the camera at her, depress the shutter release button slightly and hold it down. This will lock the focus on her. Keeping the shutter release button depressed, recompose the picture to your liking (3) and then press the shutter release button fully. The subject is now sharp and the background out of focus, even though at the moment of taking the shot the auto-focus sensor was on the background.

a system called auto-focus lock or AFL (see above). Imagine your subject is standing next to a pale-coloured wall and you want them to be to the left or right of the frame. The auto-focus sensor is only seeing the wall and cannot focus. With your eye to the viewfinder, turn the camera sideways so the sensor covers the subject. Press the shutter release button halfway to activate the auto-focus mechanism without taking the shot. Keep your finger in this position on the shutter release button but move the camera back to your desired composition. Press the shutter release button fully and take the shot. Alternatively, if your camera has manual focusing, switch off the auto-focus. Many digital compact cameras have a feature called face recognition, which as the term suggests focuses the lens on the face.

Shutter speed

On many cameras, especially the cheaper ones, it is not possible to change the shutter speed. However, on more expensive models the ability to change the speed will greatly enhance the photographer's creative ability.

On most cameras with this facility the shutter will range from about 1 second up to 1/1000th of a second. There will also be another setting on the shutter speed dial – the letter B, which stands for bulb. On sophisticated DSLRs, the shutter might be as slow as 30 seconds at one end of the scale through to 1/8000th of a second at the other. Setting the shutter speed dial to one of these settings determines how much light is let through the lens onto the film. So what is the point of having a camera with changeable shutter speeds?

Imagine you are at a fixed point beside a motor racing circuit and the camera is pointed across the track. You have set the shutter speed to 1/60th of a second. A racing car comes along the track and as soon as it is in front of your camera you take a shot. The result will be that the car will come out blurred and all details in its bodywork and wheels will be lost, while the background and foreground will be sharp. Now imagine that you do exactly the same thing but adjust the shutter speed to 1/500th or 1/1000th of a second. The result now will be that the car will be sharp and all of its detail visible. The same will be true of the background and foreground. A fast shutter speed will 'freeze' motion whereas a slow shutter speed will not. The problem here is that the action

might have been frozen so effectively that it is difficult to tell whether the car is moving or not. By using a slower speed but 'panning' the camera, it is possible to keep the car sharp but blur the background. This will give a far better feeling of speed and movement.

Another reason for a fast shutter speed is when you are using it in combination with the aperture setting. Imagine the weather is fine and it is a bright day. You are photographing a person against an uninteresting background. Your exposure meter tells you that the correct exposure is 1/125th at f16. If you set the camera to this combination the exposure will be correct but the shot could be uninteresting because too much will be in focus. By choosing a faster shutter speed, say 1/1000th, you will be able to open up the lens to f5.6. This will put the background out of focus and isolate the main subject against it.

If your camera has a B setting you will be able to take long exposures. If you set the shutter speed dial to this setting and depress the shutter release button, the shutter will remain open for as long as your finger remains on the shutter release. The problem here is that keeping the shutter release depressed like this puts more strain on the battery and will reduce its life more quickly.

Many cameras with built-in metering systems use a variety of methods to read the light and set the exposure. Some models have a facility known as shutter priority. This means you can select the shutter and the camera automatically sets the correct aperture.

Freezing action

The camera's shutter determines how much light is allowed to pass through the lens onto the film or sensor by varying the time it remains open. This is quite different from the aperture, which determines the amount of light allowed to pass through the lens onto the film by varying its size, i.e. f2.8 or f16.

The shutter can also control the sharpness of moving objects and reduce the amount of camera shake visible on the finished shot. In picture (1), taken with the shutter set at 1/1000th second, the tomatoes appear static. In fact, it is difficult to judge whether they are falling at all. In (2) the shutter was adjusted to 1/500th second. Here the tomatoes are still acceptably sharp with only a hint that they are falling. In (3) the shutter was set at 1/250th second and the tomatoes have started to blur. This is even more visible in (4) where the shutter was set at 1/125th second. Here we can now see that the tomatoes appear to be going reasonably fast.

By the time we get into the lower range of shutter speeds the tomatoes begin to blur dramatically. At 1/60th (5) they almost fill the entire frame as they move across the subject plane. This is even more pronounced at 1/30th second (6) where we can see that the tomatoes have moved through the entire frame. This blurred action increases in (7) 1/15th second and (8) 1/8th second. By the time the shutter is set to 1/2 second (9) the tomatoes are so blurred they have virtually disappeared from the frame.

A slow shutter speed can be used to your advantage if photographing a scene where there are a lot of people moving around but you don't want them to appear in your picture. If you use a suitably slow shutter speed it is possible to get them so blurred that they will not appear in your shot at all.

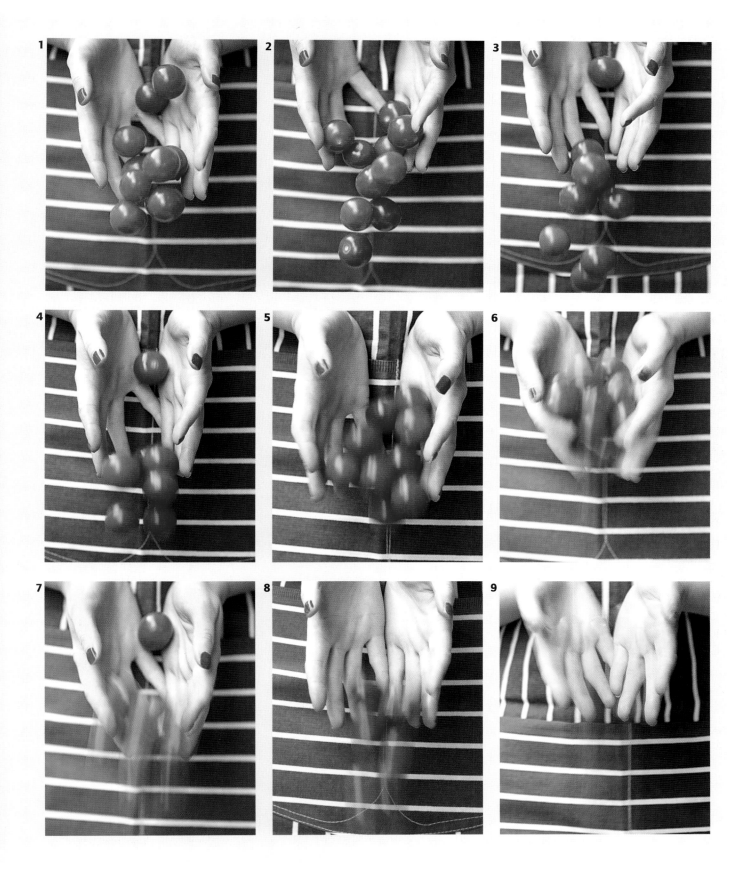

Aperture

Like the shutter speed, the aperture of the lens determines how much light reaches the film. While shutter speed can freeze a moving object, aperture controls the plane of sharp focus. As well as the main subject, there are other areas of sharp focus. Together these are known as depth of field. This is the area in front of and behind the subject that the lens has been focused on. This zone of sharp focus varies with the aperture and lens.

Imagine shooting a subject 3m away. If the camera has a standard lens set to its maximum aperture of f1.8, very little in front of or behind the subject will be in focus. If you stop the lens down to, say, f8 the area of sharp focus will increase and more foreground and a greater area of the background will be in focus. If a smaller aperture, such as f22, is chosen, a greater area in front of the subject will be in focus and maybe all the background.

If you need maximum depth of field you will need to use a slower shutter speed because with a small aperture less light passes through the lens. So, if an exposure of f8 at 1/125th is correct, the shutter speed for an aperture of f22 will be 1/15th (at this speed use a tripod to avoid camera shake). When using wide-angle lenses, depth of field is greater at all apertures than with a standard lens. Using an aperture of f8 with a 28mm wide-angle lens will result in more of

the shot being in focus than the same aperture when using the standard lens. This means you can place your subject close to the lens and still keep the background in focus. The trouble with many digital cameras is that because the sensor is so small depth of field is far greater than that with full frame cameras even when using wide aperture settings.

The reverse is true with telephoto lenses where depth of field is less, even with smaller apertures. This can be used to creative effect, especially in portraiture. For instance, placing your subject in the foreground and using a large aperture, thereby throwing the background out of focus, will help highlight your subject. An added bonus with a large aperture is the need to use a fast shutter speed. With a telephoto lens, you can keep the shot sharper, as the camera will not be as prone to shake as with slower shutter speed.

With SLR cameras you can see how much depth of field is possible by pressing the depth of field preview button. This will close the lens down to the chosen aperture so the total area of sharp focus is visible in the viewfinder.

Many cameras with built-in metering systems use a variety of methods to read the light and set the exposure. Some models have a facility known as aperture priority. This means you can select the aperture and the camera automatically sets the correct shutter speed.

Depth of field

The correlation between aperture and depth of field is shown in these pictures. Understanding this is a vital step in creating striking photos. In picture (1) a 28mm wide-angle lens was used with the aperture set at f2.8. A great deal of the picture is in focus with only a slight fall off on the very front of the bench and in the far distance. When the lens is stopped down to f8 (2), more of the picture is in focus, or sharper. When the lens is stopped right down to f22 (3), all the foreground and the background are in focus.

When the lens is changed to a 50mm standard lens and an aperture of f2.8 (4) used, it can be seen that far less of the picture is sharp than with the equivalent aperture used in (1). As the lens is progressively stopped down, first to f8 (5) and then to f22 (6), more of the picture becomes sharp but it still doesn't compare to the sharpness of the wide-angle lens.

The different degrees of sharpness is exemplified when using a long lens such as the 200mm in (7). Here, very little is sharp either side of the model. Even stopping the lens down to f8 (8) less is sharp than with the previous two lenses. At f22 (9) more is sharp but there is still no comparison with (3).

Which is the best picture?
These shots illustrate why the facility to change the focal length of your lens can be used to creative effect. In (1) it is difficult for the eye to concentrate on the model since so much of the picture is in focus. Whereas in (4) the use of a wide aperture has put the background out of focus so the eye more readily concentrates on the model. In (7) the background is completely out of focus and only the model is sharp. Apart from concentrating our attention on her, the background has taken on a mottled effect that creates a pleasing backdrop to the picture.

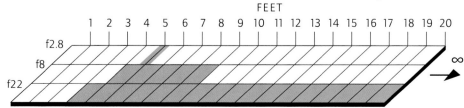

FEET

Light and colour

Because we take it for granted, many of us never really consider the light when we are about to take our photographs. Of course, we make the assumption that there is enough light for the film or sensor to record an image or we use flash or some other artificial light if there appears to be too little. However, it is rare that the light is so low that photography is impossible. What we should consider more than the quantity is the actual quality of the light available when we want to take our shots.

Although we perceive daylight as 'white light' it is, in fact, made up of all the different colours of the rainbow or spectrum, ranging from red to violet with five other distinct bands in between – orange, yellow, green, blue and indigo. Naturally, these colours do not stop rigidly next to one another and we can divide them into three main colour bands – red, green and blue. If we projected them in equal intensity onto the same spot the result would appear white.

However, throughout the day the quality of light changes. On a clear day the sun, when it rises, can be quite red or, as we would say in photographic terms, 'warm' in colour. The same is true in the evening. But at midday, when the sun is at its highest, the light is cooler, or bluer.

This variation in the appearance of light is measured on a scale known as degrees Kelvin. In photography it is called colour temperature. These degrees range from approximately 3,000 degrees Kelvin (K) – an average domestic tungsten light bulb – through to about 8,000 degrees K in the shade under hazy or overcast skies.

On digital cameras there is a white balance setting. Apart from setting it to auto (AWB) and letting the camera make up its mind what the K setting should be, we can also set it manually for greater creative control. With colour film, the packaging usually states that it is for use in daylight and flash, but in actual fact the daylight the film is balanced for is around 5,500 degrees Kelvin or the average summer sun at midday. A difference of just a few degrees either side will cause the pictures to be either redder or bluer.

If taking pictures at sunset, when the light is warmer, it can look very evocative and the reddish cast helps to create a good atmosphere. However, when taking a photograph under hazy or overcast skies, the result can look cold and extremely uninteresting.

The reason for this is that the film will record even the slightest shift in colour temperature, whereas our brain automatically will adjust our eyes to the prevailing light conditions.

A difference in colour will be reproduced on film at different times of the day, as will a difference in shadows. Someone once remarked that 'photography is memories made of shadows'. This is true, because when we look at a 'good' photograph, it is good because the shadow detail works. If we look at a photograph where the shadows are harsh and also obscure the main point of the picture, then we do not notice the picture and tend to forget it.

At the beginning and end of the day the shadows are long. At midday, when the sun is at its highest and brightest, the shadows are short. If the contrast

between the light and shadow is too harsh, some areas of the photograph will be very dark, with detail obscured and some areas so light that the detail will be burnt out. Our eyes can accommodate this variation in contrast, but the camera, or more correctly the film, will not.

Understanding how light will affect film in the way colour is cast and recorded and to see how long, or short, a shadow will be are probably the most important steps in beginning to 'see' good photographs.

▲ **The colour of light**
The colour of light changes throughout the day. In the early morning it is warmer than at midday. The same is true in the evening, as can be seen in this shot. The low position of the sun has created strong shadows and spectacular highlights in the clouds.

▶ **Looking for colour**
Our life is made up of colour. Whether we are indoors or outside, up at dawn or out at dusk, wherever we look colour is what registers first and foremost. It could be the colour of the sky or the paint on a door, the leaves of a tree or a rocky cliff face. Just as our brain interprets what our eyes see, so the camera can create a picture on film or a digital image on CCD. By being aware of the variations in colour and texture, even in our day-to-day environments, we can become discerning photographers by just looking more closely.

Exposure and auto-exposure

Apart from those at the cheapest end of the market, it is now almost impossible to buy a camera that doesn't have some sort of built-in metering system. The higher up the range you go the more sophisticated these systems become. With many of these cameras, the manufacturers would have you believe it is impossible to take an incorrectly exposed picture. However, technology can be fooled and the way you saw a shot may look totally different in a photograph, as the auto-exposure mechanism reads the scene differently.

With digital photography you will have the benefit of seeing your shot on the camera's LCD and being able to study the histogram. If it is incorrectly exposed you can dump it and make the necessary adjustments to get the correct exposure. Even if your shot is under- or over-exposed it can be corrected in the computer, but it would be much better to get it right from the outset.

If your camera has built-in exposure control it will probably work by taking an average reading over the entire frame. However, if your subject is standing against a very bright background the auto-exposure will make its calculations predominately for that background. This means your subject will be under-exposed and appear very dark in your shot. Alternatively, if the background is very dark and your subject quite light, the reverse will be true and the camera will give more exposure to the background and your subject will be over-exposed. On cheaper cameras there will probably be no alternative and no override, so thought will have to be given to each shot.

If your camera has centreweighted metering, either as a norm or as an alternative to average metering, then this method will prove to be far more accurate. With centreweighted metering the exposure reading is biased towards the central part of the scene. If your subject is in the centre of your frame, whether or not they are against a bright or dark background, the meter will read more accurately for them and not the area behind them.

If your camera has auto-exposure lock (AEL), it will enable you to move in close to your subject so it is the only area that the meter reads. Alternatively, point the camera at your subject, press the AEL button (this may be an independent control or operate when the shutter release button is pushed halfway) and then, while keeping your finger on the shutter release, recompose your picture before taking your shot by pushing the shutter release button fully.

With SLR cameras the method of metering is 'through the lens' (TTL). It might give you the choice of average or centreweighted metering and 'spot' metering. This is where only the centre of the frame, perhaps just 3 per cent, is read. As the meter is reading the light coming through the lens it will automatically compensate for different lenses or filters.

Metering systems of the most modern cameras are even more sophisticated, with such features as 21-zone evaluative metering and 3D-colour matrix metering, which takes into account the subject's colour. Your camera might have a program mode, which is where you can set the mode for different situations, such as landscapes, portraits or action photography. The camera will then set the exposure reading method for those given situations. Another aspect to bear in mind when calculating your exposures is the film's latitude.

◀ Under-exposure

The exposure data of a digital image is displayed as a histogram on the camera's LCD. In this example the levels are bunched to the left and 'blocking in', showing under-exposure.

◀ Over-exposure

The levels in this image are bunched towards the upper end of the histogram or to the right in the LCD. This indicates that the brighter parts of the image are burning out and over-exposing.

◀ Normal exposure

The levels are spread evenly through the histogram, showing an even spread of tones. The levels bunched in the middle show a good exposure for an average image.

Getting the correct exposure

Sometimes it is best to bracket your exposures to be sure of getting one that is absolutely spot on. This is especially true with colour reversal film, which has a lot less latitude than colour negative film, or when shooting digitally.

This range of exposures, from over- to under-exposure, shows that although pictures 3 and 5 are acceptable, it is only in picture 4 that the exposure is completely correct. Pictures 1, 2, 6 and 7 are unacceptable.

◀ Camera meters

Built-in camera meters can be easily fooled. The pond water on the left was very dark and the camera's meter took most of its reading from this area, resulting in the rest of the picture being over-exposed. By going in close and using the camera's AEL setting, a true reading of the horse and sky has been taken.

This is its ability to replicate an acceptable image when it has been over- or under-exposed. With colour reversal film this is less than with colour negative.

Of course, there is an alternative to all these methods or it can be used in conjunction with them – a hand-held meter. With this you will be able to read the light actually falling on the subject as opposed to that being reflected from it. This is known as the incident light method and is extremely accurate.

Effective flash

Virtually all cameras now have some sort of flash built in. This is usually positioned on the camera body, next to or near the viewfinder, or as a pop-up unit on the top of the camera. The exceptions to this are the professional cameras at the more expensive end of the market. It is the absence of flash in these models that gives us an idea of the worth of the built-in unit.

There are few of us who have been to a football match or a concert, for example, who haven't witnessed the sporadic flash of cameras being fired from within the audience. There must be a sense of disappointment when they review their picture on the LCD screen or their film is processed, as at best the only image to be recorded will be of the person standing directly in front of the camera (who will probably be burnt out) with small dots of stage lighting or floodlights in the background. The reason is that these built-in flash units are only capable of illuminating a subject that is probably no more than 3m away from the camera. Even if they were capable of illuminating the stage, the quality of light would be bland and cold. The ambience of the stage lighting would have been lost and the atmosphere of the event, which is what inspired us to take a shot in the first place, reduced to a mere record of the space it took place in.

▶ **Diffusing flash**
We can see that the first shot (top right) has been taken in available light and is under-exposed, requiring a degree of flash. Because the subject is close to the camera in the second shot (right) the flash has burnt out the face. By diffusing the flash (bottom picture) the photograph is now correctly exposed and the shadow on the wall acceptably soft.

Flash synchronization

Most SLR cameras have a recommended shutter speed for flash photography. This is usually 1/60th or 1/125th second. Some might be able to synchronize at 1/250th second. The problem if you use a faster shutter speed is that the camera will not be able to synchronize the shutter to the flash and less of the picture will be exposed as the speed is increased.

In picture 1 the camera was set on the manufacturer's recommended setting of 1/60th second. The picture is perfectly exposed. In picture 2, shot at 1/125th second, the model's sweater is just beginning to go dark at the bottom of the frame. This is more apparent at 1/250th second (picture 3) where one third of the picture has been unexposed. In picture 4 only half the picture is exposed when the shutter is set at 1/500th, and in picture 5 at 1/1000th nearly all the shot has been under-exposed.

Another common problem with the built-in type of flash is 'red eye'. In low light conditions the eyes' pupils dilate or become larger. This causes the flash, at the moment the shot is taken, to enter the subject's eyes and reflect off the red blood vessels at the back of the eye.

Although many cameras have what the manufacturers call 'anti-red eye' or 'red eye reduction mode', they do not work particularly effectively. Furthermore, they are meant to work by firing a series of small flashes before the shot is actually taken. The purpose of this is to reduce the amount of the eyes' dilation. However, because there is a delay between you composing or seeing the shot and the camera actually taking it, the moment can pass and the fleeting facial expression that looked so animated just a few seconds ago has been lost. It is not really possible to reduce red eye if the flash unit is near to the subject and is on more or less the same plane as the taking lens of the camera. It is only by having a separate flashgun, held to one side of the camera, that you will be able to eliminate these drawbacks.

An additional benefit of having a separate flashgun is that it will be far more powerful than the built-in variety. Many of these flashguns are of the dedicated variety. This means that your camera will still be able to read the amount of flash required through its TTL metering system. More than likely you will be able to tilt and swivel the flash head, enabling you to 'bounce' the flash off another surface, such as a white ceiling or wall. This will give a softer, more diffused light than direct flash (see the box below), resulting in a more flattering photograph. Although this method can sometimes cause shadows to appear under the eyes, many flashguns have a small fill-in flash window just under the main flash head to help to eliminate these.

Bounced flash

When the flash unit is built into the camera, it often creates an unsightly shadow to one side of the subject, such as can be seen below top. If it is possible to bounce the flash, a much more flattering light can be achieved as can be seen below bottom.

Outdoor flash
In picture 1, shot on a cold winter's day, the young girl's face is slightly under-exposed. Using the camera's auto flash setting (picture 2) has given a little more light on her face but has turned the background black, making it look like nighttime. By using a slower shutter speed (picture 3) to give more exposure to the background, the shot has now been evenly lit.

Selecting a viewpoint

For many people, taking photographs can be a hurried affair and you can tell from the results that very little thought has gone into choosing the best possible viewpoint. Instead of moving around the subject to explore the possibilities of a different angle, or getting down for a lower viewpoint, or standing or climbing to a higher viewpoint, they just stand where they were first aware that a shot might be worth taking, or take it out of a car window, and simply hope for the best. The excuse seems to be that because they can't move the subject, there is nothing they can do about the final composition of the photograph.

If the subject, such as a building or tree, for instance, is in a fixed position then your only option is to explore all available angles. Take your time and be patient. When you look though the camera's viewfinder try to remember the following points.

Does the subject fill the frame? If not, is the impact of the subject diminished by unwanted detail? Perhaps it would be better for you to get closer or find a position that will enable you to use other detail to lead the eye to the main area of interest so that it does not become lost in the background. Does the subject necessarily have to be in the middle of the frame? Without even having to move your feet, the picture may be enhanced by placing the main subject slightly to one side of the composition. You can do this by simply turning the camera one way or the other, or perhaps by getting down on one knee and shooting from a lower viewpoint.

▲ **Repositioning**
Shifting your shooting position by only a small amount can make all the difference to your photographs. When shooting these sunflowers I originally thought that the shot on the left was the best viewpoint. However, I noticed that there was some unwanted detail behind the main flower. By positioning myself just slightly lower I eliminated this and now the sunflower dominates the picture.

In the unlikely event that you feel you have exhausted all potential viewpoints, remember that the time of day, when the sun is in a different position, may dramatically affect an otherwise mundane view. At the beginning and end of the day, when the sun is low, it may highlight your subject while other areas are in shadow. By planning ahead you can make sure that you are in position at the best viewpoint to take advantage of this lighting.

If you are photographing a person, your task is that much easier because they can also shift position. It is surprising, therefore, to see so many photographs where a tree, telegraph pole or some other intrusion appears to grow out of someone's head. Or that the chosen viewpoint is so far away that the main subject is lost on the horizon or surrounded by unwanted detail. By choosing a viewpoint closer to the subject, it may actually be possible to use the subject to block out unwanted detail.

The focus of interest

One of the biggest pitfalls in photography is to try to include too much in the shot. It is a trap that many photographers fall into, resulting in unwanted detail where the essence of the scene viewed with the naked eye is lost. Examine these two examples shot in Provence, southern France. It was spring, the leaves of the tree were fresh and the blue wildflowers sparkled in the long grass. The shepherd's hut, made of local stone, was in good condition. I wanted to capture this sense of spring and tranquillity and put the focus of interest in the foreground.

Taking the image
At first I included both hut and tree but, after further consideration, I decided that having them both in the foreground meant it was unclear where the focus of interest lay. Without moving position I panned the camera to the right so that the hut was cut out of frame.I re-took the shot with the tree in splendid isolation. With hindsight I am pleased that I took this extra trouble as the shot without the hut is far more indicative of the sense of place than the one in which

I tried to get as much in as possible. Taking a few moments to think about what the camera sees rather than what the naked eye sees is one of the best rules in achieving better photographs.

▶ **Angle of view**
When photographing people, the angle can totally alter how they appear in the frame. The shot on the far right was taken from a high viewpoint, which makes the girl look diminutive. By taking a lower viewpoint (right), she now appears to have far more presence as she looks down confidently into the lens.

Filling the frame

How many times have we had the experience, when being shown a friend's photographs, of not quite seeing the point of them, until you suddenly realize that there, somewhere in the distance, is a diminutive figure struggling to be seen in an otherwise tedious shot that is completely devoid of any other interest. Filling the frame is one of the first steps in achieving arresting photographs.

The most obvious way of filling the frame is to move in close. It is interesting, therefore, that most people when taking their shots seem to keep moving backwards. With some cameras there is a disparity between what the viewfinder sees and what actually comes out, but that is no excuse for moving an inordinate distance away from the subject. If it is not possible to get closer to the subject, try changing the lens or

zooming in so the frame is filled. If that doesn't work, consider changing position to include some compositional detail to one side of the frame or the other. Can the subject, if shooting a portrait, use a tree, for example, to lean against? This will add a more natural feel to the shot as well as filling an area of the frame.

Another way of filling the frame is to decide whether your shot would look better framed as a landscape or as a portrait. It is amazing that so many people seem to think that photographs can only be taken when the camera is held in the horizontal or landscape position. When you think about it, most people's faces fit neatly into the frame of a camera when it is being held in the portrait or upright position. But this is not limited purely to people shots – even with landscapes or

▲ Landscapes
Even when photographing landscapes you can fill the frame. Here a long lens was used to photograph this line of trees (top picture). It has compressed the picture and has totally filled the frame. Although a different approach was taken for the picture above, the frame is still filled with interesting detail. The gate fills the foreground and leads the eye into the middle ground of fields and trees. The hills and the radiant blue sky and clouds make an interesting backdrop to complete the frame.

◄ ▲ Cropping
Sometimes a shot can be improved at printing stage by cropping and filling the frame with just part of the original image. There is nothing wrong with the shot of the girl above, but by cropping in tight and filling the frame, a far more intimate portrait has resulted.

photographs of buildings it is well worth experimenting with the different ways to frame your shot.

Of course, if you are shooting with a digital camera, it will be relatively easy to crop your shots once they have been downloaded into your computer, and you can also have conventional film cropped when you have your prints made, but both of these methods are time-consuming and, in the case of the latter, expensive.

The other thing to bear in mind is that the more you enlarge either digital or conventional film, the more clarity you will lose and the size of the pixels (or the film's grain) will become more perceptible. With digital photography this will be a problem as pixels do not look very attractive. With film, however, grain, when used in the right context, can add greatly to a photograph's overall impact.

▶ Blurring the background

When going in close try to open up the lens so that the depth of field becomes minimal. This will help to concentrate the eye on your main subject, in this case the girl and her dog.

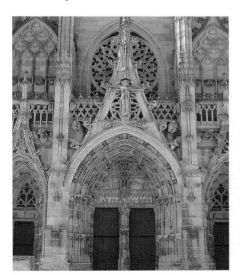

▲ Architecture
Often it is the detail of an historic building that makes for an interesting picture, such as this doorway to a church in northern France. If the viewpoint had been further back then the detail of the architecture would have been lost and it is possible that although more of the church might have been in it would not have filled the frame in the same way.

▲ ▶ Change of viewpoint
It is always worth considering your viewpoint and the focal length of the lens you are going to use when filling the frame. The picture on the right is a pleasing still life. However, if you change your viewpoint and lens, then the overall shot (above) has far more impact.

Perspective

Whether they are prints or transparencies, photographs are two-dimensional. To prevent your finished picture from looking flat and uninteresting, a three-dimensional sense or perspective needs to be added.

Perspective helps to create a feeling of depth in a picture. Without this depth, the results can look very dull. Perspective can be created by using naturally formed lines to create 'linear' perspective.

Wide-angle lenses, with their greater depth of field, help you get in close to the subject while keeping the background sharp. They also give the illusion of greater space between objects as they recede from the camera. The opposite is true with telephoto lenses, where the sense of depth gets compressed and the distance between near and far subjects diminishes. This

space between foreground, middle ground and background is essential if a picture is to have life. One of the problems with using a wide-angle lens is standing so far away from the subject that the foreground recedes into the background. Don't be afraid to go in close to your subject. This will make it appear bold and startling against a more distant background.

If we stood in the middle of a road and looked along it the edges would appear to meet at a distant point, as though they were converging. This is linear perspective and is apparent even when viewed with the naked eye.

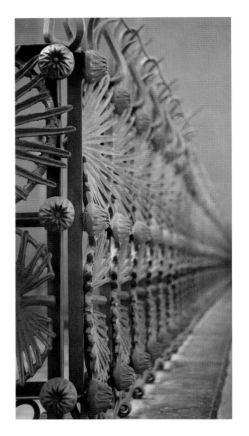

► **Wide aperture**
This shot was taken with a wide aperture of f2.8. It has reduced the depth of field greatly. However, it has also created a strong sense of perspective as the railings recede into the distance.

Landscape or portrait?

You can alter the sense of perspective by the way that you choose to frame your photograph. Look at these two shots of the Grand Canyon. In the landscape version the emphasis is on the sky. While it has an interesting cloud formation, it does nothing to draw the eye in to the picture and the canyon itself is completely lost.

However, by slightly changing the viewpoint and choosing a portrait format the emphasis has been changed. The clouds are still interesting, but by increasing the amount of foreground interest the picture now has a far greater sense of perspective. The walls of the canyon in the foreground drop away and the eye looks through the narrow gully. It is then drawn through this gully to the

walls of the canyon in the far distance. The space created by framing the scene in this way adds depth and atmosphere.

This is a good example of how important it is to view every conceivable angle to get the best shot. Often it might not be until you examine all your shots together that you will be able to edit out the best one.

Though we know the road is straight, because it appears to taper, that exaggerates the perspective and gives the feeling that the road goes on for ever. Again, by focusing on something close, such as the centre lines of the road, perspective can be enhanced by seeing these lines go from one large strip to one continuous band. The lower your viewpoint the greater this effect. However, we could use trees, for example, at the side of the road for similar effect.

When photographing buildings it is sometimes necessary to point the camera upwards to be able to get the whole subject in. However, this will result in the building appearing to taper toward the top. This effect is known as converging verticals. Although it may give a false perspective to the building, it can dramatically add to the photograph.

▶ Framing devices
The arch in this picture acts not only as a framing device but also helps to draw the eye into the picture. We see three essential elements of a good composition: the arch in the foreground, the cypress trees and gardens that form the middle ground, and finally the mountains in the background. Together they create a true sense of perspective.

▶ Viewpoint
By taking a low viewpoint in this shot of a straight road, the receding white and yellow markings help to create an illusion of distance that gives the shot great depth. You can create this sense of perspective by carefully assessing your viewpoint.

Foreground composition

The composition of a photograph can be enhanced by giving thought to the foreground. A point of interest close to the camera can lead the eye into the picture or can be used as a framing device. Many amateur photographers make composition mistakes by not observing what is right in front of them. For example, it is all too easy when a spectacular scene comes into view when driving or walking to just point and shoot. It is only when we see our final prints that we are disappointed with the results. This could be because that view across a lake with the picturesque village on the opposite side is now a great swathe of dull water with blurred buildings in the distance. Or a view from a hilltop that seems to stretch for miles comes out as with a mass of sky and no memorable features. Take time to look for a feature in the foreground or choose a different viewpoint other than just standing at normal height.

By considering the foreground we can use it to our advantage to hide untidy objects or ugly intrusions in the background of the picture. Such

▶ **Viewpoint**
A low viewpoint was chosen when photographing this dandelion. By placing it in the foreground it takes on great presence while the tree in the background, which we know is far larger, diminishes in importance but makes an effective backdrop.

◀ **Wide-angle lens**
By combining a wide-angle lens with a low viewpoint, the foreground detail in this dry desert picture has been emphasized. However, it also leads our eye into the photograph, greatly adding to the dramatic perspective of the composition.

▲ **Capstan curves**
By placing this capstan in the foreground of this picture a strong sense of foreground composition has been created. Note how the curves of the capstan echo the shape of the building in the background and by going in close greatly exaggerate its size.

a framing device might be a tree or arch in the foreground that will help hide unwanted detail and lead the eye into the picture, creating a sense of depth. However, care must be taken with exposure when objects are included in the foreground. Check that such objects are not in shadow compared to the middle and background area of the shot. If this is the case and it comes out under-exposed the result will be highly unattractive. Another way to use foreground interest is with perspective. Take, for example, a ploughed field or a road. By choosing a low viewpoint we can emphasize the furrows or tarmac, which will meet at a point of convergence. This foreground interest will lead the eye to the horizon or to the next element of detail.

We can use equipment to our advantage as well when looking for foreground interest. By choosing a wide-angle lens we can keep objects or people, close to the camera, in focus. This is because such lenses have a greater depth of field than standard or telephoto lenses.

▼ Posing
I wanted to keep a sense of place when framing this picture of a young Masai girl, so I posed her to one side of the frame but kept the main group still visible in the background.

Selecting a background

Whether you are taking a photograph of a person, object or landscape, the background will play a considerable part in its success. When looking at your finished shot, your eye will be confused as to the purpose of the picture if the background is so busy your main subject becomes indistinguishable from it. The background should act as a backdrop to set off your subject in the same way as a stage set in a theatre. Imagine that the backdrop was so busy that the actors were camouflaged by it. It would make for a tedious production and you would quickly lose interest.

Many people think that they have no control over the background, if the subject is a landscape for instance. Of

course you cannot move mountains or uproot trees. However, you can move and often a few inches either way will help to eliminate unwanted background detail. Alternatively, you can change the focal length of your lens. A telephoto lens will enable you to crop out unwanted areas of background and give the impression of compressing the background, by seeming to bring it closer. A wide-angle lens, with its greater depth of field, and a low viewpoint can keep both foreground and background sharp. It will also help to lead the eye into the picture and therefore the background.

Weather can also create interesting backgrounds. Think about how a storm

▲ **Filling the frame**
Filling the entire frame with the fishing nets that this fisherman was repairing in a port in Goa, India, has helped to create an interesting background. Careful positioning was required so that unwanted detail was eliminated.

can suddenly blow up with dark thunder clouds filling the sky in the background. This is especially true if the foreground is still lit by bright sun highlighting buildings and foreground trees.

Another way we can use natural phenomena in a landscape photograph is by looking out for distant hills that make a valley on the horizon as if it is two curtains being drawn back.

Of course, potential backgrounds are everywhere and it could be one that we see every day without giving it a second

▲ Choice of lens
A medium telephoto lens was used for this picture of an old woman's hands. By using a wide aperture the depth of field has been reduced, making the background out of focus. This has helped to draw the eye to the hands.

► Texture
The texture of this wall and doorway has created an interesting background for this street scene of an old bike. Although the shot does not make a great statement, it does typify many a traditional French village scene.

▼ Studio backgrounds
Many backgrounds in professional photographic studios are just plain rolls of coloured paper. By choosing the right colour they can produce effective background results that highlight the subject in the foreground.

thought. This could be a weathered stretch of fence or wall. It might even be a doorway or the side of building.

In photographic studios you will often see wide rolls of paper that are known as 'colorama'. These come in long rolls and a multitude of colours. When suspended from the wall or ceiling and then run out along the floor the person or object placed on them looks as though they are floating in space. In some studios where these are a permanent fixture they are known as infinity coves.

With digital photography it is possible to shoot a range of backgrounds, then drop your subjects into them by using a program such as Photoshop. Many professional photographers now use this method since it cuts down on the expense of having to take models away to a far-off location.

► Spontaneous backgrounds
Sometimes when we are taking photographs backgrounds create themselves, such as this shot of a participant in a carnival. The combination of backlighting and shallow depth of field have created just the right backdrop to show off her colourful costume.

Against the light

Some of the best and most effective pictures can be taken when shooting into or against the light. This method is sometimes known as 'contre-jour' and many famous photographers have used it to great effect.

The most important point to remember when shooting against the light is to get the exposure right. This might seem an obvious thing to say, but if you are relying on your camera's metering system it can under-expose your shots and if, for instance, your subject is a person, they may appear as a silhouette on the final print.

Many cameras have a back light setting which will compensate for this situation by giving more exposure than would ordinarily be the case. Alternatively, it might have a program mode for different situations including back lighting. Another method, when shooting into the sun, is to use fill-in flash. This requires a certain amount of experimentation to perfect, but once mastered will produce excellent results.

If your camera does not have these settings or you do not have a flashgun with you, it might be possible to reflect light back into your subject's face by using a reflector. This does not necessarily have to be a custom-made one. It could be improvised quite easily by using a white towel or any other light coloured material.

Probably the most effective landscapes, when shooting into the light, are those where there is a certain amount of water involved, such as the sea or a lake. This is because the water produces strong highlights and shadow detail. As opposed to when photographing

people, these situations are best exposed for the highlights. This method will add drama and atmosphere.

When shooting into the light, study the subject carefully and try to look at it from different viewpoints. It is amazing how just a few metres one way or another can completely change the atmosphere by reducing or increasing

▼ **Early morning light**
These two young women were photographed in the early morning when the light was still quite low. It is possible to see that the shadows on the ground are coming almost directly to the camera. This type of lighting creates a wonderful halo effect in their hair.

Basic Techniques • **73**

the amount of back light. Remember, too, that in the early morning or the evening, the sun is much lower in the sky than at midday. This means that it could be shining straight into the lens and causing flare, which will ruin your pictures. To avoid this, you will need to shield the light by using a lens hood. (This should be used at all times anyway!) However, with the sun this bright, a lens hood might not be adequate and you will need to hold something larger above the lens, such as your or a friend's hand.

▶ **Gentle shadows**
This calf had the light directly behind her. It has created a gentle light on her ears as though the sunlight is actually shining through them and also gives a soft halo appearance that can be seen on the crown of her head.

Viewpoint

Viewpoint can determine how much back light appears in your shot. In the shot above the sheets of fresh rubber are entirely back lit. On the right, the viewpoint has changed by about 90 degrees, resulting in a less intense light that is not as effective in showing the translucency of the rubber.

▲ **Ebb tide**
In this shot against the light the exposure was measured for the highlights. This has resulted in a dramatic foreshore pattern that enhances the wet sand and the gentle receding tide. A fast shutter speed has helped to 'freeze' the water.

Wide-angle and telephoto lenses

Nothing will increase the creative control that you will have with your camera more than the ability to change the lens. With SLR cameras these could range from fisheye through to ultra-telephoto. With 35mm film cameras or full-frame DSLRs, what we would refer to as the 'standard' lens would have a focal length of 50mm. This has an angle of view roughly the same as that of the human eye. However, if you are changing from a film camera to a digital one the chances are that your lenses won't provide the same angle of view unless you have a full-frame digital model. This is because the sensors in digital cameras are much smaller and so a 50mm lens will be the equivalent of a small telephoto. Camera manufacturers use different sizes of sensors, so with Fuji, Nikon, Pentax and Sony you will need to magnify the focal length by 1.5 to get the 35mm equivalent. Therefore, 50mm will become 75mm, 100mm will become 150mm and so on. For Canon it's a magnification of 1.6 and for Sigma it's 1.7. Because of this variation we will keep to the 35mm standard.

When purchasing lenses it is worth considering buying the 'fastest' lens you can afford. This term refers to the 'maximum' aperture. A lens with a maximum aperture of f1.4 is faster than one with an aperture of f2.8. This means that the former will perform better in low light situations than the latter.

A shorter focal length, such as 28mm, will have a greater angle of view, enabling you to get more into the picture, whereas a longer focal length, such as 200mm, will have a narrower angle of view,

▲ **Market stall**
Using a small aperture, f16, has meant nearly all the foreground of this stall is in focus. The camera, which was fitted with a 24mm lens, has been pointed downwards to emphasize the fish, while the stallholder still appears quite prominent in the picture.

reducing the amount you get in the picture. These three lenses – 28, 50 and 200mm – would be a good starting point from which to build your system. An alternative might be to purchase a single zoom lens that went from 28 to 200mm. However, this type of lens will probably be quite slow, with a maximum aperture of f3.5–f5.6 depending on the focal length you adjust it to, and the optical quality quite poor. Depending on your budget, a 16–35mm, 28–70mm and a

70–200mm, all with a maximum aperture of f2.8 across the range, will give you a lens for virtually every shooting situation.

Wide-angle lenses have a greater depth of field than standard or telephoto lenses. This means that you will be able

The difference between wide-angle and telephoto lenses

These two pictures illustrate the difference between a wide-angle and telephoto lens not just by how much is in the picture but by the way you can control the area of sharp focus. The picture on the left was shot with a 21mm wide-angle lens. The pumpkin in the front was only a few centimetres from the lens and the others stretch out into the background and remain quite sharp. The distance between the pumpkins looks as though they are some distance apart.

In the shot on the right a 200mm telephoto lens was used. Not only has this compressed the picture, making it look as though all the pumpkins are close to one another, but they have also been put out of focus so that it is only the front one that is sharp.

to photograph objects that are extremely close to the lens while retaining the sharpness of objects in the background. In landscape photography this can be put to good effect by having some natural phenomena, such as a plant or rock formation in the foreground, which might fill as much as half the frame, while the rest of the picture stretches to the horizon and is still in focus. When taking this type of shot it might be necessary to take a low viewpoint by either kneeling or lying on the ground.

The most important point to remember when shooting with wide-

▶ Rural scene
The greater depth of field provided by a wide-angle lens has helped keep this wooden fence in the foreground sharp. It has also meant that a greater area of vivid blue sky has been included, enhancing the overall tranquillity of the rural scene.

angle lenses is not to let their ability to obtain a wide view diminish the main subject importance. This is an easy mistake to make and often, when looking at the final print, we find that we can hardly distinguish the most important details because so much has been included in the shot. Always make sure that your foreground interest remains strong.

In as much as wide-angle lenses will include a lot of information, telephoto lenses can be used to cut out, or at least cut down, on the amount of what gets included in the frame. As well as bringing distant objects closer, telephoto lenses are excellent for portraiture as well as isolating detail.

Telephoto lenses give less depth of field than wide-angle lenses, even at small apertures. This can be used to great effect by putting the background out of focus. This is especially effective when shooting portraits, as any unwanted detail will simply become a blur of indistinguishable colour. This will keep the focus firmly on the subject's face and produce a far more flattering shot.

Telephoto lenses

Beside making backgrounds more attractive by softening the focus, telephoto lenses can be used to bring things nearer. In these two pictures the top one was shot using a 200mm telephoto lens. By contrast, the bottom picture was shot on a 400mm telephoto lens and much more of the background has been cropped out. Lenses such as these, or longer, will need some form of support such as a tripod or monopod to avoid camera shake, which can be a real problem at these lengths.

Although it might appear useful to have such a long lens the cost will probably prove prohibitive.

▲ **Shift lens**
A wide-angle 24mm shift lens was used in this picture of the Golden Gate Bridge. By using the shift facility the twin towers have been kept upright. With a standard wide-angle the camera would have had to be pointed upwards, creating converging verticals.

▲ **Weathered rock face**
Wide-angle lenses can be great for showing the scale of natural phenomena such as this rock face. Make sure the foreground does not become bland and uninteresting. Always look for something that will help to lead the eye into the picture.

Another asset with a telephoto lens is their ability to compress the picture. An example of this is if you are photographing a road with a line of telegraph poles or the columns of a building stretching away from the camera. In this case it might be an advantage if all the detail was in focus and this would necessitate using a small aperture to give as much depth of field as possible. This might mean using a tripod since the smaller the aperture the slower the speed and with telephoto lenses it is difficult, at the best of times, to keep the camera steady, especially when using lenses with a focal length of 300mm or more. However, as there are no hard and fast rules when it comes to creative photography, it might be equally advantageous to use the limited depth of field that telephoto lenses offer at wide aperture and make just one of the columns or telegraph poles sharp while the others drop out of focus. Always check your depth of field because detail in the viewfinder might not be apparent until the photograph has been taken.

◄ **150mm lens**
Using a wide aperture, F2.8, has ensured that the background in this portrait has been kept out of focus. This means that it does not distract from the girl who is the focus of interest. The backlight adds to the feeling of a tropical environment.

▲ **Spring**
One of the great things about telephoto lenses is that they enable the photographer to fill the frame. This shot of an apple orchard was taken on a 200mm telephoto lens. A low angle was chosen and the lens has compressed the space between the trees so the blossom dominates.

Fault finding

Black edges to corners of picture
Lens hood too small for lens or other lens attachment such as filters
Use correct lens hood and do not double up filters with wide-angle lenses

Rough panorama
Edges of shots showing
When stitching shots together to form a panorama shot, remove the edge lines in Photoshop with the clone tool

Moiré
Repetitive patterns can often be too much detail for the camera to read
Use a camera with a higher resolution, or crop in so the pattern isn't so close together

Film only partially exposed
Camera back opened before film is rewound
Check that camera is empty or film rewound before opening camera back

Picture orange all over
Wrong white balance
Change white balance setting for tungsten light, to avoid an orange cast

Corrupt image
Fault occurred and image has been read incorrectly
Take the shot on more than one flash card

Picture hazy
Flare caused by sun
Move your subject and make sure a lens hood is fitted

Feint image on film
Film over-exposed
Lens jammed open or faulty meter reading

Picture shaky
Camera shake
Use a tripod or other support when shooting at slow speeds

Low quality setting
Low quality setting has been used here, so cropping in creates a very poor image
Always shoot with RAW files; these will ensure the best quality prints

Digital error
Fault occurred and image cannot be read
This is an irreparable fault, so back up important images on film as well as digitally by taking more than one frame

Exposure compensation
A general exposure setting has exposed the background instead of the foreground.
Set your camera to meter only the centre of the image, or move to a location without backlight

Picture generally dull
Flash underpowered for area to be photographed
Check manufacturer's guide before using flash

Smudged area of picture
Dirt or grease on lens
Keep lenses clean and store carefully to protect from dirt

Picture burnt out
Flash too close to subject
Check manufacturer's guide before using flash for close-ups

Dark area of picture
Finger over flash
Check grip before taking your shot

Picture blurred
Auto focus not working or lens incorrectly focused
Check auto-focus setting or align rangefinder correctly

Colour cast
Using a golden reflector has given the face a yellow colour cast
Use a white reflector to neutralize this effect

Dirty sensor
Dust can fall onto the camera's sensor when changing lenses
Have your sensor professionally cleaned, be careful when changing lens

Noise
There isn't enough information, so noise can appear
Use a lower ISO or take two separate images, one exposed for highlights and one for shadows and composite together

Photographing People

Probably the subject that we photograph more than anything else is one another. From the beginning of life to old age, the human face and form have fascinated generations, both as photographers and viewers. In contrast to our grandparents' generation, we can now photograph our children at birth knowing it is possible that their entire lives will be recorded on film or, more likely, as an electronic image to be viewed by successive generations. Whatever means we use for photography, many of the same rules of composition and exposure apply if we are to achieve the very best from our equipment.

Head and shoulder portraits

When most people think of a head and shoulder portrait, it is the school, graduation or passport photograph that comes to mind. On this basis it is not surprising that so many portraits resemble 'mug shots', with the rigidly uncomfortable sitter looking as though they would rather be anywhere other than in front of the camera. This is a great pity since it is a person's face that attracts us probably more than any other feature. Faces, young or old, smooth or wrinkled, have the ability to show surprise and sadness, humour and happiness, anger and joy, despair and calm. To capture these aspects on camera is one of the most rewarding aspects of photography.

Although there are no rules as to the best equipment for taking these portraits, a medium telephoto lens

◀ **Dull weather**
Even on a cold, overcast day it is possible to take effective head and shoulder portraits. The idea behind this shot was to make the elements work to the photographer's advantage by making the model look snug in her hat and fur-trimmed coat. A wide aperture has pushed the dull background out of focus, making a more pleasing backdrop.

▶ **Using a reflector**
The beret this French market stallholder was wearing cast a deep shadow across his face. By using a small white reflector, placed just under his chin, the shadow has been softened as light is bounced back into his face.

Posing

A small change in position can alter the look and mood of a shot. By leaning her face on her hands (above), the young girl looks relaxed and informal. For the shot on the right, she sat with her body at 90 degrees to the camera and then turned her head to the camera, giving her an air of confidence.

▶ **Reflector**
When shooting head and shoulder portraits outdoors it can be advantageous to keep the sun behind your subject, so that you get a highlight on the hair, and then use a reflector to bounce light back onto the face. A gold reflector was used in this shot.

▼ **Features**
This girl had amazing hair and I wanted it to feature as much as possible. A small amount of backlighting has created highlights in her hair, while a top light gives a sheen to her tresses.

▲ **Telephoto lens**
If you use a telephoto lens or set your zoom to the longest focal length and use a wide aperture setting, the depth of field will be reduced. This will make your subject stand out since they will be sharp but the background will be blurred.

would be a good choice. Not only will you be able to get in close to your subject without crowding them, but there will be no danger of you casting your own shadow over them. This is especially relevant when taking outdoor portraits in bright and sunny conditions, or photographing children who might be inhibited if you were too close to them.

If you use a much more powerful telephoto lens and a wide aperture, the background will go out of focus, creating a far more muted backdrop. This avoids unwanted detail encroaching into the shot, detracting from the main area of focus – the person. This type of lens also has the ability to fill the frame and home in on a particular feature, such as the eyes. If a wide aperture is chosen, such as f2.8, and the lens is focused on an eye, leaving the focus on the rest of the face to drop off slightly, the impact can be quite arresting. If you are shooting head

and shoulder portraits outdoors in bright sunlight, be aware that your subject may squint and so look out for unwanted shadows, especially around the eyes. If your model is wearing a hat, be careful that an ugly shadow is not cast over the face. If the hat is a problem, other than removing it altogether, either try tilting it backwards or use a reflector to bounce light back into the shadow areas. This reflector could be something as simple as a book or newspaper – it doesn't necessarily have to be a custom-made photographic reflector. Another alternative is to use fill-in flash. This will have a similar effect as the reflector, providing you have the combination between flash and daylight correctly balanced.

Always look for a different angle. Even the slightest adjustment of viewpoint can alter the impact of your portrait. For instance, if you take a high viewpoint and look down on your subject, they will invariably seem vulnerable. A low viewpoint, where they appear to be looking down on you, will give them an air of confidence and assurance. It is nuances like this that the discerning photographer is aware of. As well as having your subject look straight at the camera, get them to pose in a more relaxed fashion, such as leaning on their hands or a wall. If shooting more than one person, posing is crucial and care needs to taken with the area of sharp focus, especially when using telephoto lenses and wide apertures.

▲ **Portraits of strangers**
As well as taking portraits of your own family and friends, great opportunities for taking effective head and shoulder shots can be found with complete strangers while travelling in different countries such as this portrait taken in Thailand. Most people are flattered if you ask whether you can take a shot of them so don't be nervous or shy.

See also

▶ **pp 54–55** Aperture
▶ **pp 62–63** Selecting a viewpoint
▶ **pp 92–93** Lighting for outdoor portraits
▶ **pp 98–99** Backgrounds
▶ **pp 134–135** Telephoto lenses in portraiture
▶ **pp 150–151** Using props

Full-length portraits

Many of the considerations given to taking a head and shoulder shot are applicable to photographing people full length. The most important thing is to create a relaxed and comfortable atmosphere while being clear in what you want to achieve.

The reason you are shooting a person in a full-length pose is probably due to their outfit, as well as their character. If this is the case, place them in appropriate surroundings so the background adds another dimension to your picture. If shooting indoors, perhaps the room is also going to be an important part of the picture. Full-length shots do not mean your subject has to be standing upright. The term implies you are including the whole body but your subject could be sitting, kneeling or lying down.

When posing a person full length, try to get them to do something with their hands so they are not just hanging by their sides. This is not to say a shot in this position might not work but it could look awkward with many people. If they are in a room, ask them to lean against the doorframe, either with their hand on it or their back against it, with their face turned to the camera. If they are in a working situation, can the tools of their trade be put to good effect? Often it is the most simple yet effective props that are overlooked.

Most people want to look tall in their full-length portraits. The way to ensure this is to take a low camera viewpoint and the angle will exaggerate the length of their legs. This is especially true when using a wide-angle lens. Conversely, a high viewpoint will have the effect of

◄ The unexpected shot
The opportunity to take a full-length portrait often happens by chance, as shown by this shot taken in a Tunisian souk. By taking a low camera angle, the dominance of this shepherd within his surroundings has been increased. Always be on the lookout for the unexpected.

◄ Posing
Many people can find it awkward when posing for the camera. To make for a more relaxed position I got this young Himba girl to lean gently against a tree and I placed two other women slightly behind her. I deliberately kept the focus on the young girl but the other two, while out of focus, give a sense of place.

▲ **Be prepared**
When travelling I always keep the camera at the ready as you never know what might happen. I photographed these two women, who were working on a building site, in Jaipur, India. Their saris were so colourful that they made the perfect subjects for a full-length portrait.

▲ **Lighting**
When the sun is bright it can create a problem with harsh shadows and make people screw up their eyes. This was the case here so I moved this young couple to an area of overall shade. This has created an even light and is much more gentle on their faces.

▶ **Candid portraits**
Always be on the lookout for candid pictures. This full-length portrait is attractive because it has captured the girl in a world of her own as she peers into the clear waters looking for sea life.

foreshortening the body. However, depending where your camera viewpoint is in relation to your subject's face, an interesting and unusual picture could result.

If the person is seated, there will not be the same problem with foreshortening of the legs unless you go in extremely close with a wide-angle lens. If you are including the room and shooting from a high viewpoint, make sure that you place the subject in the foreground, otherwise they will become of secondary importance and their surroundings could completely submerge them.

If using flash, try to avoid ugly shadows falling behind your subject, especially if they are close to a wall. If using available light, make sure the picture won't suffer from camera shake when using a slow shutter speed. If this is the case and you do not have a tripod, support the camera against something solid. If you do have a tripod and are shooting indoors, set up the camera and arrange the room to its best advantage in advance by continually referring to the camera's LCD or viewfinder. This means that when you are ready to take your portrait, your subject won't have been kept waiting unnecessarily and you will be able to sit or stand them exactly where you want them. It will then just be a matter of tweaking the picture before you are ready to take the final shot. This can create a much more relaxed atmosphere and is a more professional way of working.

When composing a full-length portrait remember the rule known as the 'golden section' or the 'golden triangle'. This has been used by artists since Ancient Greek times. It states that

▼ Wide-angle lens
Wide-angle lenses can be problematic when taking full-length portraits, as facial features can become distorted and the result not very flattering. However, in this shot of a rock climber it works to good effect and you get a real sense of her being high above the ground below.

your subject should be placed at the intersection of imaginary lines drawn vertically and horizontally one third of the way along each side of your picture. Of course rules can be broken, but if you are just beginning photography, following this rule of composition will give you well-balanced pictures.

See also

▶ **pp 26–27** Additional lenses

▶ **pp 62–63** Selecting a viewpoint

▶ **pp 92–93** Lighting for outdoor portraits

▶ **pp 112–113** Candid portraits

▶ **pp132–133** Wide-angle lenses in portraiture

▶ **pp 136–137** Using reflectors

◀ **Simple poses**
This shot was taken in a room with just one light coming from the side. A large white reflector was placed to the right of the girl to soften the shadows. Often it is the most simple lighting set-ups and poses that make the most effective photographs.

▼ **Wide-angle**
In order to get all this painter's studio in the shot I used a wide-angle lens and stood on a stepladder, looking down on him. I wanted him to look relaxed so I posed him with his feet up and had him look up to the camera. This has created an informal shot of him and his working environment.

Group portraits

As with photographing individuals, the same basic rules apply to shooting groups, i.e. posing, lighting, background and expression. However, it always seems inevitable with groups of people that someone will blink when you take the shot, not be looking where you want them to, pulling a face or making some unnecessary gesture.

If you are photographing a formal group of people, such as at a wedding, the first thing you need to do is stamp your authority on the group but balance it with a degree of joviality. The last thing you want is to upset the guests before you have taken a single shot but if you can't get them to respond to your directions then it could make for a chaotic shoot! It would be useful to have an assistant so they can keep an eye on the first people to be positioned, making sure that they do not wander off while you position the remaining guests. The best way to organize such a group is to position the bride and groom, then their respective parents followed by close relations and, finally, other guests. Distribute these guests evenly so that there is a degree of symmetry to the overall composition. Make sure that you have the taller members of the group towards the back so that shorter people are not obscured.

With a large group, it will be an asset to work with a tripod. This will mean that once you have chosen your viewpoint, you can position the members of the group accordingly and continually check by looking at the LCD or through the viewfinder. Another advantage when using a tripod is that once the group is finally settled you can

▲ **School's out**
This group of Thai schoolchildren were sitting on a bench under some palm trees. I used this to my advantage since it was a very bright day and, without this element of shade, dark shadows from their hats and under their eyes would have been unavoidable.

▶ **Colourful dress**
I photographed this group of women walking towards the camera in India. Their colourful dresses work well in the very light surroundings and each one of their faces is visible. As they were moving towards me I chose the tracking focus mode on my camera to keep them constantly sharp.

make sure they have your attention by looking straight at them, rather than looking through the viewfinder. A cable release would be a good idea here, as not only will it make for a smoother shutter release but also you will be able to fire the camera without having to look at the LCD or through the viewfinder. Take several frames of the same group, as there is always going to be someone not looking the right way.

In some cases a high viewpoint may be better, as this will give you the advantage of being able to position people so that all their faces are clearly visible. Unless you have taken some steps with you, look around and improvise. It could be your car or a wall that will give you the height advantage. If using flash, check that it will be powerful enough to expose the people at the back of the group correctly and not at the expense of over-exposing those at the front. This is something that you should have complete confidence in before you contemplate taking a shot such as this.

▶ Be spontaneous

Always be on the lookout for the spontaneous shot. These two young girls had just got out of the bath when I took this shot. Remember that a group can consist of two people just as much as one hundred.

▶ Bargain sale

This unusual looking group were having a yard sale at their home in Florida. I wanted to include as many objects as possible, so I went in close with a wide-angle lens, but made sure that the people did not recede too far into the background.

Lighting for outdoor portraits

Because daylight is the most natural source of light, many of us do not consider its ever-changing qualities.

The colour temperature of daylight in the early morning or late afternoon causes photographs to be warmer or to have an orange cast, whereas the same shot at midday will be cooler or bluer in appearance. Bright sun in the middle of the day will also create harsh shadows under the eyes and may cause your subject to squint. By contrast, dull weather, particularly with an overcast sky, can cause outdoor pictures to be flat and lifeless with little shadow detail. Your camera will record this light with a blue feel and skin tones will look quite cool.

If the sun is very bright, move your subject into overall shade so the light is more even and more comfortable for your subject, or turn your model round so they have their back to the sun. This will give a pleasant backlight to the hair. Remember to compensate in exposure as your camera exposure meter will read the light coming from behind and not the light falling on their face. If you don't, your subject will be under-exposed and come out as a silhouette. Many cameras have a built-in backlight compensation setting that will calculate the exposure automatically for this technique. An alternative is to use a reflector to bounce light back into the face, or to use fill-in flash. Adding an 81A filter to your lens on an overcast day when the light is cool will help to warm up the skin tones.

See also

▶ **pp 40–41** Digital capture
▶ **pp 54–55** Aperture
▶ **pp 58–59** Exposure and auto-exposure
▶ **pp 72–73** Against the light
▶ **pp 82–85** Head and shoulder portraits
▶ **pp 136–137** Using reflectors

▼ **Background light**
For this portrait I moved the subject into an area of relative shade so that he would not be screwing up his eyes on what was a very sunny day. I took advantage of the sun reflecting off a coloured wall, making an interestingly lit background.

▲ **Using a reflector**
This couple were shot against the light, which has created a nice halo on their hair. A reflector was used to bounce light back onto their faces and to balance the exposure, ensuring an evenly lit shot.

▲ **Candid portrait**
This young boy was photographed while completely engrossed in washing a car. The backlighting from the sun shows up the water droplets on his hair and the shadows on his face are just soft enough to make the shot acceptable.

◄ Slow shutter speed
This shot was taken in the evening when the daylight was dying quickly. I used a 28–70mm lens set on 70mm, which allowed me to get in just close enough to fill the frame.

▼ Using shade
This is another example of using shade to advantage. Notice the way the daylight is giving a very even light to this model's face. If she had stepped just a little further back then the light would have been very harsh and not at all flattering.

▲ Correct exposure
This boy was photographed against a very dark background. Because he is fair I knew the meter in the camera could get confused and take most of its reading from the background. This would have resulted in over-exposure.

Available light

The term available light refers to the light the photographer can use without having to supplement it with an additional light source. For instance, this could be light coming in through a window or doorway or simply from a candle. The benefits of using this type of light are that your shots can be wonderfully atmospheric and the setting of a particular mood much easier to achieve than with flash. If you are using a fast film or your ISO is set to 400 or higher, the grain or noise is going to be more prominent than with a slow film or a lower ISO setting.

With this type of light the important point to remember is that the light levels will probably be quite low. For this reason a faster than normal film or ISO setting might be necessary and a tripod would be useful. Some type of reflector would also be a good idea. If you are shooting in a room where the window faces north, no sun will ever directly shine through it. This means that you will be able to use a diffuse light that will give beautiful soft shadows. This is the light favoured by many painters and their studios were always built with these north-facing windows (of course, this is only applicable to the northern hemisphere – the reverse is the case in the southern hemisphere, where to achieve the same quality of light it is the south-facing window to be on the lookout for). If the light is too cool in these conditions and you are shooting in colour, it might be beneficial to use a warm-up filter such as an 81A or to make adjustments once you have downloaded your shots.

If you are in a room where the light is more directional, i.e. it is shining quite brightly through the window, you could diffuse it by placing tracing paper over the glass or by hanging a thin fabric such as muslin in front of it.

If you have a proper photographic reflector made of a diffusing material, this could also be placed over the window to soften the light. At the same time you might want to 'flag' the light. This term refers to blocking off some of the light by using the curtains, if there are any, or by using black card or paper. This is a common technique in a professional photographic studio.

If you are using artificial light indoors, such as normal domestic tungsten bulbs, you will need to use tungsten-balanced film or adjust the white balance. If you don't, then shooting in this type of light may cause your shots to come out with a bright orange cast. If your camera is already loaded with daylight film or that is the only type you have, you will need to place an 80A filter over the lens. This is dark blue in colour and will correct the

Using a reflector

When photographing a person with the available light coming in through a window, sometimes one side of their face will be too dark (see right). An easy way to solve this problem is to use a reflector to bounce light back into the shadows. This gives a more flattering light as can be seen in the example below.

▲ **Mixed lighting**
The lighting in this bar was daylight and fluorescent light. I loaded the camera with daylight balanced film, as I felt this was the dominant light source. The result is perfect and there is no hint of a green cast, which can occur when shooting in fluorescent light.

▲ **Billboard light**
In this shot the girl was lit with just the available light coming from the billboard. The light was tungsten and the daylight balanced film has recorded it with an orange cast. In this case it is quite acceptable but for true colours the camera should have been fitted with an 80A filter.

▲ **Push processing**
This shot was taken on 400 ISO film rated at 800 ISO. The lighting was a mix of daylight, fluorescent and tungsten. As the film was black and white I did not have to worry about a colour cast. The film was pushed one stop in development.

▶ **Window light**
I positioned this young girl against a door and lit her by the light coming through a small window to my left. I used a reflector to my right to bounce some light back onto her.

▲ Candlelight
Cameras have the ability to capture a scene even when the light is minimal, as can be seen in this photograph of a girl holding a candle. Her face looks quite warm while the rest of the shot falls of into shadow. A shutter speed of 1/4th of a second was required to record the candle flame.

film, as stated on the film packet, will probably be irrelevant as there will be a certain amount of reciprocity failure. There should be a guide for this on the inside of the packaging the film came in. If there isn't, it might be a case of trial and error with different films before you become confident in this type of light.

With fluorescent tubes your pictures will come out with a green cast whether you are using daylight or tungsten balanced film. There is a range of different filters to correct this cast but as there are many different types of fluorescent tubes you will only know the right filter by testing them or using a colour temperature meter. This piece of equipment will tell you exactly what the level of the light is in degrees Kelvin (K). It will then convert this information and, depending on whether you are using daylight or tungsten balanced film, tell you exactly which colour correction filters are required or the degrees K to set your white balance to, to get the right colour balance. The drawback here is that these meters are quite expensive and, unless you are intending to do a lot of photography in artificial or mixed lighting, the cost will probably not justify the purchase.

Another form of artificial light is floodlights or photofloods. These have fallen from favour over the years in preference to flash with its greater power and more comfortable working conditions, as this does not generate the same heat as photofloods. However, photofloods do have the benefit of letting you see exactly what the light is doing and where it is falling. If anyone ever doubted the quality of these lights in portraiture, then a study of the great Hollywood photographers such as George Hurrell will soon convince them otherwise!

orange cast. However, it will also mean you have to increase the exposure to compensate for the light that it absorbs. As the intensity of domestic light is far lower than daylight, you may find that exposures have to be quite long, which will necessitate using a tripod.

Another point to bear in mind when shooting film in these lighting conditions is that the ISO rating of the

◄ **Wedding pipes**
I shot this bagpipe player in a marquee where a wedding was being held. The translucent quality of the marquee acted like a giant diffuser so that wherever I moved, the light was always even.

See also
▶ pp 18–21 Film and DSLR cameras
▶ pp 34–35 Film
▶ pp 136–137 Using reflectors
▶ pp 242–243 Specialist filters

Wall of light

I photographed this girl standing between two walls of light. Because I had no idea what type of light source lay behind the wall panels, I set the white balance on the digital camera to automatic. This has ensured perfect skin tones in the finished photograph.

Backgrounds

◄ **Studio backgrounds**
Most professional photographic studios use long rolls of heavy-duty paper known as coloramas. These are available in a variety of different colours and provide seamless backgrounds that run down the wall and across the floor. I took this spontaneous picture of a young boy as he happened to be leaning against them.

When photographing people, the background often determines whether the shot is going to be a success or failure. If the background dominates the picture we could well lose sight of the person. On the other hand, perhaps the background can tell us something about the person we are photographing. In this case we need to achieve a subtle blend between background and subject.

In a professional photographer's studio there will be a range of backgrounds, or coloramas. These long rolls of paper come in a range of colours and although they could be thought of as quite bland because they are simply flat colour, they can be lit in such a way to give them depth. Also, if the subject is professionally made up, so that the face is striking just on its own, this type of background is ideal. A quick study of fashion magazines will illustrate how popular this type of background is, with white probably the most prevalent.

When it comes to shooting outdoors, we have to take from our surroundings and make the background work for us. In some cases this is quite easy. If we are somewhere with above average sunshine, we can often make the light work for us by looking out for the patterns it makes on walls and doorways. This might take the form of sunlight shining through the branches of trees, thereby making a dappled light pattern on a wall. This can look very attractive and also add to the picture by adding the element of light and warmth. If you are posing your subject against a surface with this type of light you will need to take care as to exactly

Viewpoint

When we see a potential shot, we are often so concerned that we will miss the opportunity if we do not act quickly that we fail to spot basic flaws in the composition. Compare these two photographs. In the one taken from a low viewpoint (above), the background is very cluttered and confuses the eye, which makes it difficult to concentrate on the girl who, after all, is the point of interest. By taking a higher viewpoint (right) and eliminating the unwanted detail, the emphasis is very much on the girl and her expression.

where the light is falling. What you do not want is part of the dappled light falling harshly over their face. It might mean that they only have to move very slightly one way or the other.

Another element to look for if your subject is at work is to try to get a hint of the workplace into the shots. This will help to give a sense of place as well as providing information on the subject's employment and environment. Often the background is already in place and all we have to do is to change the viewpoint to see it at its best. This could mean crouching down low or getting up much higher. Always be on the lookout for the unexpected and unusual – the simplest everyday textures can make the most brilliant photographic backgrounds. It's just a case of keeping your eyes open.

▲ Unusual backgrounds
This Tunisian boy and his camel were photographed in a souk. The camel makes an ideal background for him to pose against and the colours work well together. Always be on the lookout for an unusual background to put your subject against.

◄ Dappled light
The dappled light, caused by the sun filtering through the trees, makes an attractive background for this young girl to pose against. Care must be taken in these situations that there are no strong pools of light that might fall across the subject's face.

See also
► **pp 48–49** How the camera 'sees'
► **pp 56–57** Light and colour
► **pp 62–63** Selecting a viewpoint
► **pp 64–65** Filling the frame
► **pp 92–93** Lighting for outdoor portraits

Weddings

As we have seen with photographing groups, it is probably the shot of the bride and groom with their relations and guests that will be the most demanding photograph. However, to shoot a wedding successfully, there are more than set piece photographs.

If you have the opportunity and can be at the bride's home before the wedding, there is the possibility of getting some wonderfully informal shots of the preparation, not only of the bride herself, but also of the bridesmaids and the bride's mother and father. Once the bride is ready, try to get a portrait of her at her best. Remember to think about the light. A shot with her by a window, using the available light and perhaps a reflector, will look far more evocative than one with full-on flash. If there is time, photograph the bridesmaids too. Remember these people are only going to get married to each other once and you want to be sure that you have covered every conceivable angle.

At the church or venue where the wedding is taking place, photograph the guests arriving. Always be on the look out for the informal and unexpected. Try to get a shot of the best man and groom. When the bride arrives with her father, be in position to get that shot. Remember that on a day like this the bride will naturally be a little nervous

and won't want to hang around for you while you find the best position to take the shot. If you have the priest's permission, try to get some shots in the church and when the actual ceremony is over, photograph the bride and groom signing the register. Finally, when they are walking down the aisle, make sure you know where to stand and at what point the bride and groom will be in the optimum position for your shot as they walk towards you. It will now be up to you to organize the various groups before everyone leaves for the reception.

Again, keep an eye open for the informal and unexpected.

At the reception try to get the bride and groom to yourself so that you can get some relaxed pictures of just the two of them. Find somewhere where the available light is flattering and romantic and if there are attractive grounds at the reception venue these may provide an appropriate background. After all this, return to the guests for more informal shots and then maybe you can have a glass of champagne yourself.

See also

- pp 56–57 Light and colour
- pp 64–65 Filling the frame
- pp 90–91 Group portraits
- pp 92–93 Lighting for outdoor portraits
- pp 112–113 Candid portraits
- pp 138–139 Using fill-in flash

◀ **Fill-in flash**
This shot of the bride and groom was taken with just a small amount of fill-in flash. It has added a sparkle to the shot, which was taken in the late afternoon when the light was beginning to fade and look quite cold.

▶ **Building an album**
As well as the more formal shots of the bride and groom and their immediate families, be on the lookout for other shots. These might be as simple as a floral display or a napkin. It is surprising how useful these shots can be when you are putting together an album of the day.

Victoria. Richter

Babies

If any photographic situation calls for a greater degree of sensitivity than usual, it is when photographing babies. Imagine if you were just a few days old and a dark, foreboding shape cast a shadow over you followed by a huge flash as a picture was taken. For this reason, try to work in available light with very young babies. This may mean using a faster than normal film, which could result in more grainy pictures but at least flash will not be required.

If the baby has just been born or if you are photographing its birth and this is taking place in a hospital, it is likely that the lighting will be fluorescent. This will give a green cast to your colour film, whether it's daylight or tungsten balanced, so use a filter to get a more natural result, or if shooting digitally alter the camera's white balance accordingly. If using black and white film this is not a problem as it is not sensitive to colour temperature changes.

If recording the birth, remember your photography is the least important part of the proceedings and the safety and health of the mother and baby are the priority. A moderate telephoto lens will put you in the action while keeping a physical distance from those involved. Only if everything has gone smoothly should you move in close and then only if you are sure it's wise to do so.

When the baby is older and at home you may want to do a more formal shot for family and friends. Again it would be preferable to shoot with available light, perhaps daylight coming through a window balanced on the shadow side by using a reflector. Always look out for that special glance or expression.

▲ Capturing expression
Babies change rapidly and it is essential, if you are to build a record of their development, to take plenty of pictures at regular intervals. Their expression can change in a flash, which is why you need to always have the camera ready to shoot.

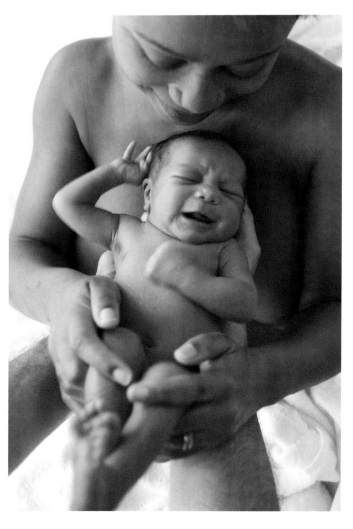

◀ Family portrait
To get away from the stereotypical picture of the mother and father with their newborn baby, I photographed them with the father's hands coming into the shot holding the baby for the mother, whose hands are also cradling the child. It makes a tight intimate group.

▶ Extension tubes
Babies have the most delicate features and I wanted to show this in a photograph. This baby was asleep and had her hand resting on a soft toy. I put an extension tube on the camera and focused in close on her hand so that it was sharp while the rest of the shot, although discernable, goes into soft focus.

See also
▶ **pp 54–55** Aperture
▶ **pp 94–97** Available light
▶ **pp 108–111** Families
▶ **pp 128–131** High key and low key
▶ **pp 234–235** Extension tubes and bellows

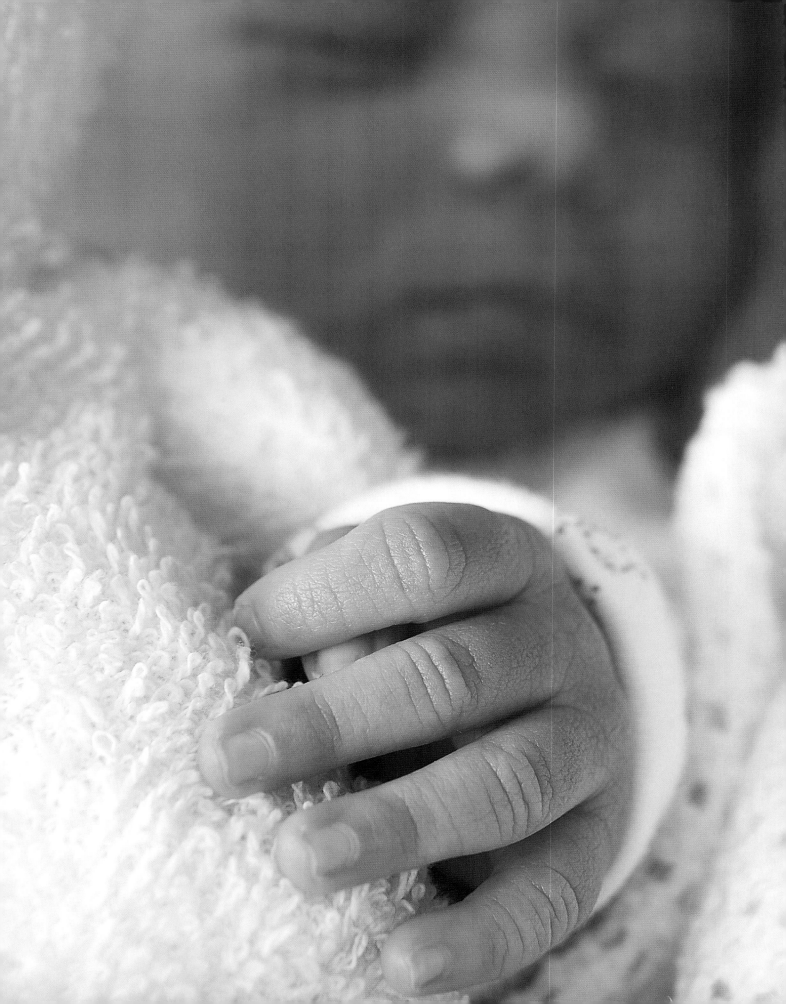

Younger children

hotographing younger children or toddlers can produce great results but because at this age few are going to either understand your requests to 'hold it' or stay still for very long, you will have to work quickly and be on the lookout for the unexpected. With these limitations in mind, it would be advantageous to use a camera with a zoom lens, as this will enable you to get in close without crowding the child while zooming out should you want to get more of the surroundings in the shot. Selecting a low viewpoint will put you on the same plane as the child and will produce far more interesting results than taking pictures from a standing position and looking down on them.

Consider the light and its direction carefully. You can't ask a child of this age to turn round or move if there is an ugly shadow falling across its face. However, if the child seems quite happily occupied and the sun is behind them, you may have time either to use fill-in flash or to get someone else to hold a reflector in position so that some light can be bounced back into the child's face. Failing to do either of these might result in a disappointing photograph with the child coming out as a silhouette or very dark.

By using a wide aperture you will minimize the depth of field, especially if combined with a telephoto lens. This will mean that the background will go out of focus, thereby emphasizing the child. It will also mean that you can use a faster shutter speed and capture the action more confidently.

Remember that children tire easily and become bored quickly. If you don't get the shot in their time, you are unlikely to get it in yours – unless it's an album of wailing expressions that you are after!

▶ **Point of focus**
Most of the time I think it is best to get down to a child's level so that you get a better perspective on their world. However, this picture is the exception to that rule and the child's eyes look stunning as she stares into the camera.

See also
▶ **pp 26–27** Additional lenses
▶ **pp 52–53** Shutter speed
▶ **pp 54–55** Aperture
▶ **pp 74–77** Wide-angle and telephoto lenses
▶ **pp 92–93** Lighting for outdoor portraits

Capturing the moment

Younger children and toddlers are always on the move and to photograph them well means that you need to be constantly alert so that you will capture them in a variety of different situations and moods. It would be advantageous to use a 70–210mm zoom lens, which will enable you to get in close, even when standing at a distance. However, it will also give you the opportunity to zoom out and get down to their level if, for instance, they are involved in an activity on the ground. Use a fast shutter speed to freeze movement and a large aperture to blur the background so it does not become a distraction in your photograph.

Older children

Older children are far more likely to be receptive to having their picture taken than their younger brothers or sisters. With this in mind, and because children are naturally curious, it can help if you let them handle the camera and perhaps even take a few shots themselves. This will help to break down any inhibitions they might have and make them less aware of you.

Children usually have short attention spans and if you are planning a specific type of picture, forethought and speed of picture taking will be of the essence. The last thing you should do is to fiddle with the camera controls or lenses while the child gets bored and irritable. If this happens, you will probably have to abandon the shot for a while. If you become annoyed, you will probably lose the opportunity, not only now but perhaps in the future, as children have an uncanny knack of associating objects – in this case you and your camera – with bad or unhappy experiences.

Setting the ISO to 200 or using the film equivalent will enable you use a telephoto lens without the need to worry about camera shake even if your lens does not have IS. This will give you plenty of scope for going in close while maintaining a distance from the child.

Always be on the lookout for a different angle. Although the children

See also
▶ **pp 26–27** Additional lenses
▶ **pp 54–55** Aperture
▶ **pp 62–63** Selecting a viewpoint
▶ **pp 70–71** Selecting a background
▶ **pp 74–77** Wide-angle and telephoto lenses
▶ **pp 92–93** Lighting for outdoor portraits

▲ **Keep it simple**
Sometimes it is the simplest of shots that is the most effective. I shot this girl just looking straight to the camera in the studio against a plain white background. It is the symmetry of her face that makes the picture work so well.

◀ **Using a long lens**
A long lens is great for capturing those fleeting moments. Here I used a 70–210mm zoom lens on 210mm. The day was quite sunny, which could have created problems if I hadn't used a lens hood. This is the one accessory you should always carry.

might be moving about, try to consider the background. You don't want a great shot ruined by unwanted detail behind them. On the other hand, if you spot an interesting opportunity, move them in front of it and use it to your advantage. On very bright days use fill-in flash or a reflector to soften the shadows. This could easily be improvised by using a white towel or a book rather than a custom accessory.

▼ Choosing backgrounds
Always be on the lookout for an interesting background. This was a temporary painted hoarding in a park that I felt complemented the colours of the boys' clothing and also provided them with something they could casually lean against.

◀ Selecting the viewpoint
As this boy was getting out of the swimming pool, I asked him to pose on the steps. By taking a higher viewpoint and slightly looking down on him, there was only water in the background, which contrasted well with his skin tone. A large aperture meant that the focus is definitely on the boy, as the water drops out of the area of sharpness.

Families

Photographing families, either individually or in groups, makes fascinating documents, not just for the immediate members and their relations, but also for friends around the world. With digital photography and email, the immediacy of sharing your latest photographs means that everyone can share in an event almost as soon as it has happened. Never before has it been so easy to record a family's life, in the case of some members from birth until death, that will make a truly historical document for generations to come.

So where do you begin with your family photographs? Pregnancy or birth? Formative years, first day at school, holidays and special events? The list of opportunities is endless and there really isn't a beginning other than to start as soon as possible.

Photographing a woman when she is pregnant, either with or without her partner, can result in some particularly poignant and tender pictures. By taking a picture every month, you can create a record of the physical changes she is experiencing as the baby grows, which could make a fascinating opening for a baby album.

If you are shooting on film, choose colour unless you have a specific shot in mind that particularly lends itself to black and white. The reason for saying this is that you can always scan your colour photographs at a later date and print them in black and white, whereas if shot this way to begin with you will never have a colour record. However, if you

◀ Father and son
Shots where the parents are involved in an activity with their children always make good pictures. Here is a good action photograph of a father and son on holiday, with the boy taking control of the speedboat. A fast shutter speed kept the shot sharp.

▶ Bedouin family
I shot this Bedouin family in the Sinai Desert, Egypt. They were pleased to be photographed and posed in a relaxed manner for the camera. A series of shots like this from different countries could make a fascinating album on the world's families.

▶ **Family groups**
Photographing family groups can be difficult, as it is essential that you have everyone's attention and that everyone has the right expression and eye contact. For this reason it is best to shoot quite a few shots and edit after the session.

▲ **Grandparents**
When you are building a photographic record of your children it is always important to include the grandparents. This shot was taken in available daylight coming in through a window. A small reflector bounced a small amount of light back into the shadows.

◀ **Black and white**
I thought all the shots from this session worked well in black and white as opposed to colour. If I had been shooting digitally I would have had the choice of either. This is a great advantage because with film I would have had to keep changing from one to another.

are shooting digitally, this will not pose a problem since you can always convert them to black and white in Photoshop.

Try to shoot in available light for these first pictures. Not only will it create a better mood, but also the baby won't be subjected to brilliant bursts of light that a flashgun would create. If you are photographing the parents and newborn baby together, think about the

pose. For example, as well as the parents smiling at the camera, have them look at the baby instead of the camera. This will draw the viewer's attention to the baby first and create a very intimate feel.

As time evolves, try to have a camera at the ready for all events, including the unexpected. Even a phone camera or one-use camera, kept permanently in the car for example, will produce a

reasonable result that will be better than not having the shot at all.

When it comes to photographing the family you have the option of using the camera's self-timer so that you can also be in the shot. In this mode always take several frames, as you will never be sure until the film is processed or you review the images on the camera's LCD that everyone is looking how you want them to.

If your camera is auto-focus make sure that the sensor is over a member of the group. If it is on the distant background then the entire family group could come out totally out of focus. This is why, when photographing a family group, it is good to try and frame it as tightly as possible. This will help to create a feeling of intimacy.

If you are using flash make sure that one member of the family does not cast a shadow over another. This is a problem you should look out for even in strong directional daylight. If this is the case, place the group in a different position or move them to an area of overall shade. You could then use the bright daylight to backlight them. This always looks attractive, especially on the hair. However, make sure that you use the camera's backlight setting or use a small amount of fill-in flash. You do not want the camera's exposure meter to record the bright background, thereby turning the group into silhouettes.

Holidays always provide a wealth of opportunities for family pictures, especially when this involves some action

 Colour
This mother from Ghana, West Africa, was walking through a village with her young son. I loved the vibrant colour of her clothes and asked her if I could photograph them. She was delighted, especially when I gave her a Polaroid of the two of them.

where one or more of the family is involved in an activity. Take care of the camera when you are at the beach. Sand is a real problem and always manages to get into the equipment no matter what precautions you take. The same is true of seawater. Always be on the lookout for the unexpected and don't waste time looking at the camera's controls or the moment will have passed by the time you are ready to take the shot. In this situation always have the camera set on its most reliable exposure mode so that you can take a shot at any time.

Grandparents also provide great opportunities for family portraits. Remember they might not be there as the child gets older and it is as important to have a record of their extended family just as much as their immediate ones.

See also
▶ **pp 18–21** Film and DSLR cameras
▶ **pp 34–35** Film
▶ **pp 52–53** Shutter speed
▶ **pp 90–91** Group portraits
▶ **pp118–119** Studio lighting set-ups

◀ Mother and daughters
This shot of a mother and her daughters makes a tight and intimate portrait. Although the shot might look posed, it happened quite spontaneously while I was working in the studio. Always be on the lookout for these unexpected shots.

Candid portraits

The term 'candid' basically means portraits of people taken when they were unaware of your presence. This doesn't mean that you are setting out to spy on people but rather to portray them in the most relaxed and revealing way possible. One of the greatest exponents of this type of photography was the great French photographer Henri Cartier-Bresson. His black and white photography, nearly all shot on a 35mm Leica camera, is revered around the world for its tightly ordered composition and his trademark gift of capturing the 'decisive moment'.

It is easy to see why Cartier-Bresson chose a camera like the Leica. It is virtually silent in operation, has superb optics and is compact – you are hardly likely to remain inconspicuous using a 6 x 7 medium format camera. Your greatest asset, having chosen your camera, is patience. It might be necessary to wait some time for the person you are shooting to get into the

position or portray the expression that will make the shot. It would be advantageous to use a telephoto lens, which means that you can keep your distance, while at the same time get them framed tightly. Remember, you are not going to be able to move the subject of your attention. If, for example, the light is wrong and perhaps their face is in deep shadow, you will not be able to ask them to move. It will be

◄ Events
Events such as carnivals provide countless opportunities for candid photographs. A zoom lens in the range of 70–210mm is an excellent choice. Setting the camera to shutter priority will enable you to use a fast speed while the camera takes care of the aperture.

See also

up to you to find an angle where the light is more favourable.

If you are at an event where there are crowds of people, look out for candid shots amongst the crowds. These people might not be related to you but could be the basis of a stunning shot you could enter into a competition at a later date. An event such as this allows you to become submerged into the crowd so as not to be conspicuous. However, remember that the stunning girl you are pointing your camera at might have her big boyfriend standing behind you or, in this day and age, photographing children who are no relation to you might create the wrong impression.

◄ Street life
It is impossible to walk down a street and not see a scene that would make a great shot. This man doing a crossword while his dog looks at, well, other dogs makes an amusing portrait.

▶ Children
Children make great subjects for candid shots. Often it is just a case of sitting still and observing them going about their business. Here it is her pensive expression that makes the photograph.

Black and white portraits

For portraits, black and white is a perfect medium, as the eye concentrates on the subject, lighting, composition and tonal range and is not distracted by a bright colour. On some digital cameras there is a setting for shooting black and white. However, if you shoot in this mode you will only be able to print in black and white, whereas if you shoot in the colour mode you can always convert to black and white at a later stage. Of course, if you shoot on film choose one to suit the situation.

If using available light, it would be wise to use a fast film or up-rate a medium film. Although this will increase the grain, it will not necessarily detract from your finished print – it could well increase the atmosphere. If grain is a concern to you, get your film processed in one of the many fine grain developers. Remember that black and white films have far greater latitude than colour films and will give you a greater margin of error, but you should still aim for the correct exposure.

When shooting indoors with artificial light at slow speeds, use a tripod. If you have lighting, such as electronic flash, start with just one light and build it up if necessary. If the flash is too powerful for the shot, i.e. you want to use a wide aperture, you could use the flash unit's modelling lights as your light source. Most units have variable intensity and work like a dimmer switch so you can alter the intensity of the light without having to move it nearer or further from your subject.

▲ **Getting the right expression**
Often it is a black and white portrait of a child that makes a far more interesting picture than a colour version. In this case, having the young boy hold a ball above his head reveals a sparkle and vitality in his expression that might not have been so apparent if shot in colour.

See also
▶ **pp 34–35** Film
▶ **pp 94–97** Available light
▶ **pp 106–107** Older children
▶ **pp 120–123** Further lighting techniques
▶ **pp 128–131** High key and low key

▲ **Push-processing**
I was photographing this Michelin-starred chef in the south of France. All the food photography was shot in colour but I felt that it was more appropriate to photograph him in black and white. I chose 400 ISO film, which I pushed to 800 ISO but still retained fine grain.

▶ **Close-ups**
I wanted to do a close-up of this model because his face has such strong features. I used one light from the side with a white reflector on the other to bounce light into the shadows. I chose a high viewpoint and focused on his eyes. This low key approach works well in black and white.

Hair and make-up for photography

Many of us have had the experience of plucking up the courage to ask a stunningly gorgeous person we have spotted in the street if we can take some photographs of them, only to find when we get them in front of the camera that the session just doesn't work. The reason for this is that some people simply have a natural rapport with the camera, and often it isn't the type of person that would sweep you off your feet when you first catch sight of them.

So what makes this difference between being photogenic or not?

Very often it comes down to the hair and make-up. Top fashion photographers would never consider taking a shot before the team of make-up artists, hairdressers and stylists, who have probably spent years perfecting their craft, had got to work. Prior to shooting, perhaps days in advance, they would all meet with the art director of the magazine or advertising agency to

discuss the required look and the feel to be reflected in the shots. Of course, in reality, there are very few of us who have this army of experts at our disposal. However, there are some basic rules that will help you to achieve a striking look and produce photographs that are far more glamorous than the everyday shot.

The type of make-up, which might look striking in the street, office or at home and which a lot of women wear

Make-up for photography

1 For photographic make-up that will portray a natural look and achieve symmetry, start with a base of liquid foundation close to the tone of the model's own skin and a powder to even out skin tones and create a matt canvas.

2 Define the eyebrows to create a frame for the eyes using an eyebrow brush with suitable colour. Rest the brush or pencil against a soft pad to avoid marking the foundation.

3 An alternative to the brush is to use an eyebrow pencil, which may be easier for a make-up novice.

4 Apply eyeshadow to emphasize contours of the eyelids, remembering that light tones will highlight an area whereas darker shades will make them recede.

5 To add extra definition to the eyes, a dark eyeliner can be smudged subtly along the rim close to the lashes.

1

2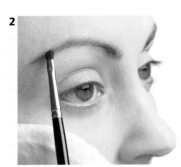

3

4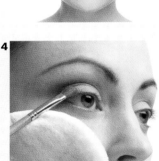

5

6

7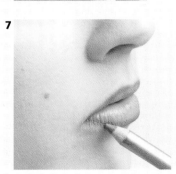

8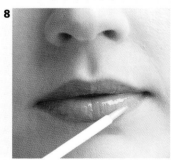

9

every day, may not translate particularly well in front of the camera. Often it might be too shiny and reflect badly when lit.

Try to remember that the camera is unforgiving. Unlike a movie that pans or cuts from one scene to another, the still photograph is just that – a still moment that will not pan or cut but is there forever to be studied in minute detail. So if that hair parting is not straight, it will be there for all to see. That blemish on the skin, hardly noticeable in real life, stands out like a sore thumb; the eyeliner that has been applied crookedly and unevenly; the

lacklustre hair that wasn't washed prior to the shoot and has lost its sheen; the slight chip in the nail varnish – look at all these elements in great detail before you start shooting.

If you do not know anybody who is a professional photographic make-up artist or you cannot afford to hire one, discuss the type of look that you want to achieve with your model. Look at examples torn from magazines as a reference. Many professional models are very adept at doing their own make-up, as they have had experience working with make-up artists and will have picked up hints and tips.

Men, too, need to think about how they are going to look in front of the camera. What is applicable to women – hair, skin blemishes and nails, for instance – is equally important for men. A great portrait of a rugged hunk leaning on his hand is going to look terrible if his fingernails are broken and dirty and his hair is dry and dull.

See also

► **pp 56–57** Light and colour
► **pp 82–85** Head and shoulder portraits
► **pp 118–119** Studio lighting set-ups
► **pp 128–131** High key and low key
► **pp 152–153** Close-ups

6 The next step is to apply the mascara to the eyelashes. If you want a more natural look only apply the mascara to the top lashes. After applying the mascara, comb the lashes through with a clean mascara brush to prevent clogging.

7 Define the lips by using a lip pencil as close to the natural colour of the lips as possible to even out and enhance the mouth shape. This step may be easier if a light smear of lip balm has been applied first.

8 Fill in the lip area with the chosen colour, blot with tissue and re-apply for a denser and longer-lasting coloration.

9 Finally, use a blusher brush colour to apply to the apples of the cheeks to create a healthy natural glow to the complexion. The final shot shows a clean and natural effect that will photograph well under studio conditions.

Studio lighting set-ups

Many aspiring photographers are daunted by the idea of taking portraits in a studio setting. However, the great advantage is you have complete control over the lighting.

Studio lights can be photofloods and spotlights or flash. The former have fallen in popularity since they get very hot and are expensive to run. Their advantages are that you can see exactly where the light is going and its intensity. Although these units have what are called modelling lights, they are only a guide to the final effect and not a completely truthful rendition. They run at much lower temperatures than photofloods. The range of reflectors, umbrellas, soft boxes and optical attachments is vast.

When using this lighting for the first time it would be best to use a model who will be patient as you discover exactly what each light does. A small adjustment to the light can completely change the feel of the final shot. Study what happens every time you move a light. The advantage of shooting digitally is that you can always look at the camera's LCD to check the lighting. Alternatively, if your camera supports it, you could tether the camera to the computer and look directly on the monitor.

Once you start positioning your lights, always return to the camera and see the effect from the camera's position. Do this with every adjustment.

See also

Different lighting set-ups

1 For a simple but well lit portrait, start with one light. This is known as the key light. With your model facing the camera, position this just to the right of the camera and high enough so the light creates a shadow between the nose and upper lip.

2 When you are satisfied with the position of this light you can add another. This one is known as the fill or fill-in light. Place this to the left of the camera so that it 'fills-in' the other side of the face. You will need this light at a lower power than the key light. It is vital to avoid a double shadow on the nose.

3 Now you could add a hair light. This will give a pleasant sheen to the hair and add body and highlights.

4 In this shot a reflector has been placed under the model's face. This has softened the shadow under her chin and the eyes. For the final shot opposite, two lights have been directed towards the background to keep it pure white. The overall feel of this picture is one of soft and even lighting that brings out the model's 'peaches and cream' complexion. It is a simple set-up but the final result is highly effective.

Further lighting techniques

Once you feel confident with using studio lights you can start to become more adventurous. This does not mean that you have to buy more lighting but rather experiment by trying the lights in different positions to obtain different effects.

If you start with one light, as demonstrated on the previous pages, but place it in different positions you will start to see the endless possibilities that are available to you. With your model facing the camera, try putting your key light down low and quite close to your model. Now point the light up to their face at quite a steep angle.

Return to the camera position and note the effect. This should look quite ghostly, with the shadows running up the face rather than down. If you now take a low camera angle so your model is looking down on to you, it should give them a menacing, slightly eerie quality. Now position the light directly over and about 1m (3ft) above their head and point it straight down. The shadows will now run downwards, forming dark areas in their eyes and under the nose and chin. Although this will also have a haunting quality to it, the ambience of the light will give a totally different effect.

If you take this single light and now move it almost behind your model, you will get what is known as 'rim' lighting. This is where the light looks as though it is painted just along the outline of their body or face. If you were then to place a bright reflector, such as a mirror or a sheet of silver foil, to the opposite side but in front of your model, so the light is bounced back on to them, you will create a theatrical effect. Look at what happens to the light if you move or tilt the mirror or foil. You will find that you can direct the light to wherever you require it, creating different effects quite easily.

Light and mood

When you have familiarized yourself with studio lighting, you can experiment with a host of different effects. These shots of two young models show how different lighting has changed mood and appearance more than anything else.

In the top left shot I used one light coming from the side. This has created a strong shadow that creates more of a moody look than if I had lit her face-on. In the shot, top right, I changed the background and moved the light further round. This gives a more seductive appearance.

In the bottom left shot the background has been slightly under-exposed to turn it light grey. If the model had been further from the background I could have turned it even darker. The bottom right shot has been lit with a directional light so that his shadow falls on to the background.

All these shots have been taken using one key light and reflectors. Imagine the permutations of having more lights.

Another way you can change the quality of the light is by placing a honeycomb attachment over the light's reflector. As the name suggests, this is a metal grid with lots of tiny holes in it. This will make the light more concentrated and directional and help to reduce spill. This is when the light flares around its edges. There are different types of these honeycombs and it is only by experimenting with them that you will find the one that best suits the light for the shot that you have in mind.

As well as fitting this type of grid, you can also fit barn doors to the light. These can either be used in conjunction with the grid or on their own. Barn doors have four moveable flaps that can be angled to control the light that spills onto an area of the shot that you do not want to light.

When using these lighting reflectors the light will be quite harsh. To soften it you could put a diffuser onto the front of the lighting reflector. Alternatively, improvise by using a piece of tracing paper either over the light or just in front of it. Remember, the further away from the light the diffuser is placed, the softer the light will be.

A different way of changing the light is to place coloured gels over the reflectors in the same way you might use the diffuser. Obviously, this will change the colour of the light but the effects can be quite dramatic, especially where different colours merge.

If you have a focusing spotlight, you will be able to use an extensive range of gobos. These are small metal discs that have various patterns cut out of them. Some of these might be quite random while others, for example, recreate the glazing bars of a window, a tree or the flames of a fire. Spotlights have a focusing lens at the front of the lamp

▶ **Going in close**
This photograph was taken with a light coming in from the left. No reflectors were used but the light has defined the model's cheekbones and there is just enough definition in the shadows to make the shot work.

▲ **Using mirrors**
By placing a mirror under this girl's face a strong light has been reflected upwards. This can produce dramatic and at times eerie results. Other materials such as aluminium foil could be used to obtain the same type of effect.

▲ **Backlight**
For this shot the light was placed behind the model and pointed back towards her. This has given good modelling and the white pillow she is lying on has acted as a reflector, bouncing light back into the shadows.

▲ **Bounced light**
The background in this picture was lit with two flash heads to keep it brilliantly white. Two additional heads were then bounced into large white polystyrene reflectors placed on either side of her. This has created a soft high-key look.

housing that operates in much the same way as a slide projector. The gobo slips into the spotlight between the lens and the light source. The pattern is then projected onto the surface or the person and can be softened or sharpened by focusing the lens. They can be used in conjunction with coloured gels or doubled up. You can, of course, make your own for a completely unique look. As well as these effects, the spotlight can be used to direct a beam of light, of a variable diameter, at a specific point.

Another attachment is a snoot. This is a conical device that fits over the front of the light. It creates a circular beam of light but it cannot be focused. A beauty dish is also useful. This is a large, white, round metal dish with a baffle placed in front of the flash tube, giving a soft light. You can put diffusers on the front to soften the light even more.

Another light that has gained favour is the ring flash. This circular light fits around the lens and creates a completely even illumination with flat rendering of details. The only shadow detail that is visible is a soft one around the model.

It is important to remember with all these lighting effects that you want to create an ambience that suits the person and the type of shot required, as well as experimenting with a new approach.

▶ Gel lighting

Many portraits can become more effective by the simplest changes in light. I had positioned the model in front of a glass brick wall, which I had lit from behind. Then I decided to alter the background light by putting a blue gel over it. This altered the background quite noticeably without having to move a single light.

See also

▶ pp 82–85 Head and shoulder portraits
▶ pp 114–115 Black and white portraits
▶ pp 118–119 Studio lighting set-ups
▶ pp 128–131 High key and low key

▶ Forties look

This shot was a multi-lighting set-up and I wanted the feel of a Hollywood-type portrait from the 1940s. I positioned my key light slightly to the right of the camera and pointing down onto her face. This created a strong shadow under the nose. My next light, the fill in, was placed to the left of the camera to soften the shadows. Next I positioned a light with a snoot to add body to the hair and, finally, another light with a snoot was projected onto the background to create a shaft of light.

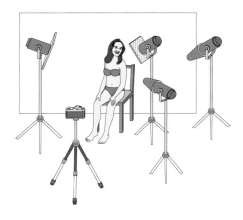

In the workplace

For many people, the world of work is either somewhere they can't wait to get away from or they would rather be doing anything else but their everyday job. For the observant photographer, however, the working environment offers a wealth of photographic opportunities, both in their own place of work or locality, and while travelling all over the world.

It is probably easiest to divide photography of the working environment into two categories – the formal and informal. The former could be a portrait of the chief executive of a multi-national company or of someone leaving work after a lifetime's service. In either case, you will want to portray something of their working environment to give your shot a sense of place. Expression will be important and should reflect their position and status. To this end, background will also play an important part.

One of the most famous portraits of a person and their work is the one taken of the great engineer and inventor Isambard Kingdom Brunel. This shot was taken in 1857 by Robert Howlett, a young London-based photographer, when photography was still in its infancy, yet it is still held up as one of the most definitive images in this category of photography. So why has this image endured for so long and what can we learn from it?

The first thing that strikes us is how comfortable and confident Brunel looks, from his top hat, the cigar hanging nonchalantly from his mouth, his hands plunged into his high pockets, down to his trousers and boots. These are quite dirty but their appearance is obviously of little concern to him and reinforce the fact that he is quite at home in the working environment. Add to this confident air and a striking background

▼ **Early evening light**
These waiters were standing outside a famous San Francisco restaurant waiting for diners to arrive. They made an informal group of workers and I just had time to shoot them in the available early evening light. If I had used flash it would have killed the shot.

▲ Isolated figure
I saw this workman suspended in a boson's chair high above ground, when this building was under construction. Rather than zoom in close on him, I used a 24mm wide-angle lens to isolate him within the intricate design of the structure.

▶ Formal portrait
For this portrait of a senior banking figure I had to deal with three different light sources – daylight from the windows on the right, tungsten in the room and the flash he needed to be lit with. As flash and daylight were the dominant sources, I used daylight balanced film.

of huge anchor chains, and we can begin to see why this portrait of a person's work has taken on iconic status. Obviously, fashions have changed, but we can still use all the ingredients that Howlett put together – dress, expression, props and background – in our photographs.

If you are travelling, then there is a wealth of photographic opportunities of people at work. These could range from people in shops and restaurants to others working in fields or markets. The first thing to do, especially in a foreign country, is to gain the confidence of the person you want to photograph. Apart from putting them at their ease, you never know what their status might be or if they are allowed to pause for the photograph.

If they agree, look for the best viewpoint. Is it straight on or would it be better if taken from a higher or lower viewpoint? A lot will depend on the background. If it is unsuitable, see if you can move them to somewhere more applicable to the shot you have in mind. Do you need to move or turn them round to take advantage of the available light or can you better position yourself to do this? Perhaps you need to use some fill-in flash or get someone, such as a travelling companion, to position and hold a reflector to bounce light back in to the areas that require it. As for props, are they using tools in their work or is it just hands-on? Whatever it is, try to get some movement into your shot. The woman picking tea in India (shown opposite) was working so quickly that her hands have come out quite blurred. However, this adds to the shot and shows how hard she is expected to work.

If taking a more formal shot, perhaps indoors, consider how it is going to be

◀ **Hands on**
These two shots were taken in a pottery. To get in close for this shot of the potter kneading the clay, I used a 150mm lens and a small amount of diffused flash balanced with the daylight.

▼ **Perspective**
Changing to black and white, which I thought was better suited to this potter, has resulted in a gritty image. The board he is holding the finished pots on adds a fine perspective to the composition.

lit. If using the camera's flash, will it be powerful enough and will it create an ugly shadow behind the subject? If you want to include the whole room with maybe the subject in the foreground, can you light the rest of the room without the lights being seen or will the ambient light be enough? If using the room lights as the main source and tungsten-balanced film, do you have a correction gel to put over the flash for some 'fill'? If not, they will come out looking very blue.

All this might seem like a never-ending list of potential problems, but many of the answers – filters, gels, flashgun, and so on – can be carried in your camera bag along with the rest of your kit. It is simply a case of being prepared.

◄ **Tungsten light**
I had to photograph this shopkeeper in his specialist food shop in Provence, France. The shop was lit with tungsten light, but with just a little daylight entering through the window. I needed to use some fill-in flash on him and so I used a gel over the flash to balance it with the shop lights.

See also
▶ **pp 46–47** Holding the camera
▶ **pp 60–61** Effective flash
▶ **pp 94–97** Available light
▶ **pp 114–115** Black and white portraits
▶ **pp 138–139** Using fill-in flash
▶ **pp 256–257** Mixed lighting

▶ **Action shot**
To get this shot of the metal worker I had to use the camera on a tripod. This was necessary since the shutter speed required was 1/4th second and any faster would have meant that the sparks would have not come out. Flash was used to light him and care was required so that it did not flare on his visor.

▲ **Tea picker**
There are always lots of opportunities to photograph people at work when travelling. This tea picker in southern India was working so fast that her hands have blurred in the photograph. However, this brings across the frenetic nature of her working conditions.

High key and low key

◀ Children
Young children are well suited to high key photography. This two year old was lying on a roll of white colorama background paper. She was lit by a single soft box fitted to a flash head, and the point of focus was on her bright blue eyes.

High key pictures are those where the tonal range of the print is primarily at the light end of the scale. Conversely, low key photographs refer to those where the tonal range of the print are mainly at the dark end of the scale. High key photographs are not to be confused with high contrast prints, which have extremes of tones with very little in the mid-tone range. Low contrast prints have a narrow range of tones, which is probably due to under-exposure rather than a deliberate technique.

Normally a photograph is judged on its tonal range across the scale. In black and white photography this would include rich blacks, clean whites and a range of greys. However, this doesn't always produce striking photographs and the rules therefore need to be bent from time to time.

Softness and delicacy are the essence of high key pictures, and to achieve them you will find that a soft light is nearly always necessary. I use either a soft box or a beauty light with a diffuser, or project the light source through one or more layers of tracing paper. As an alternative to tracing paper,

◀ The figure
To light this shot two flash heads were directed at white reflectors and bounced back onto the model. Two lights on the white background made sure that the shot was kept white and soft, creating a totally high key picture.

▶ Make-up
This model's make-up was deliberately pale to match the white coat and hood she was wearing. The idea was to create a feeling of the winter's snow and cold. For this reason, the lighting was kept very soft and even with minimum shadow detail.

you could use a material like muslin, which is relatively inexpensive and can be used over and over again. Depending on the degree of softness that is required, either use a light on the hair or behind the head. You also need to over-light the white background slightly. However, you do not want to create flare so this needs to be done carefully. Then use a variety of reflectors to soften the shadows as much as possible. These will probably be white, although light gold or silver sometimes work well.

The opposite is true when you shoot low key pictures. Most photographers usually use black velvet for the background, as this gives a much richer black than the normal photographic black background paper in your final print. Try using directional lighting, which means putting a honeycomb grid over the light sources. This will control the degree of spill, but you could also

▶ **Multiple lights**
For this portrait I used one key light placed to the right of the camera and a reflector to the left to soften the shadows. Another light on a boom added body to the hair. This lighting set-up has resulted in a dynamic, masculine portrait and is a classic example of a low key picture.

use barn doors or a simple flag.
If you are shooting a portrait, begin
with one light, which you could place
behind the subject and to one side.
This creates what is known as a rim
light. Using reflectors, white boards
for a soft effect, or mirrors for a harsher
one, position them so you have the
detail in the shadow side. For deep
shadows, place a piece of black card
or a black board next to your subject to
absorb any stray light and stop it being
reflected back on to your subject.

Of course, there are situations where
you will use more than the one light,
but it is amazing what can be achieved
with just one light source and a couple
of reflectors and flags. It is also a good
exercise in observing how light works.

When calculating your exposure for
low key lighting, take the reading for
the highlight area of the shot. If you
take the reading for the part of the face
in deep shadow, your shot is likely to
come out over-exposed.

▲ **Reflected light**
This girl was lit by a single soft box positioned
slightly behind and to her left. I then used two
white boards to reflect light back into her face
but controlled the amount until I had achieved
the mood I was after. Although this is a low
key shot, there is nothing hard about the
finished picture.

▲ **Beauty dish**
For this shot I chose a high viewpoint and lit
this model in a similar way to the one pictured
on the left, but used a light called a beauty
dish. This gave a crisper effect than the soft
box and worked particularly well on the eyes.
A silver reflector was used to bounce light back
onto the face.

See also
▶ **pp 62–63** Selecting a viewpoint
▶ **pp 114–115** Black and white portraits
▶ **pp 116–117** Hair and make-up
▶ **pp 118–119** Studio lighting set-ups
▶ **pp 120–123** Further lighting techniques
▶ **pp 152–153** Close-ups

Wide-angle lenses in portraiture

Different lenses play an important role in creating striking portraits of people. While we might assume that the best portraits are taken with standard or telephoto lenses, it is surprising to find what can be done with a wide-angle lens.

When using these lenses in portraiture remember they can easily distort and create unflattering pictures. Full faces, huge noses or eyes that seem to pop out of their sockets might at first look funny but the joke will soon fade. Depth of field is greatly enhanced, so pay attention to background detail.

If you take a low viewpoint when using a wide-angle lens of a person standing they will appear to have much longer legs than in real life. For some people this can be flattering, but for others it could make them look anorexic. Conversely, if you shoot them from a high viewpoint, not only will they look short but their legs could look like stumps. However, with careful use some of these irregularities can be beneficial when creating a striking shot.

▲ Hands at work
Using wide-angle lenses in portraits can create problems by distorting people's faces. Here, I have avoided that, although the sculptor's hands do look large. However, they convey a sense of strength to him and his artwork.

▶ Viewpoint
A degree of moodiness was required when photographing this young man. His head is lit with strong side lighting, throwing one side of his face into deep shadow. A high viewpoint provides the focus on his eye, resulting in a slightly menacing look.

▲ Facial features
The 28mm wide-angle lens used to take this portrait has created a stunning shot. Care has to be taken when using such a wide-angle lens to make sure it does not distort facial features.

Take care not to cast your own shadow over your subject since you will probably be close to them. If using flash, check it has the spread for wide-angle lenses – some units only have coverage for 35mm and so if you are using a 28mm lens the light coverage will fall off at the sides of the frame. Also, when using flash close to the person's face the background may be unacceptably dark, as the power needed for the foreground will be much less than for further away. A lens hood or filter may cause vignetting. However, with its extreme angle of view, flare from the sun could enter the lens if you do not use a hood or sunshade. If shooting groups of people make sure they don't look as if they are standing miles away from the camera, with a lot of unwanted foreground detail in the picture.

▲ ▶ **Extreme wide-angle lenses**
I took this shot above with a 35mm lens but thought it looked too ordinary, so I positioned myself low on the ground and used a 17mm extreme wide-angle for the shot on the right, which makes a much more dynamic picture.

See also
▶ pp 26–27 Additional lenses
▶ pp 62–63 Selecting a viewpoint
▶ pp 82–85 Head and shoulder portraits
▶ pp 86–89 Full-length portraits

Telephoto lenses in portraiture

While a wide-angle lens can distort a face and make it look fuller, a telephoto lens can have the effect of compressing the picture. A favourite lens with many photographers, the medium telephoto lens is an absolute must not only for taking flattering head shots but full lengths as well.

The first asset of this lens is that when used at a wide aperture the background detail will be completely out of focus. This concentrates the eye on the subject and makes for a far more attractive portrait than if the background was in focus with distracting detail. Remember that with a longer telephoto lens, say 300 or 400mm, there is the risk of camera shake, especially at slow shutter speeds. If you are using one of these lenses at their widest apertures you will have the shutter set to a higher speed. This will help to eradicate camera shake, but it would still be best to have the camera on a tripod or monopod.

Another way of controlling the background is to frame your subject much tighter in the viewfinder than when using a wide-angle lens. Because there will be a distance between you and your subject, you will not have to worry about casting your own shadow over them. If using a reflector to bounce light back into their face, you can position this closer to them, as it will be cropped out by the tighter framing.

▼ **Framing your subject**
A professional photographer will often frame their subject to one side of the viewfinder. This is so that the photograph could run over two pages in a magazine or book. The girl would appear on the left with the blurred background on the right, with the type running over it.

This lens can also bring your subject closer to you. If you have posed your model in a landscape setting, they might be lost in the overall scene. By zooming in or using your telephoto lens you can bring them closer to your viewpoint without having to move position yourself. This will also have the effect of bringing the background closer. Remember that the further away your subject is from the camera, the less control you have over the depth of field and more will be sharp, both in front of and behind the point of sharp focus.

If using a zoom lens with a lens hood, make sure it adjusts for the focal range of the lens or vignetting could occur when using wider-angle focal lengths.

Filling the frame

Telephoto lenses are useful for bringing distant subjects closer. In the top picture, taken on a 50mm lens, it appears that the shot is of the tree. It is only on closer observation that we realize there is in fact a girl leaning against the tree trunk. Of course, we could have the picture selectively enlarged but that would increase the grain or noise and the result might not be very flattering. By using a 300mm telephoto lens (bottom photograph) the girl takes centre stage and there will be no need for such an extreme enlargement.

▲ Reducing depth of field
When taking portraits you want the centre of focus very much on your model. For this reason, telephoto lenses, with their short depth of field, are ideal as they can throw the background out of focus while retaining complete sharpness on your subject.

See also
▶ pp 26–27 Additional lenses
▶ pp 36–37 Processing film
▶ pp 82–85 Head and shoulder portraits
▶ pp 98–99 Backgrounds
▶ pp 262–263 Effective use of grain

▶ Relaxing your subject
To photograph this young boy I chose a 150mm lens. This enabled me to fill the frame with his face without having to go in so close that he might have felt uncomfortable. Keeping a distance between yourself and your subject is an excellent way to relax your subject.

Using reflectors

Often when photographing a person outdoors, the light is so bright that they cannot help screwing up their eyes or they squint so badly that the end result looks extremely unattractive. Another tricky lighting situation might be on an overcast day, where the light is low, and their skin tones look cold and flat. We can rectify these problems quite easily by using a reflector.

A reflector is any piece of material or surface that can be used to reflect light onto or at the subject of your photograph. This could be a purpose-made photographic reflector, which can be purchased at any well-stocked photographic dealer. These come in a variety of shapes and sizes. When not in use they fold up into a manageable size and are carried in a small pouch. Some come with an expanding frame over which the reflective material fits. The reflective material could be just single-sided and in white or silver, or double-sided such as gold on one side and white on the other. Having two different surfaces can be a real asset in many different situations. When using a large reflector, you will either need an assistant to hold it or have a stand handy to support it.

If your subject is posed with their back to the sun and their face in shadow, a reflector held slightly to one side of the camera will bounce the light back onto the face. If you use the white

▲ ▶ Even exposure
When photographing people wearing hats, it is almost inevitable that the brim of the hat will cause a shadow to fall across their face, as can be seen in the picture above. If we were to give more exposure, then the rest of the picture (his hat and shirt) would be over-exposed. By placing a small white reflector under the man's chin, enough light has been bounced back into his face to keep the exposure even.

side of the reflector the effect will be
a much cooler light than if the gold side
were used, which will bathe the skin in
a warm glow, giving the appearance
of a slight suntan.

Of course, it is not necessary to buy
a purpose-made reflector and you could
quite easily improvise by using any
object with a light surface, such as
paper or fabric. If you are taking a
close-in head shot, even the light
bouncing off a newspaper or the pages
of a book could act as a fill-in. These
tricks are useful if you find yourself
having to take a photograph without
a proper reflector to hand.

Remember that when it comes to
taking your exposure reading you
should go in close and read from the
person's skin, otherwise your shot
might be incorrectly exposed. Be
careful not to cast your own shadow
onto your subject and make sure that
when you take your reading the
reflector is in the same place as it will
be when you take the shot. The benefits
of using a reflector in this way are that
you can see the effect immediately and
adjust the intensity and direction of the
reflected light to your liking before
you take your photograph. The
important point to remember is that
you do not want the reflected light to
be so strong that it has the same effect
on your subject's eyes as you are
trying to correct.

See also
▶ pp 58–59 Exposure and auto-exposure
▶ pp 72–73 Against the light
▶ pp 82–85 Head and shoulder portraits
▶ pp 92–93 Lighting for outdoor portraits
▶ pp 94–97 Available light

▲ ▶ **Against the light**
Often when shooting against the light your subject will be in shadow, as can be seen in the top picture. By using a gold reflector just the right amount of light has been bounced back onto the girl's skin to give her an even glow.

Improvised reflectors

By lying down on the floor, I could look up into the face of this young girl lying on a sofa with the light coming in through a window behind her. I immediately realized I could use the book she was reading as a reflector to put more light back into her face rather than using a custom-made reflector or fill-in flash.

Another example of working with an improvised reflector is this photograph of a young girl who was playing in the garden and sitting on a white towel. Although the shot is back lit (you can see where the sun hits the top of her head), the towel reflects back a sufficient amount of light to balance the exposure.

Using fill-in flash

The difference between using fill-in flash and reflectors is that with reflectors you can immediately see the effect that they are having. With fill-in flash the result will not be apparent until you have checked on the camera's LCD or, worse, had your film processed. This is not necessarily a problem, as once you become more familiar with the technique you should be able to use this method with confidence on every occasion.

So why would you use flash on what appears to be a well lit sunny day? The main reason is that bright sun can cause unattractive shadows in the eyes and under the nose and chin. By using a small quantity of fill-in flash, these shadows will be eliminated and softened. Another situation for using this technique is when the person you are photographing is in shadow but the background is in bright sun and you want to retain the detail of the background. If you expose for the background, the person will be under-exposed and come out as a silhouette. On the other hand, if you expose for them the background will be over-exposed and the detail burnt out.

The secret of using fill-in flash is to use the flash at a slightly different setting to the one manufacturers advise.

◀ ▼ **Against the light**
I wanted a different angle for this shot of a team of young footballers so I lay on the ground and looked up at them. This meant shooting against the light, in this case a bright sky, and it was inevitable that their faces would come out under-exposed (left). By using fill-in flash (below) I have retained the colour of the sky and all their faces are correctly exposed.

Even dedicated flashguns that calculate the amount of flash required for any given shot will need to be overridden. The reason is that they will balance the flash perfectly to the daylight, and the result will look slightly artificial.

Imagine that the daylight reading is 1/60th at f11. However, our subject has dark shadows under the eyes and nose. The camera is set to this exposure but we need to set the flash to give half (1:2 ratio) of this exposure or even a quarter (1:4 ratio). This would mean that the flash would be set to give an exposure of 1/60th at f8 or f5.6 respectively. In other words, less flash output than the daylight. The shot is then taken at 1/60th at f11 and at this combination the background will be perfectly exposed and the amount of flash falling on our subject will be just enough to soften these shadows and make for a more flattering portrait.

If you are using a camera with built-in flash it may not be possible to do this and you will have to rely on the camera's fill-in flash mode if it has one. This might emit too much flash power and make the shot over-lit. With a separate flashgun you should be able to adjust the power of the flash manually or adjust its compensation control. When shooting digitally you will be able to check the LCD to ascertain the correct amount of fill-in flash.

Because daylight continually changes it is impossible to say exactly what the combination should be and only practice will perfect this.

See also

▲ Getting the right balance
In these two shots the sun was directly behind the model. I could have used a reflector to bounce light back onto her but decided to use fill-in flash. In the shot on the left it is quite clear that the side of her body facing the camera is in shadow. By using the flash as a fill-in this shadow has been eliminated. However, the flash is just a little too strong and there is now a certain artificiality about the shot. It will take practice to perfect the technique of using fill-in flash.

Fill-in flash

If your subject is wearing a hat or another object is obscuring their face, such as the board this surfer is carrying, it is likely that it will cause a line of shadow to fall across their face (above left). The simplest way of correcting this is to use a certain amount of fill-in flash. In the shot on the left the board is causing the surfer's face and body to be in shadow. By using flash, set at two stops lower than the normal setting, just the right level of light has been directed at the subject (above right). This has eliminated the shadows while the exposure for the background remains perfect.

Tone, texture and form

Ever since people started drawing, the human body has received more attention than any other subject. With the invention of photography, capturing the beauty of the human form proved a similar obsession.

Before you embark on this type of photography, consider what style of nude pictures you want to achieve. As well as studying other photographers' work, it will be useful to look at the work of painters. Even the most abstract or expressionistic painting can lend ideas for light and line, texture, tone and form. Don't be afraid to copy poses and angles used by other photographers. Some that look graceful, sensual and simple are often difficult to achieve and only experience will help you get it right.

There are no rules about what type of equipment is best for photographing the nude body. The best answer is to use what you are familiar with. If you are shooting digitally you will have all the benefits of being able to review your shots as the session progresses. This can give you a great advantage over film, as you will be able to show and discuss with your model areas such as posing. This should ensure that you get the desired result. Having said that, film, too, is important in nude photography. Fine grain medium black and white films, carefully processed in specialist developers, will produce beautiful prints with a wide range of tones. This type of exhibition printing can in itself add to the sensuality of the final image. However, if you choose a fast black and white film and push process it to enhance the grain, the result will be a completely different style of eroticism and sensation. Colour will add yet another dimension but strangely enough, considering that we live in a world made up of colours, it can be more difficult to work with when trying to convey an image of eroticism than with black and white.

▲ ▶ **Light and form**
Light plays a crucial part in defining the shape of the nude body and can be used in its own right to create interesting shapes. For both these shots the model was lit from the side by a single light. When she is in the corner of the room her body casts a shadow onto the wall, creating a pleasing silhouette. When I moved her to the centre of the room, the shadow is far more gentle, leaving the eye to concentrate on the sensuous curves of her body.

◀ **Wide-angle lenses**
In this shot I asked the model to lie on the floor and I chose a low viewpoint. By using a wide-angle lens I have elongated her body but the effect works. By posing her thigh and arm at the same angle, a shot of strong sculptural lines has been created.

What is of greater consideration than the actual camera equipment is the quality of the light you intend to take your shots in. Whether it is artificial or daylight, the way you control it will determine whether your pictures are striking or mediocre. With artificial light, such as a single studio flash unit, you will be able to achieve a huge variety of effects. A single light placed almost directly behind your model will draw the most revealing line along the contours of their body. Brought further round to the camera, so the light is almost directly to one side of your model, will produce strong shadows. With careful positioning, strong directional light will emphasize a variety of different body areas, from a woman's breasts to a male model's toned stomach. Brought further round so that it is close to the camera and directed through a diffuser, an almost shadowless soft light will result. When printed as a high key picture, the result could be a highly romanticized image of sensuality.

Posing your models and positioning them into the sculptural shapes that will look erotic in your final prints is an area where experience will really count. Also it is the rapport between photographer and model that is so important here. It can be the model's input as much as the photographer's that can keep the momentum going on a shoot. Finding a good model with whom you can work with in this way will really help in developing your style of erotic photography. Once your images have been downloaded into the computer, all manner of manipulations, retouching and printing techniques will be possible; however, getting what you want in camera is still the most important factor.

◀ **Strong light**
When photographing this male model I used a single light with a beauty dish coming at right angles to the camera. The light was flagged so that it did not spill onto the white background and a large silver reflector was used to throw light back into the shadows.

See also
▶ **pp 114–115** Black and white portraits

▶ **pp 120–123** Further lighting techniques

▶ **pp 128–131** High key and low key

▶ **pp 262–263** Effective use of grain

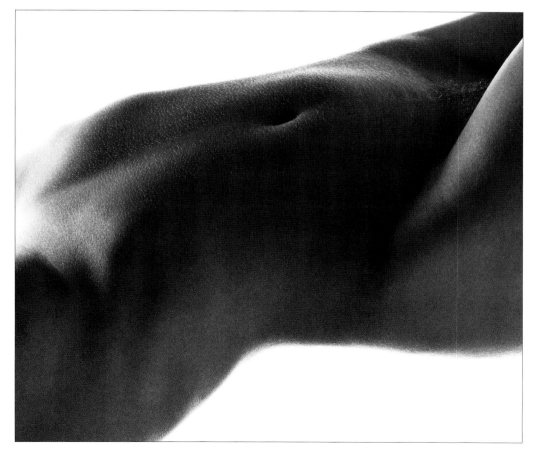

▲ Two rear lights
For this full length study I lit the model with two lights coming from behind. Although I used a reflector to bounce light back, I kept this to a minimum so that I retained some of the shadow detail on her body.

◄ Changing the angle
When I photographed this girl, she was standing up and stretching her arms upwards. Although it made a pleasing shot, I felt it was enhanced by printing it as though she was on her side. Always look for new ways of presenting your work.

The body indoors

When photographing the naked or semi-naked body indoors, attention to lighting, composition and pose are paramount, as well as many other details that are easy to overlook if you have not had much experience with this area of photography.

Having chosen your model, it is important that they are fully aware of the type of pictures that you have in mind. This is applicable to both female and male models. One reason for this is that you do not want them to wear any type of tight clothing that will leave marks on the body. This will include most underwear and anything that is elasticated, such as jogging bottoms, watchstraps and tight belts. The last

thing you want is to have to wait hours for these marks to fade. It might seem a small point, but a wide elastic mark around the waist of a perfectly toned body will look extremely unattractive. Some blemishes can be hidden with foundation or camouflage cream, but even this can be time-consuming and not necessarily effective.

Another important point to bear in mind is body make-up, such as fake tan. Lots of people wear this and think it gives them a healthy glow, but if it is not applied properly it can look streaky and extremely unnatural. If this is the case, it could take some time to remove and could even leave blemishes on the body. It would be far better to use

▶ **Simplicity of pose**
It is sometimes the most simple of shots that gives the best results. I was photographing this girl on a bed using just the daylight coming in through the window. A low angle has given the feeling of an intimate shot while her pose makes her look relaxed.

a gold-coloured reflector to give a warmer light and the appearance of a tanned body. If you are using available light you should always make sure you have a variety of different reflectors as a matter of course.

Make sure that the room you are shooting in is warm so goose bumps don't appear on your model. Create a calm, unflustered atmosphere and, above all, handle your camera equipment confidently. The more professional you appear, the more your model will grow in confidence, which will lead to establishing the rapport between the two of you that is essential for these types of shots to be successful.

When posing your model, look out for any unattractive folds and creases in the skin. Try to find original angles and if you are using a wide-angle lens, look carefully at what it does to the body shape. This does not mean that you should avoid any distortion as these can be made to work in a creative way.

Experimenting with ISO

Having posed and lit your model, many people might think that there is nothing else that can be done. In certain cases this could be true but it is surprising just how many variations can be found that will enable you to change the feel of a shot. In the photograph on the left I had posed the

model against a brick wall and lit her with flash balanced for 5,200 K. In the shot on the right, to try something different I re-set the ISO to 3,400 K, which would be the setting for tungsten light. This has resulted in a blue cast, which gives a steel-like appearance to the finished photograph.

See also
▶ **pp 34–35** Film
▶ **pp 86–89** Full-length portraits
▶ **pp 94–97** Available light
▶ **pp 134–135** Telephoto lenses in portraiture
▶ **pp 136–137** Using reflectors
▶ **pp 292–295** Digital toning and lith

▶ A different angle

I was photographing this girl indoors when I suddenly saw her from the top of the stairs as I looked over the banisters. I used a 150mm lens so that she fills the frame and eliminates a lot of unwanted floor area. Always be on the lookout for a new and different angle.

◀ Against the light

I photographed this girl against the large windows of a loft apartment. I placed two large white polystyrene reflectors on each side of the camera so that they bounced light back onto her. The result is a soft and natural looking shot, using the minimum amount of equipment.

The body outdoors

All the things that apply to photographing the body indoors are just as applicable to shooting outdoors, but also bear in mind the time of year and where you propose to take your shots. It is not a good idea to do a shoot in a well-known beauty spot during school holidays when there are likely to be prying eyes watching every move you make. Remember that in some countries taking pictures of this nature is not seen as art, but an affront to morality. It can't be emphasized enough that care needs to be taken and you should always respect another country's traditions, especially when it comes to morality and religion.

Before the session, have a good idea of the style of photographs you want to achieve. This avoids your model waiting around and turning an unattractive shade of blue in what might be the freezing cold. Take tear sheets along to help explain what you are looking for. Taking your time and perfecting a particular pose will be far more productive than trying to get as many different positions as you can. As you become more experienced your shooting rate will increase, as will your ability to create new poses.

Try to make the shots look convincing. If in an area of rocks, for example, that take on sculptural forms, can you place your model amongst them so that they too will echo these forms? Observe what happens to your model's body when they curl up in an embryonic position. Does their backbone become prominent and sculpted? Can you keep this shape in the foreground of your shot while the rocky terrain stretches out in the background? Perhaps a low viewpoint will help by increasing the monumental appearance of their pose. This is particularly true of the male form. If you are near water, can this be used to emphasize texture when it comes into contact with the skin? This might look particularly striking with back lighting. Remember that part of the body might work better than the whole, so don't be afraid to go in close.

See also
▶ **pp 18–21** Film and DSLR cameras
▶ **pp 66–67** Perspective
▶ **pp 92–93** Lighting for outdoor portraits
▶ **pp 98–99** Backgrounds
▶ **pp 132–133** Wide-angle lenses in portraiture

▲ **Low viewpoint**
Taking a low angle and including the parasol has created an interesting shot, conveying the feeling of heat and light. Her tanned body and pink bikini contrast well with the blue sky.

▶ **Strong light**
Taking advantage of strong sunlight has resulted in creating interesting shadows on this model's skin. The white pillar she is leaning against helps with the composition and contrasts well with the curves of her body.

▲ **Perspective**
A low viewpoint has helped to exaggerate the perspective in this shot by making the rock strata appear to flow away from the camera. A 24mm wide-angle lens has also added to this effect by making the body look as though it is moving against the rock.

▼ ▶ Black and white or colour?
Viewed in isolation, both shots work well. In the colour version the model's body blends well with the colour of the rocks. However, in the black and white shot his muscle tone looks far more defined and he has a sculptural appearance. Shot digitally it is easy to view both versions and select the one you prefer prior to printing. If using colour film, you can make a black and white print or scan the transparency or negative to produce a black and white print.

More than one model

The great thing about having more than one model when you are taking nude photographs is that it gives you far more scope for sculptural and monumental potential. The idea of interlocking and intertwining bodies conjures up all sorts of possibilities that would not be possible if you were working with just one person.

Nature itself echoes many of these forms and the observant photographer will always be on the lookout for such references. It is a good idea always to carry a simple point-and-shoot camera that you can use as a notebook. For example, you might be on a walk and notice the shapes formed by the twisted branches of a tree or its roots pushing through the ground. Even the most basic shot of details like these will be a future reminder of how you saw them

and how you can put these shapes to use in a future shoot. In a sense this is no different than how any other artist works. Most painters and sculptors keep these visual notebooks to which they refer at a later date. A visit to any major exhibition by an internationally respected artist will include this reference material. It is a good habit to get into and you will be surprised at how useful the discipline is. You might even get a worthwhile shot in its own right from this way of working.

It goes without saying that your models should feel comfortable and at ease working together when doing this type of photography. If they are going to embrace one another and have their naked limbs intertwined, you want them to look relaxed with one another rather than inhibited. This is equally

▲ **Glass doors**
This shot was entirely backlit with the light coming from some full length glass doors. I used two large reflectors placed either side of the camera to fill-in the shadow areas.

▶ **Soap patterns**
By photographing this couple in the shower I have used the suds created by the soap to form an interesting pattern on their skin. I used available light with one large reflector.

▲ **Against the light**
These two models were photographed against the light so they were in shadow. It only required a small reflector placed near to the camera to bounce light back onto them and keep the exposure within an even latitude.

true whether you are using two models of the opposite sex or of the same sex. For this reason it is probably best that they know one another well, perhaps be in a relationship, or that this type of modelling is something they have done professionally.

If you are shooting outdoors and the sun is bright, pay careful attention to how the shadow of one model falls on the other. It might look fine to the naked eye but on film, especially colour

which has less latitude, the end result might look ugly and intrusive.

If you are using available light outside, you might be working with the lens set at its widest aperture. If this is the case, try to put this to good use with differential focusing. A feature of one body focused pin sharp can look very effective against the backdrop of another body, especially when it is slightly out of focus and has taken an amorphous form.

See also

▶ pp 62–63 Selecting a viewpoint
▶ pp 66–67 Perspective
▶ pp 92–93 Lighting for outdoor portraits
▶ pp 132–133 Wide-angle lenses in portraiture
▶ pp 136–137 Using reflectors
▶ pp 146–147 The body outdoors

◀ **Big foot**
In this shot I focused on their feet as their bodies recede into the background, and the intertwining limbs lend a sense of eroticism to the picture. I used a 45mm lens. Any wider and their bodies would have looked unnaturally 'stretched'.

Using props

A ny item that we deliberately include in our photographs that aids the overall composition and final look of the picture could be classified as a prop. This could be as simple as a hat or a more complicated arrangement of items that tell us something about the person we are photographing. These could be to do with the person's work or their home. Another way we may use a prop is to give the person that we are photographing something to hold. This will make them appear more relaxed and natural in front of the camera.

Many professional photographers have what are known as prop stores or cupboards in their studios. The area of photography they specialize in will determine what is kept in such a store. For instance, a food photographer might have a variety of crockery and cutlery as well as tablecloths and napkins, saucepans and kitchen utensils, whereas a photographer who shoots glamour might have a variety of shoes and swimming costumes, lingerie and hairpieces. In the course of a shoot it might just be that the very item the photographer already has in their store is the perfect prop for a particular shot. This can be the case even when a photographic stylist has been hired to

find all the items required for that particular day's shooting.

Photographers will often be on the lookout for props and some of them might be found items rather than purchased from a shop. For instance, a walk on the beach might uncover the most amazing piece of weathered driftwood. Depending on its size, it could be used for a model to recline on, or to support food items in a still life photograph. Material or fabric shops are another source of props. It is amazing what remnants of fabric can be used for, from draping around a model to using as an entire background.

Making the most of props

Many amateur photographers think they are incapable of creating professional-looking pictures because they do not have a large studio with lots of lights and a vast array of backgrounds or scenic artists to create them. While it might be true that some shots are created in this way, others can be taken with the bare minimum of props and lighting. Here, a backdrop was

painted onto a small piece of canvas to represent foliage and a few leaves were scattered over the floor. A single beauty dish on a boom was positioned behind the model while a single reflector was placed to the left of the camera to bounce light back. Once the unwanted detail has been cropped out of the frame, who is to know exactly how it was shot?

▲ **Old rope**
Not all shots are planned in advance. When I was shooting this model on a beach I felt the shot needed a prop. Looking around, I found this piece of old rope that had been weathered by the sea which I thought fitted perfectly with the pose and surroundings.

Once you become observant in this way, it is amazing what you start acquiring, often with no specific use in mind other than one day maybe you will use something you have had for a considerable time.

Many photographers find it difficult to throw any of these items away, even when they might have fallen out of fashion. This is especially true with clothes and accessories. But if you think about it, today's fashion is tomorrow's period piece and in that context all the items for a very good retro shot might be languishing in a photographer's prop cupboard right now.

See also
▶ pp 82–85 Head and shoulder portraits
▶ pp 98–99 Backgrounds
▶ pp 120–123 Further lighting techniques
▶ pp 136–137 Using reflectors
▶ pp 240–241 Ring flash

◀ **Simple props**
The idea here was to make the girl look as though she was defying the realms of probability by being able to hold up this rigid steel beam. It is in fact made of plywood and has been painted to look like the real thing. Many effective props like this are relatively easy to make.

Close-ups

The body lends itself to close-up photography brilliantly. There is hardly a feature of the human form that does not look effective when shot close in and certain areas of the body can take on an almost abstract or sculptural feel.

If using a macro lens or extension tubes, when in close make sure you do not cast your own shadow or that of the camera over the area you are shooting. This is easy to do at these distances and could ruin a potentially great shot. When using extension tubes you will need to give an increase to the exposure. This is because the light has further to travel when it enters the lens to the film plane. If your camera has TTL this will not be a problem. If it doesn't you will have to gain experience by trial and error to know what the compensation factor should be. In any case it is always

best to bracket your shots, as a few frames wasted here or there is far better than losing the shot entirely.

Another aspect of close-up photography that you will need to pay attention to is camera shake. Because depth of field at these distances is going to be minimal, you will probably use a small aperture. This will mean a slower than average shutter speed, which could lead to camera shake and therefore blurred pictures. Try to support the camera on a tripod and use a cable release. Of course, if you do use a wide aperture, the background will fall off quite dramatically. This could create a great abstract picture so do be open to a variety of exposure and focusing modes.

An important point to remember with this type of photography is that when you are in as close as this, every

little blemish and spot will show up. You are not photographing for a medical journal so look carefully before you shoot. Remember that with an SLR you are seeing the shot through the viewfinder at wide open. When you take your picture the camera will stop down and more of the shot will be in focus. This is why it is important to use the camera's depth of field preview mode to see how the shot will come out and whether anything unsightly is going to be in focus.

See also

▶ **pp 18–21** Film and DSLR cameras
▶ **pp 28–29** Accessories
▶ **pp 50–51** The viewfinder and auto-focus
▶ **pp 234–235** Extension tubes and bellows
▶ **pp 268–269** Slow sync flash

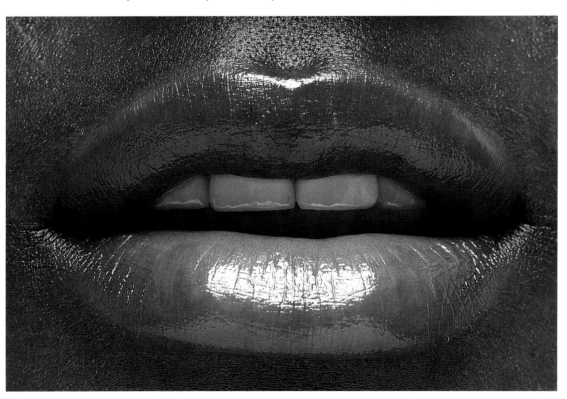

◀ **Extension tubes**
To get this close will require extension tubes. The lens was 150mm (6in) from the lips and stopped down to f22. A single flash head above and a white reflector under the chin provided all the light needed for this shot of perfect lips.

▶ **Slow sync flash**
Here, slow sync flash was used. The shutter was set at 1/15th second and the aperture at f11. This meant there was some movement of the camera and this has been recorded with the available ambient light. The result is a very sensuous close-up.

Travel Photography

Today travel is as commonplace as it is varied. Whether it is to a foreign country for a holiday or business purposes, or to another region of our own country, we now travel further than ever before. As well as different physical features or architectural styles, there is also the difference in climate that travel brings. This gives us unprecedented photographic opportunities to record what we see and find, not only for our own memories but also to relate to others and, perhaps, create an historical document for future generations.

Spring

Spring provides an abundance of subjects to photograph and the light can be bright and crisp without the haze of a hot summer's day. However, what looks photogenic one day can wilt and fade by the next. To capture it at its best means careful planning, precise timing and a dependency on the weather. If you are familiar with an area and know roughly when the first flowers bloom, plan to photograph them as early in the season as you can or if you know someone in the vicinity, ask them to keep you posted on the progress of the scene.

Try to be in position before the sun is up, partly because there are few people around, but mainly because the low morning sun filters through the trees, creating dappled light or casting long, interesting shadows. The sun often rises rapidly and in 20 minutes the quality and feel of the light can alter dramatically and the scene that first attracted you is now a pale image of its former self.

Another reason for an early start is detail. Excellent shots can be taken with a macro lens, enabling you to go in close on flowers covered in dew or a spider's web spun from one flower to another. At this time of the morning the wind can be virtually non-existent. This is excellent for long shutter speeds, as any movement in your subject will create blur.

See also

▲ Foreground interest
Wild flowers burst upon the landscape in spring in a profusion of colour, shown here in the Alps of northern Italy. Pointing the camera downwards and cropping out an uninteresting sky emphasizes the foreground and puts the focus of interest firmly on the flowers.

◀ Close ups
Flowers are at their freshest in spring, so it is worth going in close. Choose a macro lens or fit an extension tube between the camera and lens. Pay attention to the background since unwanted detail will ruin the shot. Here, the sky contrasts perfectly with the yellow broom.

▶ Wide-angle lenses
Another approach to emphasize flowers is to use a wide-angle lens. Here, a 21mm ultra wide-angle lens combined with a low viewpoint has made the flowers appear to flow away from the camera, creating a great sense of perspective.

Summer

The problem with taking pictures in summer is when the sun becomes so hot that a heat haze builds up, making photographs of landscapes look flat and dull. Even in early morning, if the weather has been like this for a while, there can be an annoying haze, often not lifting until a thunderstorm and rain clear the air. However, this should not deter the observant photographer as many photographic opportunities occur in midsummer that do not happen in other seasons.

For example, lavender is at its peak from June to mid August in the south of France. These plants, although cultivated, stretch in great swathes though the Provençal landscape. They can be shot either from a low viewpoint so the delicate detail of the flower can be seen in close up with the rest of the field sweeping into the background, or from a higher viewpoint so the furrows enhance the photographic perspective and the vivid lavender colour can be seen against a radiant blue sky. Look out for similar occurrences with other plants and flora around the world.

If the weather is clear, a polarising filter will darken a blue sky and help white clouds to stand out brilliantly from it. Remember that it is best to shoot mid morning to get the most from this filter. At midday, when the sun is at its highest, the effect of the polarising filter will be minimal or non-existent. This filter also helps to give a vivid blue hue to seas.

Look out for changes in the sky when storms occur. These can often act as a dramatic backdrop, dark and foreboding, when set against a brilliantly sunlit foreground. If haze is a problem, look at the scene in a different way. For instance, can you go in close and make a feature of detail? Crop tightly. Don't be afraid to use the telephoto or zoom lens. If the area is in your locality, can you photograph it in all four seasons to show the differences that take place throughout the year? The summer is a time of year when there is a lot of rural activity. Be on the lookout for it – a field of golden wheat can soon become a field of stubble if you don't act quickly.

▲ Using the background
Choosing a slightly high viewpoint and cutting out the sky has resulted in these poppies almost filling the background. A wide aperture has lessened the depth of field and, together with careful framing, has put the emphasis firmly on the beehive, bringing it immediately to the eyes' attention.

▶ Low viewpoint
Use the natural contours of the land to frame your photo, such as in this undulating field. A 150mm medium telephoto lens has helped to compress the field of lavender and a low viewpoint has emphasized the perspective of the hillside in the background.

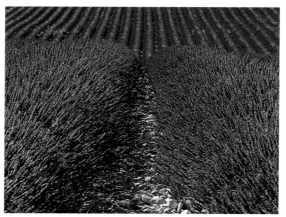

See also

▶ Emphasizing the sky

Summer is the season of blue skies and the
best way to emphasize them is to use a
polarising filter. This will also enhance the
colour of the sea and bring out a greater range
of hues. Remember to increase the exposure
when using this filter.

▼ Speed of thought

Summer skies can quickly become stormy
with dark thunder clouds. Here, they make a
dramatic backdrop to the church bathed in
foreground sunlight. Speed is of the essence in
these situations, as the light can quickly change
and the dramatic quality of the shot lost.

Autumn

The autumn is a season rich in colour. However, it is probably the shortest of the seasons when it comes to taking photographs. It can also be made shorter still by natural forces such as the weather. If the summer has been very wet, this can stop the leaves from turning colour in their full glory until they are actually about to drop, and a couple of days of high winds can quickly strip a tree of all but the most stubborn foliage.

For these reasons the photographer needs to be alert and get the shots as soon as the possibilities present themselves. If the weather gets better, you can always take more and perhaps improve on what you have already shot. However, if it doesn't you could end up without any shots at all and then you would have to wait until the next season to capture the scenes.

The colours of autumnal trees look brilliant, especially if you can contrast them against one another. For instance, a tree whose leaves have turned gold can look beautiful when photographed against a backdrop of evergreens. You might want to consider using a telephoto lens in this situation. If there is sufficient distance between the main tree and the background and you use a wide aperture, it might be possible to throw the background out of focus. This would result in blurred but muted colours, which would then frame the main tree. Another opportunity to keep an eye open for is a group of trees that have changed to provide leaf colours which contrast with each other, such as copper against golden or brown against red.

▲ **Colour contrast**
The intensity of autumnal colours contrast well with one another. It is best to catch them while you can, as the season passes rapidly. Here, the different coloured leaves are highlighted against a radiantly clear and crisp blue sky while the church makes a perfect backdrop.

▲ Perspective

These lavender plants make as striking a shot as when they are in full summer bloom. The low autumn light has helped to bring out the rich autumn hue and the furrows, which are in deep shadow, lead the eye straight into the picture. The blue sky makes a perfect contrast.

Besides these types of shots, be on the lookout for details. As well as leaves on branches, you might find potential shots at your feet. Often these can make great close-up pictures. Not only can you shoot them where you find them but also it may be beneficial to gather them up and take them indoors to photograph as a still life. You will be able to arrange them as you want and without worrying that the wind will blow them away. You might also consider backlighting them. In this case you will see all the veins and membranes that run through the leaf. This is especially true of leaves that are slightly weathered. Another idea you might want to try is to spray them with water to give the impression of early morning dew or rain.

▶ Telephoto lens

By using a medium telephoto lens, much of the uninteresting foreground has been cut out of this shot. Nothing destroys a shot more than including too much in the frame. Here, the point of interest is the bank of trees and their changing colours.

▶ Isolating detail

Autumn leaves make great subjects for detail shots. Whether it is just one leaf or several, such as the case here, always be on the lookout for an interesting pattern. Although the top leaf is only just beginning to turn, it makes a great contrast to those it has fallen on.

See also

Winter

Winter is a great season for photographers but it is full of potential pitfalls that are easy to avoid if you know how your equipment reacts in certain situations. Cameras do not automatically override what their auto-focus and internal exposure meters tell them to do. Even the most sophisticated models can give false readings.

Imagine a landscape covered with fresh snow and a blue sky contrasting with the white foreground. When we point our camera to the horizon the auto-focus cannot work if the sensor or focusing point in the viewfinder is on the sky. It cannot focus because of the lack of detail and if the sensor is on the snow it cannot focus there for the same reason. You have two options – either turn off the camera's auto-focus and

▲ Exposure
With so many white, shiny surfaces to reflect light, exposure can be tricky in snowy conditions, especially if the camera has built-in metering. The exposure meter can think there is more light than there is and under-expose your shots.

▶ Low light
Even in the late afternoon winter sun, evocative pictures of landscapes covered in snow can be taken. This picture required a tripod, as the shutter speed was 1/8th second.

focus manually, or find an area of detail in your shot and move the focusing sensor over it so the camera can focus on this detail. Using auto-focus lock, recompose your picture and take the shot.

Because snow reflects so much light it can fool the camera's exposure metering system into thinking there is more light than there actually is. If you point the camera at a snow-covered landscape with trees to one side of the frame, the trees could come out under-exposed since the meter has read for the highlights, which are the most prominent, and under-exposed for the shadows, or the trees. Find an area of mid-tones and take your reading off that. The alternative is to bracket your exposures so you can choose the best one for your final print.

See also

▶ **pp 28–29** Accessories
▶ **pp 52–53** Shutter speed
▶ **pp 58–59** Exposure and auto-exposure
▶ **pp 234–235** Extension tubes and bellows
▶ **pp 242–243** Specialist filters

▶ **Shadow detail**
Sunshine creates shadow detail, which adds vibrancy to your shot. Blue skies, enhanced by a polarising filter, make a wonderful backdrop to what might be a monochromatic picture.

Frosty details

Besides the big landscape shot, snow provides many opportunities for going in close and getting pictures of detail. You need to be quick with pictures like this because as soon as the sun comes out the snow and ice will start to melt. In certain circumstances this might work to your advantage. For instance, the picture far right is the result of the snow melting on the previous day. This re-froze overnight and formed these great icicles.

The weather

▲ Patterns
Often what is at your feet is just as interesting as what is in front of you. On a cold day I kept noticing the leaves on the ground and the frost seemed to emphasize their features. By taking a series of shots of different leaves and mounting them together in a block, an interesting arrangement has been formed.

See also
▶ pp 56–57 Light and colour
▶ pp 66–67 Perspective
▶ pp 70–71 Selecting a background
▶ pp 162–163 Winter
▶ pp 170–171 Seas and oceans
▶ pp 194–195 Time of day

Except for in some equatorial areas, the one thing that most of us can depend on are changes in our weather patterns. Although it would seem essential that the best photographs are taken in bright sunshine, there are many opportunities for great pictures in rain and fog or mist, snow and frost. Many of these opportunities will happen without warning and it is yet another reason for carrying a camera with you at all times.

Although it is difficult to take pictures in pouring rain, there are other aspects of wet weather that you can take advantage of. For example, distant clouds, where you can clearly see rain falling, can look dramatic if caught in the right light. You might need a telephoto for this type of shot if the rain clouds are some way in the distance. On the other hand, if the rainstorm is nearer, a wide-angle lens used from a low viewpoint to make the sky more prominent can be equally dramatic.

Once the rain has stopped look for puddles or flooded areas that might make for interesting reflections. Circumnavigate these and look at them carefully. It is surprising that just a step backwards or forwards can make all the difference to the reflection and how much you see of it. The same is true from the height you look at the reflection. Remember that with pictures of reflections you need to focus on the reflection and not on the top of the water. If you do the latter then it is possible that the main point of interest in your shot will appear out of focus. This could be easily done with an auto-focus camera, as the sensor could focus

▶ Snow

Snow is at its best shortly after it has fallen and, hopefully, when the sun is shining. Here in Oregon, USA, the shot is almost monochromatic, especially with the wet black tarmac cutting a swathe through the landscape.

on something like a leaf or twig floating on the top of the puddle.

Unless the mist and fog are particularly thick, you could get some very atmospheric pictures in these conditions. Again, auto-focus cameras may have trouble focusing in these conditions and you might have to use the manual focusing setting. The light is probably going to be quite low in these circumstances and having a tripod will be an asset.

Snow is obviously photogenic, but frost is an equally good subject. The art here is to shoot early in the morning before it starts to melt, which if the sky is clear the sun will do quite quickly. Look for close-ups, particularly of leaves with frost-fringed edges.

▲ Rainbows

You need to be quick to get a good shot of a rainbow. This one formed a perfect arc over the Giant's Causeway in Northern Ireland and happened while I was getting ready to photograph the sunset.

▶ Frost

I had arrived at a restaurant in Provence, France, early in the morning to photograph food, but saw this frosty, misty scene. Within minutes the frost had melted.

Emphasizing the sky

When photographing landscapes or seascapes the picture often does not live up to the reality. We see a wonderful cloud formation or a radiant blue sky, yet on film the clouds are lost and bleached out or the blue sky becomes a pale and hazy hue of the vista we remember seeing. The main reason for this is that the difference in exposure for the sky and the rest of the picture can be considerable. The trouble with most cameras that have built-in meters or are 'automatic' is that they will take an average reading. This means that you end up with a sky that has lost its drama and a foreground that is too dark for you to see any detail.

◀ Shooting in evening light

Late evening light can produce wonderfully coloured skies that can be more subtle than a full sunset. In this case, the purple hue of the upper sky reflects well in the shallow water of the ebb tide. The low sun has also helped to create strong shadow detail in the exposed sand and cliffs. I used a graduated neutral density filter, which helped to even up the difference in the exposure of the sky and the foreground by cutting down the amount of light entering the camera from the sky portion of the picture. This filter is best used with an SLR camera where you can see the effect through the viewfinder. Of course, there is nothing to stop you combining a polarising filter together with a graduated neutral density filter for a really dramatic effect.

▲ Choosing camera angle
I was driving through a storm in Provence, France, when a sudden break in the clouds allowed the sun to come out and reveal this huge cloud formation. I angled the camera upwards to take full advantage of the sky and cropped the foreground to about one third of the picture.

▲ Using a polarising filter
I knew I would lose some detail in the clouds because the sky was so bright, so I used a polarising filter over the lens to bring out their detail. This also had the effect of making the sky appear bluer and the true drama of the scene has been captured.

See also
▶ **pp 18–21** Film and DSLR cameras
▶ **pp 28–29** Accessories
▶ **pp 34–35** Film
▶ **pp 58–59** Exposure and auto-exposure
▶ **pp 242–243** Specialist filters

The best accessories for emphasizing the detail in the sky are a polarising filter and a graduated neutral density filter. A polarising filter will help to turn the blue of the sky darker while retaining the detail in the clouds. When using polarising filters you will have to increase the exposure by about 1½ stops. This may mean you have to use a tripod or support if you want your picture to be pin sharp. If using black and white film, a yellow filter will also help to bring out the cloud detail. However, if you use this filter with colour film the whole picture will have a yellow cast. A graduated neutral density filter will help to even up the difference in the exposure of the sky and the foreground by cutting down the amount of light entering the camera from the sky portion of the picture. This filter is best used with an SLR camera where you can see the effect through the viewfinder. And, of course, there is nothing to stop you combining a polarising filter together with a graduated neutral density filter for a really dramatic effect.

▲ **Special filter**
While this was not a very bright day, I have kept detail in the sky by using a graduated neutral density filter over the camera lens. This has balanced the sky with its reflection in the water and increased the feeling of isolation.

The changing day

Daylight changes rapidly, as you can see by watching a speeded-up film of any outdoor view shot from the same spot, from just before dawn to just after sunset. The differences in the shadow patterns and the changing colour hues as the sun rises and sets are astounding.

It is at dawn and dusk that these changes are at their extremes, with skies seeming to alter their colours by the minute. These changes need equally rapid thinking on the part of the photographer if they are to take full advantage of the different colours. No two days are the same and a sunrise lost today may not look the same tomorrow. Taking this into account, it will often be necessary to get up before the sun has actually risen as it is at this time that the colours of the sky change subtly.

Only if you live in an area where the weather is reasonably predictable, such as the Mediterranean region during the summer months or the west coast of California, can you plan ahead with some confidence. In more northern countries, a clear and haze-free dawn one morning might be followed by a misty and murky one the next. However, even this type of light can be appropriate in certain situations, which goes to show that there are no hard and fast rules. Many of the most memorable and evocative shots have been taken in the most adverse conditions.

After the sun has set, the sky goes through its most volatile changes. Again, what might be an orange or red sunset today might be a much cooler one, in terms of colour, tomorrow.

When photographing sunrise and sunset, a tripod and cable release will

Early morning

Light changes most noticeably in the morning and early evening. At these times you need to be in position and ready to take your shot because the light won't wait. These two pictures, both shot at dawn, show how quickly this happens. In the top picture, dawn has broken but the sun has yet to break over the horizon. The landscape looks flat and the moon is still visible. Minutes later the sun has risen and bathes the mountains in a warm glow. Not long after this, the sun had rapidly climbed higher into the sky and the scene returned to being flat once again.

▲ **Mirror images**
Another reason for getting up early is not only to take advantage of the light but also the quality of water if it is to be included in your shot. At this time of the day it has a stillness that perfectly reflects a mirror image of its surroundings, but this lasts only for a few minutes.

prove to be invaluable assets. Where long exposures are required, it is only in emergencies that you should try to take these types of pictures by resting the camera on a wall, or with some other form of support. It is highly unlikely that, at these times of the day, a really successful picture can be taken with the camera hand held, and without camera shake being apparent.

Daylight also changes long after sunrise and sunset. The changes might be more subtle in good weather but can be very dramatic when the sky becomes stormy or overcast. Look out for dark and foreboding clouds. These often provide startling backdrops to both city and rural landscapes, especially if the foreground is highlighted by the sun.

See also

▶ **pp 18–21** Film and DSLR cameras
▶ **pp 56–57** Light and colour
▶ **pp 58–59** Exposure and auto-exposure
▶ **pp 72–73** Against the light
▶ **pp 166–167** Emphasizing the sky
▶ **pp 172–173** Rivers and lakes

◀ **Midday sun**
As the day progresses, the sun gets higher and the shadows shorter. This shot of the Corinthian Canal in Greece was taken almost at midday. Minutes later the sun would have been directly overhead and there would have been no shadow at all, making the picture look flat.

◀ **Sunset**
Getting the exposure right for a sunset picture is crucial. With some built-in exposure systems the meter records for the sun, and the surrounding areas are under-exposed. Alternatively, it is the shadow areas that get read and the intensity of the sun and sky come out over-exposed. In either case it is best to bracket your exposures.

Seas and oceans

As water covers two thirds of the planet, it is not surprising that seas and oceans fascinate us, providing an ever-changing palette for the photographer from sunrise to sunset.

Where many photographs of seas and oceans fail is with their exposure. This is not surprising as the combination of vast skies and the reflective surfaces of sand and sea can fool your exposure metering system into thinking your photograph needs less exposure than it actually does, meaning shots come out under-exposed. Another common problem is that many photographers use a wide-angle lens for this environment. In itself this is fine, but unless you frame your shot carefully it is all too easy to end up with vast swathes of foreground without any visual interest whatsoever and the background appearing so far away that very little detail can be seen. Skies, too, if overcast and without cloud detail, can look bland and ruin your shot.

When composing pictures, think about the foreground detail. On a beach of endless sand, is there anything you can place near the camera, such as a person or a piece of driftwood? If the beach is fringed by trees these could be put to good use to frame one side of your picture. If none of these framing 'tools' is available, what about the sand itself? Does it have interesting patterns formed by the wind or any undulations that would resemble a desert if shot from a low angle?

If you are up high, such as on cliffs, can you find a headland to lead the eye into the shot? If not, can you look along the cliffs, beach and sea to add a sense of perspective to the picture?

◄ **Perspective**
This rocky headland provides the perfect foreground for this shot. The white walls lead the eye to the lighthouse and give a great sense of perspective, while the choppy sea reminds us of the need for such a structure.

► **Editing**
Using a wide-angle lens has captured the full expanse of the incoming surf breaking onto this rocky coastline in South Africa. It often takes several shots to get the right effect.

◄ **Against the light**
Shooting into the sun can produce effective results, as seen here. Exposing for the highlights means the shadow areas go quite dark, which can make your picture look as if it was shot in moonlight.

See also
► **pp 66–67**
Perspective
► **pp 68–69**
Foreground composition
► **pp 72–73**
Against the light
► **pp 176–177**
Foregrounds for landscapes

Rivers and lakes

Many of the pitfalls that can occur when photographing oceans also apply to rivers and lakes. Care needs to be taken with exposure and composition, especially with lakes. Having said that, this type of scenery provides fantastic opportunities for great photography.

To capture the mirror-like surface of a lake, you will need to be in position just before the sun breaks on the horizon. It is amazing that shortly after the sun comes up, the ripples in the water's surface start to appear and those wonderful reflections of bordering hills or mountains have gone. Any shot across the water to the land on the opposite side will now probably look quite dull. To rectify this the picture will need an element of strong detail in the foreground. If using a wide-angle lens, be careful that you don't lose sight of the background, quite literally. This is easily done and thought needs to be taken with the angle you point the camera in. If using a polarising filter to bring out the clouds in a blue sky, be careful you do not eradicate their reflection in the lake at the same time.

If you are taking pictures in the snow and ice of lakes, pay particular attention to exposure. With all highly reflective surfaces it is very easy to under-expose your shot. To cut down on the risk of flare, make sure you use a lens hood.

▲ **The unexpected shot**
Late afternoon light adds atmosphere to this scene. The frozen canal and its surroundings looked quite flat, but as the winter sun made a brief appearance it changed the photographic possibilities. Carrying your camera at all times is essential for the unexpected shot.

▶ **Flowing water**
Waterfalls and fast-flowing rivers present a different photographic challenge. If the shutter speed is too fast, 1/250th second for example, the water will be static and show no signs of movement. However, if you use a shutter speed of 1/15th second or less, the appearance of the water in the photograph will look as if it is moving at speed. To get this type of picture you will have to use a tripod since holding the camera steady at these speeds will be impossible, resulting in camera shake.

See also

▶ **Early morning**

Most lakes have a stillness in the early morning that soon disappears. Taking advantage of an early start meant that this castle was reflected in the water, creating a mirror image. Later on in the day the water would have begun to ripple and the reflection would have been lost.

▶ **Low angle**

Sometimes you need to be a little more adventurous to get a striking shot. Here, I waded out in the shallow waters of this river rather than shoot from the bank. A low viewpoint and a wide-angle lens have created a feeling of great space and tranquillity.

▼ **Focus of interest**

This lagoon in Goa, India, would have looked quite ordinary without the Portuguese church on the far bank. It is often small details, carefully positioned in the camera frame, that can turn a shot from the mundane to one that is a pleasing composition.

Desert situations

It really does pay to get up early when taking pictures in a desert. You need to be in position before the sun has risen, so it is important to decide your shooting position beforehand. Work out where the sun will rise to take advantage of the extremely low light that will produce the best shadows on sand dunes. When the sun does rise, you will have a maximum of 30 minutes to get your shots. At this time of the morning it is staggering how quickly the sun rises and how fast it climbs in the dawn sky. If you do not capture this moment, haze will ruin the shots, and when the sun gets too high the texture of the sand will lack any definition and so your shots will be extremely flat. If you are in an area with lots of tourists you may have to walk some distance to find an area free from footprints. These can ruin the sense of isolation and emptiness – the emotions that make desert pictures work.

However, animal footprints and reptile tracks made by the nocturnal creatures of the desert will look good in your shots. These can form fascinating patterns in the sand and if shot low, with a wide-angle lens, become the foreground interest of your picture. Again, you really need a light that is low on the horizon to pick out the pattern that has been made in the sand. Another way to create foreground interest is to use desert plants, either alive or dead, or weathered rock. It is amazing how abstract some desert strata can be and some can take on quite surreal shapes.

A word of warning! It is easy to die in deserts from dehydration and sunstroke. If you set out before the sun is up, it will be extremely cold, but once the sun has risen, it becomes unbearably hot very quickly. If you have walked over dunes with heavy equipment you will be surprised how long it will take you to walk back in searing heat. Wear a wide-brimmed hat, take lots of water and let someone know where you have gone.

See also

▶ **pp 26–27** Additional lenses
▶ **pp 56–57** Light and colour
▶ **pp 62–63** Selecting a viewpoint
▶ **pp 168–169** The changing day
▶ **pp 176–177** Foregrounds for landscapes
▶ **pp 242–243** Specialist filters

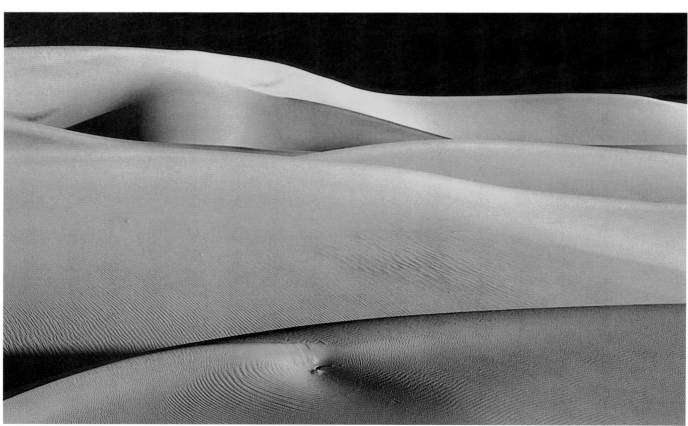

▲ Foreground detail
Even in an arid desert you can find something to make a feature of. Here I got down low and used an old, dry tree stump in the foreground so the eye is immediately drawn to it. A polarising filter helped retain the blueness of the sky.

▼ Framing
This lone Joshua tree filled one side of the frame perfectly. The intensity of the colours has been heightened by the early morning light – you can tell this was shot when the sun first came up by the length of the shadows.

▲ Wide-angle lenses
For this shot I chose an extreme wide-angle lens, 17mm, so I could get plenty of foreground detail while keeping the background sharp. The dried up sand bed makes a great feature and leads the eye into the shot.

◄ Early morning
The best photographs in deserts are taken when the sun first comes up. On this basis it pays to be in place before it gets light, as the amount of time you will have is very short indeed, perhaps only 30 minutes. If possible, look around the area the day before so you know where the light will be at its best.

Foregrounds for landscapes

One of the most important aspects of landscape photography is the attention that is paid to the foreground. It is all too easy to see a great landscape, but transferring that 'view' from how our eyes see it to how it will come out as a photograph needs a little more thought than just pointing the camera at the horizon.

What is in the foreground of our photographs can frame the overall picture or it can lead the eye into it and draw our attention to the middle ground, which might otherwise be overlooked. However, if the foreground is cluttered or badly composed, then it will detract from the overall picture and the eye will be confused as to where the centre of interest is.

Often a tree can be used in the foreground not only to frame the photograph, but also to hide unwanted details that would otherwise ruin the picture. For example, the sky might be without clouds or colour and look rather bland. Not only could you use the trunk of a tree to act as a framing device on one side of the shot, but also

▼ **Choosing the viewpoint**
Often the first view we see when looking for a good landscape shot is not necessarily the best, as we can see in shot (1). The expanse of sand without any foreground features makes the photograph bland and boring. Moving to another position (2) has filled the foreground with detail, but it is so muddled it is difficult for the eye to concentrate on any particular feature. Choosing a different viewpoint (3) has meant the foreground is less cluttered but I still wasn't completely satisfied. By including an interesting rock (4), I finally settled on this view, which had just the right amount of foreground interest.

1

2

3

4

its branches could be used to frame the top of the picture. These will cover the bland sky and add interest to the overall shot. If you adjust the viewpoint and make it higher or lower, the branches can cover more or less of the sky until they are in just the right position.

If there are no trees, there are other devices that we can use to create foreground interest. This might be something as simple as a farm gate or a textured wall. This could be in the foreground, stretching across the whole width of the picture. If we position ourselves so that it runs at an angle, the composition will be more interesting than if it is running dead straight across the foreground.

Colour and contrast can also be used to create foregrounds for landscapes. Flowers, especially in springtime, can add a welcome splash of colour to the foreground. If a low viewpoint is chosen and the camera pointed slightly downwards, we can make a real feature of them, which will lead the eye into the middle ground of the picture. This can also be used as another device to reduce the amount of uninteresting sky that might otherwise dominate the shot. Other devices that can be used to the same effect are rock formations, interesting erosion of the soil, or weathered trees.

▲ **Choosing the right lens**

When looking for the best view of this house, I started by including part of the decorative gates (1). However, the gate dominates the foreground while the area between the gate and house looks like a parade ground. By moving back (2), the immediate foreground now dominates the shot without any discernable feature. By moving back further, I thought I could use the foreground trees to help frame the shot (3) but the house seems too far away and it is difficult to find a point of interest. Finally, I changed to a medium telephoto lens (4), which helped to compress the picture, bringing the house nearer and reducing the foreground to a few trees. The shadow detail fills the foreground, giving the right balance.

See also

▶ **pp 26–27** Additional lenses

▶ **pp 62–63** Selecting a viewpoint

▶ **pp 64–65** Filling the frame

▶ **pp 68–69** Foreground composition

▶ **pp 74–77** Wide-angle and telephoto lenses

Building exteriors

Buildings provide the photographer with a wealth of opportunities. As well as looking at the buildings in your own locality, architectural styles can change when you travel to another region of the country, and it goes without saying that architecture varies overseas even more radically. Even modern buildings can be different abroad. Photographing buildings can teach us many simple lessons in the ways we look at pictures, and give an insight into what many of us take for granted without really seeing.

As buildings are permanent fixtures, the observant photographer is given the opportunity to see them at different times of the day and night, in varying lighting and weather conditions. If we are aware of the many changes such conditions bring, we can start to see ways of photographing buildings at the most favourable times and under the best possible conditions. Learning to be discerning in this way will help us look at other subjects and themes in a more critical manner and see details we might not have otherwise imagined existed.

The tendency when photographing exteriors is to point the camera upwards. The reason for this is that it is usually the only way we can fit the whole building into our shot. This always results in what is known as converging verticals. This means that the building appears to taper towards the top. If you are photographing a modern building such as a skyscraper, this can add to the dramatic qualities of the finished picture and make the building appear even taller than it really is. However, with some buildings, for

▶ **Unseen problems**
Although this house, designed by the acclaimed Spanish architect Gaudi, is highly decorative, photographing it was a problem as there were so many electricity wires and street lamps to the front elevation. I took this from across the street using a 200mm telephoto.

◀ **Creating depth**
A polarising filter has helped to retain the blue of this sky in Siena, Italy, while the random street pattern has created a sense of depth by making the buildings appear to go on forever. The green vegetation contrasts well with the terracotta buildings.

example a cathedral, this can make them look distorted, resulting in a rather unattractive finished shot.

This problem can be rectified by using a shift or PC lens (PC stands for perspective control). This lens can control the amount of convergence and photograph buildings so they are all in the frame but all the verticals remain vertical. Although this lens has other uses as well as controlling perspective, it is a relatively expensive piece of kit. Unless you are going to do a lot of this type of photography, its expense will probably not be justified. In any case, it would be worth hiring one from a professional photography store to see exactly how it works and the different things that you can do with it. If you subsequently decide to buy it, most good suppliers will then not charge you for the hire. If, on the other hand, you do not buy it, at least the hire cost will be a fraction of the purchase price and you won't have invested in what might be a redundant piece of equipment.

Another way to get this type of picture is to position yourself some distance from the building and then use a telephoto lens. This will also help to compress and bring closer other buildings behind the one you are photographing, thus enhancing and improving the background.

Try to choose a viewpoint where unnecessary clutter, such as shop signs

▲ **Stunning contrast**
I used a 24mm shift lens to take this shot, as I thought it was essential to keep all the building's vertical features straight. It curves in a sweeping motion away from the camera and the red of the exterior contrasts well with the blue of the sky.

▶ **Abstract views**
Modern buildings provide the photographer with a wealth of possibilities, as this view of the Guggenheim Museum in Bilbao, northern Spain, shows. With so many reflective surfaces, and irregular shapes, abstract views as well as the more conventional should be plentiful.

and street lighting, are cropped out of the frame, unless they make a statement or add to the composition. Study the way that light falls on the buildings that interest you at various times of day. Remember that in the early morning the shadows will be longer and the highlight details harsher. Another point to consider is urban pollution, especially the carbon monoxide emitted from vehicles. In certain cities where congestion is constant throughout the day, this can be a real problem for the photographer and, if it builds up, it can take days to disperse, causing haze to be prevalent in the pictures.

A final, somewhat bureaucratic point to bear in mind when photographing buildings and using a tripod is that some city authorities require you to obtain a photographic permit for this piece of equipment.

▶ When the sun goes down
If you are going to photograph buildings at night, try to do it in the twilight period. This is about half an hour after sunset and is when the sky goes a deep blue. Just imagine how dull these buildings would have looked against a black sky.

▶ Cloudy picture
I liked the way the walls of this building echoed the billowing clouds in the background. The camera's viewpoint creates a strong sense of perspective and the path leads the eye right into the picture.

See also
▶ pp 26–27 Additional lenses
▶ pp 62–63 Selecting a viewpoint
▶ pp 66–67 Perspective
▶ pp 226–227 Shift and tilt lenses
▶ pp 246–247 Aerial photography

Small-scale buildings

Small structures can also make fascinating photographs. Many are worth shooting for their historical value, while others make interesting compositions within a larger landscape. Some might catch our eye because we intend to use them as foreground interest for a larger shot such as a landscape, but having shot them for this purpose, we might find they are worthy of being photographed in their own right. These could be buildings such as small churches, barns or even derelict buildings or small clusters of buildings.

The important point to remember when photographing buildings of this size is to not lose sight of the scale and, if possible, emphasize it, perhaps by framing another structure next to it to show its diminutive nature. Wide-angle lenses can be used to good effect here, as we can get in close to what is positioned in the foreground while keeping the background in focus. This can make a small building look larger or make the small building even smaller.

Finding a high viewpoint can help when framing small buildings. Looking down on them can make their position in the landscape seem isolated and vulnerable. Using a telephoto lens from a high viewpoint can compress a group of small buildings in such a way that they fill the frame, so the final picture might just be a patchwork of tiled roofs.

Small buildings are not only found in rural areas. Many cities abound with modern, well-designed private homes as well as historical examples. As with so many aspects of photography, it is surprising what can be found even on our own doorsteps.

▲ Scale
The USA is famous for its signs and billboards. I particularly liked this one in Montana, as it soared over the small building at its base, making it appear colossal. A wide-angle lens has exaggerated the scale even more.

▶ Making a statement
A small building can take on a significance all of its own. In a prairie-like landscape I came across this isolated barn. It had been painted in the colours of the Stars and Stripes flag and obviously makes a vivid patriotic statement of painterly dimensions.

◀ Documentary
Religious buildings come in all shapes and sizes. I found this ancient mosque on the outskirts of a village in Ghana, West Africa. Made of mud, it is extraordinary that it has been preserved for so long. Shots like this make great educational and historical documents.

▲ **135mm telephoto lens**
High in the Swiss Alps I came across these buildings that look as if they had been placed on the hillside like a model village. A 135mm lens brought them just close enough while retaining their small scale.

▶ **300mm telephoto lens**
By contrast, I used a 300mm lens to shoot this Pueblo Blanco in south-west Spain. This has compressed the buildings and cut out unwanted detail. The uniformity of terracotta roofs and white walls makes a pleasing geometric pattern.

See also
▶ **pp 26–27** Additional lenses
▶ **pp 56–57** Light and colour
▶ **pp 64–65** Filling the frame
▶ **pp 66–67** Perspective
▶ **pp 74–77** Wide-angle and telephoto lenses

Black and white rural landscapes

Unlike colour photographs of landscapes, which can be easy on the eye and therefore easier to hide faults in their technical quality, black and white landscapes stand or fall totally on their merits of composition, tone and print quality. To this end you need to pay particular attention to these aspects and use a certain amount of ingenuity to bring them to the fore.

If you are using a digital camera and it has a black and white option you have to decide whether this is the best option. The reason for this is that if you shoot in colour you can always convert the shot to black and white later. This gives you two options, whereas if you shoot in black and white and then decide it would have looked better in colour then there is nothing you can do about it.

If you are using black and white film, or have chosen the black and white option on your digital camera, then you can use a range of filters to enhance your shots. A really useful filter is a yellow one. This will enhance the clouds against a blue sky and give your shot greater clarity. If you were to use a red filter, this can make the sky go almost black and could give a very surreal feel to your picture. You could also use a graduated neutral density filter to hold the sky back. This will help to retain a certain amount of sky detail while leaving the foreground correctly exposed.

After you have taken your shots and found that the detail in the sky is still weak, you could correct this in Photoshop, or if you are shooting on film, in the darkroom. Although many people talk about 'manipulation' when talking about digital photography, no

one ever mentions this about the wet darkroom. This is odd because bringing out the sky in a photograph, for example, follows similar techniques. In the wet darkroom you would choose a particular grade of paper and developer. This would enhance contrast just like curves would do in Photoshop. Then you might 'dodge' the sky to bring out detail just in the same way you might use the 'Lasso Tool' in Photoshop to adjust that part of the picture you want to enhance. What you should bear in mind is that whatever you choose to make your prints you should be aiming for the best possible image you can obtain.

▲ **Foreground interest**
Placing this old fishing boat to the left of the frame ensured that there was sufficient foreground interest to lead the eye into the picture. The peeling paint on the boat's hull provided plenty of the texture well suited to black and white film.

See also

▶ **pp 34–35** Film
▶ **pp 62–63** Selecting a viewpoint
▶ **pp 66–67** Perspective
▶ **pp 72–73** Against the light
▶ **pp 166–167** Emphasizing the sky
▶ **pp 176–177** Foregrounds for landscapes

▶ **Eliminating flare**
Shooting into the sun can cause flare problems, but a lens hood eliminates this. A graduated neutral density filter used on the sky ensures the foreground does not become too dark, and the exposure was bracketed for the best result.

▼ **Shadow detail**
Strong shadows provided the right degree of contrast for this picture of a snow-covered jetty. The low viewpoint has helped to emphasize the perspective, while the footprints and the snowy posts draw the eye to the very centre of the frame.

◀ **Using filters**
White clouds can often be lost in the blue of the sky when shooting in black and white. A yellow lens filter avoids this by turning the sky darker while retaining the detail in the clouds.

After you have taken your shots, if you discover detail in the sky has been lost it might be possible to correct this at printing stage. Contact sheets or machine prints are printed to an average so any one of them might not show the full range of tones that could be achieved in an individual print. The best way to judge the potential is to look at the negative. If you can see detail in the sky, then it will be possible to bring this out in the printing.

If you can find a lab that does hand printing, take your negatives to them and discuss the kind of print that you want. They will be able to hold back the sky in printing to retain the detail. The other point about hand printing is that you can choose different grades of paper. These range from 1 to 5, or soft to hard.

The harder the paper, the more contrast the finished print will have or the fewer tones. Choosing the right paper, together with experience of darkroom techniques, can totally alter the effect of your finished print and can be just as creative as taking the original shot.

If you have a computer, then you could scan the negative and manipulate the image in a program like Photoshop.

Black and white urban landscapes

Taking pictures of the environment in black and white can be particularly effective. Using this medium to capture urban landscapes can produce strong, graphic images that might not look so powerful if photographed in colour. Buildings shot in black and white not only work well as high contrast photographs, but also as images with a good range of tones. Printing, whether in the traditional darkroom or computer generated, plays a key role in determining the final look of your chosen image.

If shooting digitally I would set the ISO no higher than 200. This will keep noise to a minimum and should be fast enough in most conditions. If shooting on film the same is true and one with an ISO of 100 or 200 will give fine grain and good tonal range. If you are using the latter you might want to process the film yourself. This is not as difficult as it might seem. Any good photographic supplier will be able to sell you the equipment and chemistry for very little expense. The important item is a development tank. The smallest size will hold just one roll of film while others might hold two, four or six. The only time that you need to be in complete darkness is when you are actually loading your film into the tank. This could be done in a room with blacked out windows or in a lightproof cupboard. Once the film is loaded into the tank, all other operations can be done in normal lighting conditions. The only other equipment that you will require is a thermometer, some measuring jugs for the developer, stop bath and fix. A small length of hose, fitted to a tap, would be useful to wash the film thoroughly at the

end of the process. Once the film has been developed, fixed and washed, you will need a pair of squeegee tongs to remove excess water and a dust-free area to hang it up to dry.

Whether you shoot digitally or on film, you will still be able to output your prints on the computer. With film you will need to scan your chosen negatives. Once your shots are downloaded you can make all your enhancements and corrections before outputting your prints.

◀ **Framing the picture**
I used the branches of trees and their shadows to frame this photograph of London's Buckingham Palace. Without them I felt the sky and foreground would be too dominant and the palace would look lost, making the shot seem bland.

▲ **Graphic images**
This detail of the Grande Arche at La Defense, Paris, works well in black and white. The geometric shapes and patterns make a strong graphic image, showing the importance of going in close and looking at all possible angles.

See also
▶ **pp 26–27** Additional lenses
▶ **pp 34–35** Film
▶ **pp 58–59** Exposure and auto-exposure
▶ **pp 62–63** Selecting a viewpoint
▶ **pp 226–227** Shift and tilt lenses
▶ **pp 242–243** Specialist filters

◄ **Yellow filter**
As well as finished buildings, building sites can provide great opportunities for photography. This shot was taken at the start of building London's Canary Wharf. Such pictures taken over a period of time make good historical documents. A yellow filter has helped to retain detail in the sky.

▼ **Wide-angle shift lens**
This soaring statue in Moscow of Yuri Gagarin dominates the surrounding buildings. To exaggerate the perspective I used a 24mm wide-angle shift lens and chose a low viewpoint. The buildings still look upright and don't lean in as would have been the case without the shift facility.

Exposure

Strong vertical and horizontal lines, reflective surfaces and varied shapes and sizes are found in modern buildings, such as these at London's Canary Wharf. Wide-angle lenses are useful here as they can exaggerate converging verticals, making buildings look even taller. When looking up and including sky in your shots, take care not to under-expose the buildings. If in doubt, bracket your exposures.

Interiors

The biggest problem with interior shots is judging the light or, more correctly, the lack of it. Most of us have attempted to photograph the inside of a building we have visited on holiday, only to be disappointed with the result. This is usually because the picture comes out under-exposed, with all the grandeur and detail lost in darkness. If your camera has built-in flash, it will still be totally inadequate to light the interior of even the most modest church, let alone the Sistine Chapel. The best solution is to use available light and a long exposure.

As with photographing exteriors, converging verticals can be a problem. If you do not have specialist equipment, try to find a high viewpoint for your shot. This might be from a gallery or staircase, or you could stand on a

See also

▶ **pp 56–57** Light and colour

▶ **pp 58–59** Exposure and auto-exposure

▶ **pp 60–61** Effective flash

▶ **pp 190–191** Lighting interiors

▶ **pp 256–257** Mixed lighting

◀ **Viewpoint**
To include as much of this Victorian pumping station as possible, I used a 21 mm wide-angle lens. As the building was constructed along a symmetrical design, I chose a viewpoint to emphasize this. The area in the basement needed to be lit with flash to balance it with the rest of the interior lit with daylight.

stepladder. This higher viewpoint will enable you to include more of the interior and keep the camera level.

Be careful when using a wide-angle lens. This can 'stretch' the shot, making it look as though it were taken through the wrong end of a telescope, and leaving the background detail lost in the distance. Nevertheless, such a lens does have its uses, especially if you want to look up to show as much of the ceiling as possible.

Once you have selected the viewpoint and lens, consider the amount of light available and the type. Is the scene well

◀ Daylight
There was so much light coming through the industrial-style windows of this apartment that additional lighting was unnecessary. However, a reflector was needed to bounce some light onto the central work unit.

▲ Using flash
When shooting interiors you may need to use flash to balance the picture. If I had relied on the camera's exposure meter it would have read for the daylight coming through the windows and the room would have been in deep shadow.

▶ Mixed lighting
There were three lighting sources here: daylight coming in through the windows, tungsten light from the chandeliers, and flash. The flash and daylight had the same colour temperature while I kept the tungsten lights on just long enough for them to record and not cause a colour cast.

lit with daylight from side windows or from an atrium above, or is it artificial light from spotlights or chandeliers? If the former, is the light even? If you are taking a shot looking down a church nave, with windows on each side, it is unlikely that the daylight will be coming evenly through all windows. This means that one side of the interior would be in deep shadow, while the other could be bathed in strong sunlight. Your only remedy here is to fill in the shadow area with multiple flash, or wait until midday to see if the light is more even.

If the lighting is predominately tungsten you will need to adjust your white balance accordingly, or if shooting on film use tungsten-balanced film, otherwise all your shots will come out with an orange cast.

Lighting interiors

The mistake that many photographers make when taking pictures of interiors is making the assumption that because the built-in flash on the camera goes off, the picture will come out. Even if the room is reasonably small, the camera flash can make the final image look harsh and bright with any detail in the foreground washed out.

On the other hand, when taking photographs in large spaces, such as a theatre or sports stadium, the power of the built-in flash will be inadequate and the picture will come out under-exposed. Even if you override the flash and use available tungsten light, you might then find that your pictures come out with an orange cast unless you have set the white balance accordingly or used tungsten-balanced film.

Different colour balanced films or conversion filters should always be carried in your equipment bag. These filters adjust the balance of a particular film to the prevailing light conditions. An 80A filter – blue in colour – will remove the orange cast

▲ Using daylight
It is possible to light interiors entirely with daylight, such as in this shot. Even so, I placed two large reflectors to the left of the camera to bounce light back into the room. Although the window is slightly burnt out, I felt the atmosphere is that of a bright and airy room.

▲ Using daylight and flash
This bathroom, in a house in southern France, was bathed in sunlight. However, the immediate foreground was in shadow so I used a single flash unit to the right of the camera to balance the exposure required and soften the shadows in the foreground.

▶ Tungsten light
The sheer size of the Bolshoi Theatre in Moscow proved too great for my flash equipment so I decided to use the available light. I set the white balance to 3,400 K to match the house lights and used a tripod, as the required exposure was 15 seconds.

See also
▶ pp 34–35 Film
▶ pp 56–57 Light and colour
▶ pp 192–193 Architectural details
▶ pp 242–243 Specialist filters

that would occur when using daylight balanced film in tungsten light.

In available light the exposure is likely to be long, so a cable release and tripod will be essential to keep the camera steady and avoid camera shake. This is good practice even if your camera or lens has an image stabilisation mode.

A flashgun that you can detach from the camera would be a useful accessory. With this you can fire off several flashes into key areas of the picture. This is known as painting with flash. With the shutter set on B and kept open you will be able to fire off the flash without appearing in the shot yourself.

▲ **Using daylight, flash and tungsten**
This modern apartment was lit with three different light sources, the daylight streaming through the windows on the right being the main source. I used a flash unit to the left of the camera to lift the shadow areas to the left of the blue column (flash and daylight have the same colour balance) and switched on the room lights as this added to the atmosphere even though I had the white balance set to 5,200 K.

Architectural details

Besides the 'big' shot of a building or its interior, there is a wealth of other shots that can make great pictures. Many of these are easy to overlook because by themselves they might not be particularly eye-catching, but when put together in a series or collage, it is amazing how effective they can be.

The reason for taking these pictures is that the detail at the top of a Corinthian column, for instance, may get lost in an overall shot. By going in close you can highlight the intricacies of the carving and other details of the workmanship.

If you are shooting a detail of stained glass, you need to read the light coming from behind the window to ascertain the correct exposure. The coloured glass will reduce the intensity of the light coming through it and so you will

probably need a long exposure and a tripod to support the camera. Make sure the camera is correctly aligned. Nothing is worse than seeing a shot where it is clear the photographer has gone to the trouble of getting the correct exposure only to see the windowsill tilted one way. When photographing stained glass do not use flash. If you do, the stained glass will not record except for a big starburst on the glass!

Sometimes it is the way photographs of details are presented that can make them so striking. One interesting way is to make up a collage. This could be done with just one photograph. Get several prints made but have half of them printed back to front. When mounted together, a fascinating kaleidoscopic effect can be seen.

See also

▶ pp 18–21 Film and DSLR cameras
▶ pp 62–63 Selecting a viewpoint
▶ pp 64–65 Filling the frame
▶ pp 178–179 Building exteriors
▶ pp 186–187 Black and white urban landscapes

▶ Viewpoint

Often a shot is found by chance, such as this staircase at the Hotel Martinez, Cannes in the south of France. When I came out of the lift of the top floor, I saw that the view down the staircase was far more impressive than looking up and I knew I had found the right viewpoint.

▼ Details

In architecture, details are everywhere. Inside or out, sections of buildings or interiors, or a brick or a column, tile or plasterwork all have the potential to make a great shot, either individually or as part of a collage. Shoot several and compare them on a light-box or computer.

Time of day

Much of what has been explained about the time of day and the quality of the light in shooting rural scenes is applicable to photographing buildings. Early morning brings the advantage of the scenes being relatively quiet and free of people who might intrude into the foreground of the shot. The chances are that the light will be crisp and clear, as any urban pollution will not have had a chance to build up. Water, such as rivers, will be calmer at this time of day. If a building has a lot of detail, the sun will still be quite low at this time of day and will give good shadow detail. Later in the day the sun's movement changes that shadow detail and gives a totally different perspective.

Much of this book talks about the quality of light and how important it is in the making of good photographs, so it seems strange to start thinking of taking pictures at night when there is very little light around. Although this is

▼ **Time of day**
Few photographers really take advantage of the best time of day. In the smaller of these two shots the light is flooding in at right angles, almost burning out the wall. Two hours earlier the sun made diagonal patterns that are more pleasing and the colonnade is more evenly lit.

See also
▶ **pp 28–29** Accessories
▶ **pp 40–41** Digital capture
▶ **pp 52–53** Shutter speed
▶ **pp 56–57** Light and colour
▶ **pp 226–227** Shift and tilt lenses

true of what we refer to as 'daylight', there is still an enormous amount of other light around at night that will be strong enough to allow you to take pictures by. Some of this might be in the twilight – the time after the sun has set but before the sky is completely black – or in the artificial light that comes from buildings, street lighting or the light from illuminated billboards, or from vehicle light trails.

You will need a tripod and cable release for successful night photography. If you do not have these, it is well worth considering buying them since there are so many photographic applications that they are useful for. Because shutter speeds are likely to be longer, there is the chance that noise will increase, or if using a fast film, grain will be more pronounced.

A lens hood, which should be fitted as a matter of course, is essential for cutting out any stray light that might come from a nearby streetlight or a reflection from a shop window.

◀ **Early morning**
If your photograph includes an expanse of water it is best that you choose to photograph it early in the morning. It is at this time that the water will be at its calmest and the reflections will be at their best.

Early evening

These two shots of Las Vegas show the difference that just ten minutes can make after sunset.

The small shot on the right was taken first and, as can be seen from the red car light trails, required a long exposure. Although the photograph is correctly exposed, the sky is dull and it does not allow the backdrop to do justice to the buildings – they simply look flat and uninspiring. By contrast, the larger shot below was taken ten minutes later, by which time the sky had taken on a rich deep blue hue. The illuminated buildings now stand out dramatically against the sky, which forms a perfect backdrop.

Waiting for the right moment and being patient is just as important in photography as getting the right exposure.

▲ **Early morning**
In this bedroom shot, the early morning light streaming through the window has bathed the room in a warm glow. Although the sun looks bright, the camera still required a tripod, as the shutter speed was 1/4th second.

Carnivals

arnivals and street parades provide endless opportunities for great pictures, but they require forward planning. Decide which are the most important elements to concentrate on. With some big events it is unlikely you will be able to shoot every single aspect so it is better to concentrate on what will work. Write a list of the shots you want and work out what equipment and film you will need. If the carnival goes on into the night you may well need a tripod. However, do you want to carry it around all day in a heaving crowd?

To get a flavour of the whole day, you need to start early in the morning. Look for the setting up of stalls, preparation of floats and participants getting into their costumes. Be on the lookout for those candid shots of people sharing a joke or looking pensive while they wait.

Then there is the growing crowd with their anticipation. Many people here will also be dressed up or having impromptu dances with the stranger next to them. Children provide good opportunities for these types of candid pictures. Look out for them eating ice cream and getting messy, or crying because they are bored. All these shots are relevant when you come to tell a story in pictures.

Before the parade begins, find the best vantage point to get the key pictures. Can you get up high so the crowd will not be in the way? You want a variety of

▶ **Emphasizing detail**
I used a 70mm lens for this portrait of a carnival queen. It gives great framing and helps to emphasize the detail in her costume. A shutter speed of 1/250th second has kept everything pin sharp.

pictures, so don't think that you need to be up a lamppost all day. Can you shoot into the light? If so, look for costumes that look best with back lighting so the material appears translucent and vivid. Use a backlight compensation setting or make an adjustment to the exposure so your shots are correctly exposed.

If shooting in the evening, be careful your flash does not kill the atmosphere. A degree of slow-sync flash might be worthwhile so you can get movement into your shots rather than static pictures of revellers against a black background.

See also

▶ **pp 46–47** Holding the camera
▶ **pp 52–53** Shutter speed
▶ **pp 58–59** Exposure and auto-exposure
▶ **pp 72–73** Against the light
▶ **pp 74–77** Wide-angle and telephoto lenses
▶ **pp 112–113** Candid portraits

▲ **Retaining detail**
Although I used a slow shutter speed in this shot, it was important to retain the dancer's facial features. If I had used a lower shutter speed, her face would be completely blurred without any distinguishing features. Here the balance is just right.

◀ **Abstraction**
Because a slow shutter speed can't freeze moving subjects, it can add a degree of abstraction to your pictures. However, if you use a slow shutter speed all detail will be lost. An amount of trial and error is the best way to arrive at the correct choice of speed.

Street scenes

Besides carnivals, there is a wealth of other life out on the streets but we don't always realize that interesting shots might be right before our eyes. This is why it is so important for the committed photographer to carry a camera at all times, not just when you are travelling or on holiday. Next time you walk to work or the shops, make a determined effort to really look at your own neighbourhood. You might be surprised at just how much is going on.

Some city buildings and their surrounding pavements appear to make perfect courses for skateboarding and roller-skating. The skill of many of these performers is astounding as they leap from walls and steps, skillfully side-stepping city workers and tourists. They provide great material for action shots.

▲ **Shadow detail**
The long shadow of this French boules player makes an interesting composition. When you come across scenes like this you need to act quickly because the moment will soon pass. It was shot with a 70–200mm zoom lens, which is ideal for a range of spontaneous situations.

▶ **Night light**
This illuminated Christmas tree makes the perfect backdrop for the skaters. Although they are blurred because of a slow shutter speed, this adds to the sense of fun and spontaneity. Flash would have killed the mood and the background would have come out too dark.

◀ **Be prepared**
This bus had stopped in an isolated African village and bustles with activity, illustrating a good documentary shot. A young child plays in the foreground while someone cycles up to see what is going on. When travelling, be on the lookout for these opportunities.

If this is too frenetic for you, what about the French game of boules. It is almost impossible to visit any town or village in France and not see at least one game being played on any day of the week.

Markets form another street scene to be found worldwide. The opportunities here range from a single pitch selling flowers to a bustling street market. These are full of colour and life, and an amazing cross-section of people frequent them. Many of the traders are great characters, and provide the alert photographer with plenty of opportunities for really good portraits,

as do the shoppers. For this type of photography a couple of camera bodies would be ideal, set at 200 ISO or similar for film. On one, a wide to medium telephoto zoom would be great for getting close-up detail on market stalls while providing plenty of depth of field to make sure that people in the background are sharp. On the other, attach a more powerful zoom. With this you will be able to keep your distance and take candid shots.

Of course, many people who are on the street are not there out of choice. Whether it is morally right to

photograph them is not an issue for debate in this book. However, do we look at historical photographs taken in the late nineteenth century of abject Victorian poverty and say to ourselves that they should never have been taken?

See also
▶ pp 58–59 Exposure and auto-exposure
▶ pp 68–69 Foreground composition
▶ pp 72–73 Against the light
▶ pp 74–77 Wide-angle and telephoto lenses
▶ pp 112–113 Candid portraits
▶ pp 138–139 Using fill-in flash

◀ **Back light**
The sun was behind this stallholder at a market in Marseille and created a halo effect on her skin. The exposure required a certain amount of compensation so that she did not come out under-exposed and as a silhouette.

◀ **Flash and daylight**
There are areas in most cities that seem to attract activities like skateboarding. This young skateboarder was photographed as he took off from a wall. A small amount of flash was combined with the daylight and helped to freeze him in midair.

▲ **Street colour**
It was the colour of these women's costumes and the goods they were carrying on their heads that made me take this shot. Street markets in India, such as this one in Madras, are a photographer's paradise and abound with possibilities.

At the beach

For many people, the idea of travel is jetting off to a faraway destination and taking it easy on a white sandy beach with a beautiful azure sea lapping at their feet. For others, it is the chance to get some great shots in a country that guarantees them constant sunshine. But however good the weather, there are plenty of pitfalls for the photographer in these seemingly idyllic situations.

Sand and seawater is a killer to all photographic equipment. Taking a camera bag to the beach, whether it is canvas or aluminium, is a recipe for disaster as sand will always find its way into even the slightest opening. If this does happen, wait until you are away from the beach before dealing with it. Do not attempt to rub the sand off, as this will be just like using an abrasive on your equipment. The first thing to do is to take all the equipment out of the bag or case. Take the bag outside and shake it thoroughly. If sand still remains, blow it hard with either your own breath or a proprietary air can. If sand is on your cameras and lenses, separate each piece, take it outside and blow the sand away in the same manner. Do not wipe any of the equipment until you are sure that no sand remains.

A far better way to protect expensive equipment on the beach is to wrap each piece in a plastic bag and seal it with a rubber band. Make sure that all your lens have a skylight filter attached to them to protect the front element. Before getting equipment out, wipe your own hands free of sand so that you do not let any of the sand into the bag. As soon as you have finished with the equipment, re-seal it in its plastic bag.

◀ **Candids**
This girl was absorbed in her music and oblivious to me photographing her. It makes a good portrait, helped by the softness of the background, caused by using a wide aperture.

Sand and sea reflect a lot of light, so it is possible that your camera's metering system will be fooled into thinking there is more light than there really is. This means that your shots could come out under-exposed, especially if you are shooting a person against the sea and sky. Try to get in close to your subject so that you can take a reading of their skin tones and not the surrounding areas. Be careful not to cast your own shadow over your subject when doing this as this could result in over-exposure.

▲ **Fill-in flash**
I had been photographing these two surfers in the sea but wanted another shot to go with the action pictures. They were carrying their boards on their heads and this I thought made a good composition. I used fill-in flash to soften the shadows made by the boards.

See also

▶ **pp 18–21** Film and DSLR cameras
▶ **pp 32–33** Equipment care
▶ **pp 52–53** Shutter speed
▶ **pp 54–55** Aperture
▶ **pp 138–139** Using fill-in flash

Getting the best shots

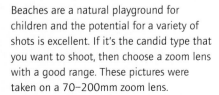

Beaches are a natural playground for children and the potential for a variety of shots is excellent. If it's the candid type that you want to shoot, then choose a zoom lens with a good range. These pictures were taken on a 70–200mm zoom lens.

Most children are perfectly content to occupy themselves in these situations, which gives you the opportunity to find a position for photography without them being aware of you. Choose a fast shutter speed and set the camera to its predictive focusing mode,

so that if they are running they will still be sharp. A camera with a fast burst rate will be an asset as you will be able to track them and then edit out the best picture after the shots have been processed or downloaded into the computer.

At the landmarks

Wherever we go on holiday there will always be landmarks and places of interest to photograph. If travelling with family or a companion, it is often appropriate to photograph one another at these places. While this doesn't present any particular problems, there are a few points to watch out for.

When looking at people's holiday snaps, it can often be really difficult to identify the person they are referring to when there is a crowd of other people in the photograph. Choose a lens that will frame all the important details, rather than one that gets so much in that nothing of interest becomes noticeable.

Try to position the person you are photographing in an area where you can see them. It is not always necessary to have your subject standing in the middle of the frame, staring at the camera. It might be the case that you are using them in your composition to give a sense of scale. If so, it doesn't really matter whether they are looking at the camera or not. If the site is so crowded that it is impossible to take your shot without getting an army of other people in it, try to use them to your advantage. For instance, this might be with a sense of irony if your landmark is a place that is noted for its tranquillity.

▶ Sense of scale
You often need to show the scale of the landmark that you are shooting, such as this photograph of Michelangelo's David, in Florence, Italy. Including a companion in the picture gives a good indication of just how monumental this statue really is.

◀ The right shot
I waited for this tram in San Francisco to be close enough in the foreground before shooting. It looks simple, but I had to wait for several trams, as other vehicles were in the way.

▼ Telephoto lenses
I used a 300mm telephoto lens to take this shot. This has compressed the picture, bringing the statue and background closer to the camera and giving the figure greater presence.

▶ Viewpoint
Every capital city has its regular events, such as this annual inspection of the Yeomen Warders at The Tower of London. Try to get a viewpoint that excludes other tourists or unsightly street signs.

You might want to place your subject in the foreground and to one side of the frame while composing your picture. If this is the case and you are using a wide-angle lens, then be careful that their face does not become distorted. Another important point to remember when using these lenses is that the real area of focus – the landmark – can become a distant object in the background of the picture. Make sure that you are close enough to it before posing your subject in the foreground.

Unfortunately, it is becoming increasingly likely that your view of a local landmark will be marred by an advertising hoarding or a cellular telephone mast. Always try to walk around and find a viewpoint that eliminates as many of these unwanted distractions as possible. Be careful that surrounding buildings are not reflecting bright sunlight into your camera lens – fit a lens hood at all times to diminish this risk.

Above all, be aware that you know where your equipment is at all times. If you don't, you can be sure that there is a pair of eyes out there watching and waiting for you to be off your guard.

See also

▶ **pp 54–55** Aperture
▶ **pp 62–63** Selecting a viewpoint
▶ **pp 66–67** Perspective
▶ **pp 70–71** Selecting a background
▶ **pp 74–77** Wide-angle and telephoto lenses
▶ **pp 242–243** Specialist filters

▼ **Wide angle**
To get this photograph of the old Roman amphitheatre at Taormina, Sicily, I climbed to the top and used a 24mm lens. I just managed to get the full width of the site in. A polarising filter was fitted to the lens to enhance the blue sky and to add definition to the white clouds.

Local colour

If you are planning a trip to another country, it is worth taking time beforehand to research what might be the best features to concentrate on. In addition to the well-known sights and customs, there might be other less obvious features that could make really good shots. Many of these scenes or details, when combined together, could make a very effective montage.

If you are going to a country such as India, you can be sure that the streets and the markets will be overflowing with life and colour. Markets will carry an abundance of fresh produce, herbs and spices that will radiate colour, while brilliant silks and other materials will overflow from stalls. A similar scene could be found in the Provençal region of France or in any number of African countries. Architectural details are another source of such images, along with richly decorated ceramics.

When you have decided which details would make an interesting set of pictures, try to get in as close as possible to them so that extraneous detail is cropped out. Try to photograph them either straight on or directly overhead. If you shoot them obliquely, perspective can be a problem and these pictures will sit uncomfortably with other images shot straight on.

Shoot in both landscape and portrait formats so that you can see what works best once you are back home and have all the images you can edit either in computer, from prints, or on a lightbox if transparencies. If you are shooting on colour negative and have prints, lay these out on a table to get the best arrangement. Keep moving the images around until you are satisfied with the overall arrangement of shapes and colours. Remember that you can still crop a tightly composed picture if it makes it work better when juxtaposed with another image.

If you scan all your prints or negatives into the computer, you could arrange them on screen. In this case you can flip them, have some larger or smaller and crop them. You will also be able to repeat some images that might make an effective border to the montage.

▶ Editing pictures

When travelling, there is so much to see and photograph that it can be difficult to display just one shot that does justice to the journey. It might be wisest to start out by photographing themes, which could be details of buildings, market stalls, items for sale or different faces. Once you have returned home you can edit these pictures either on the light-box or in the computer and make up an interesting collage that sums up the local colour and interest of the country or area that you have visited.

See also

▶ **pp 56–57** Light and colour
▶ **pp 74–77** Wide-angle and telephoto lenses
▶ **pp 192–193** Architectural details

◀ Local colour

I was attracted to this washing hanging on a line outside a house in Goa, India. I had noticed it from the other side of the square I was walking in. It works as a picture because of its simplicity in conveying a sense of local colour and the warmth of the climate.

Farm animals

Most of us live within reach of a farm, so taking pictures of farm animals should not be beyond anyone's range. Even the largest city usually has an 'inner city farm' where children can discover how these animals live. What is good about farms is that most of the animals are kept together in relatively small areas. This means that you will be able to get in quite close and not have to worry that the particular species you are photographing is going to run off. Even so, as with all animals, a degree of patience is necessary to get good shots.

As well as taking shots of groups of farm animals, look out for individual shots. This could be a forlorn face or a young animal or chick hiding under their mother's wing or coat. Try to get in close by using a telephoto lens. However, if you are leaning over a cattle pen, you might be too close and find that you will need an extension tube to make sure that you get your subject sharp. Wide-angle lenses have their place too, and a close-up of an animal's face can produce some interesting results, even if there is an element of distortion. But don't get too close!

If you are at the farm with children, try to get a degree of interaction between them and the animals, but remember, even the most placid animal can turn and bite, so don't put either the child or the animal in a situation that might cause upset or injury.

If you can have regular access to a farm, perhaps you could create a picture series. For example, this could be of a calf, lamb, or chick being born and then recording their growth over a season and their changing appearance as they grow. Unlike humans, most farm animals mature quite quickly, so it may be necessary to make your series a weekly event.

▼ Tight framing
When photographing animals it often pays to go in tight and fill the frame. These pigs were waiting to go to market and were tightly packed in a pen. I chose a 70mm lens and concentrated on one pig's face while the others surrounded it. This has emphasized the look of bored resignation.

◀ Wide angle

Going in close with a wide-angle lens can produce great results when photographing farm animals. Here, I used a 24mm lens, which was only about 200mm from the goat's nose. Obviously you need to take care otherwise you could end up with a nasty bite!

▼ Low viewpoint

When photographing relatively small farm animals, such as these sheep, it is important to change your viewpoint, otherwise all of your shots will be looking down. I knelt to take this shot so that the sheep had direct eye contact with me.

▶ Detail

This turkey's wattles makes a colourful detail against its almost monochromatic feathers. To make sure the picture was sharp I stopped down to f11 and used a shutter speed of 1/250th second.

Wild animals

With travel now possible to more and more wild and exotic places, the opportunity to photograph animals in their natural habitat has never been greater. But even for those who do not want to travel far there are opportunities for photographing wildlife nearer to home. Almost every region has a living eco system that supports wildlife and it is a matter of detective work on your part to discover where to find it. Even cities in highly developed countries now support a growing population of foxes as their natural rural hunting grounds become built up. Zoos can provide good opportunities, but even better are safari parks, which try to provide an environment that is reasonably free and natural for the animals. For photography these are an excellent location.

Wherever you go, there are some pieces of equipment that will be essential. Anything other than a camera that accepts interchangeable lenses will not be adequate. A telephoto lens of at least 200mm will be necessary if you are going to get in close enough to take decent shots of wild animals. Better still would be a 400mm. If you do not have one of these, an extender will be a good alternative. This fits between the camera body and the lens and can double its focal length, i.e. a 200mm becomes 400mm. The only problem is that this diminishes the speed of the lens.

Therefore, a lens with a fastest aperture of f2.8 will, once the converter has been fitted, be reduced to f5.6. These work with zoom lenses as well as prime lenses and are reasonably priced. They also reduce the bulkiness of the equipment you have to carry around.

As your lenses are going to be slower, it is advisable to use a faster film than normal, such as 400 ISO. This will give you the necessary speed to photograph moving animals. Also, you need to bear in mind that many animals will be lying in the shade as protection from the sun, which means that they are going to need more exposure than would otherwise be the case.

▲ Be alert
You need to be quick when photographing animals and wild animals are no exception. This meerkat appeared from nowhere and I just had time to get two shots before it disappeared out of sight.

▲ Wide aperture
I used an aperture of f2.8 which combined with a 300mm lens gives minimum depth of field. This has put the focus firmly on the eyes and nose which look bright and alert. It also blurred the background so that nothing distracts from the monkey's face.

See also

▶ Powerful telephoto

Leopards are not the type of animal you want to stand close to and for this shot I had the benefit of a 300mm lens. Although it is a large piece of kit to hold, I was fortunate that it had image stabilization, which kept the shot razor sharp.

▼ Tight cropping

After I have taken my shots I sometimes crop in very close. This can create almost abstract pictures and put the focus firmly on one aspect of the animal, in this case its eye.

Birdlife

As with photographing wild animals, birds make fantastic subjects for photography. Although we might find more exotic varieties in countries other than our own, it doesn't mean that we can't get great shots. If you are shooting in your own garden you might want to make a 'hide'. This is simply a structure that you can be in, but hidden, and has a small opening for your camera lens to poke through. After a while birds will get used to this type of structure and be unperturbed about it. If you are using a full-frame SLR, a good quality zoom lens in the region of 70–200mm would be ideal. Rather than purchase a much more expensive telephoto, consider buying a lens extender. A 2x extender will double the focal length so that a 200mm lens will effectively become a 400mm telephoto for a relatively small outlay. The downside of this is that it is at the cost of lens speed. A lens with a maximum aperture of f2.8 will lose two stops and will have a maximum aperture of f5.6. However, this should be still adequate in most conditions.

Patience is the key to this type of photography and you might find yourself waiting several hours for either the bird to come into view or be in the right position. I like to use a wide aperture when taking pictures of birds as this will give minimal depth of field. This means that once you have focused on its head, for example, the background will be completely out of focus. This will isolate the bird against the background and make it stand out with greater clarity.

Another method of photographing birds is to use a remote control. This could be an infrared trigger attached to the cameras hot-shoe or simply a long cable release. If you observe where the birds congregate you can mount your camera on a tripod and focus it on that area. Then from a safe distance you can fire off the camera when you think the time is right. If your camera allows you to shoot tethered to the computer then you will be able to see instantly whether your shots are working or if adjustments need to be made.

► **Tripod**
Because I waited an hour to get this shot, I mounted the camera and 600mm lens on a tripod. Lenses of this size are far too big to hold comfortably in your hands and it is essential to support them.

See also
► **pp 26–27** Additional lenses
► **pp 28–29** Accessories
► **pp 54–55** Aperture
► **pp 62–63** Selecting a viewpoint
► **pp 74–77** Wide-angle and telephoto lenses

▲ **Low light**
Because the light was low I had to use a slow shutter speed of 1/60th second and an aperture of f2.8. Although the 300mm lens had image stabilization, I mounted the camera on a monopod for greater rigidity.

◄ **Tracking**
Many DSLRs have a feature that allows you to track a moving object yet keep it continuously sharp. This is a real asset when the subject is moving towards you. I used a shutter speed of 1/1600th second and took the shots at a burst of five frames per second.

Pets

Unlike photographing wild animals, at least we have the benefit of being familiar with our own pets, or those of our friends. There is the famous saying in showbusiness, 'Don't work with children and animals'. But as photographers, we know that both can make delightful and rewarding pictures. There are great similarities in photographing these two subjects – they don't like being told what to do and they definitely have their own ideas about what they are going to do! So be alert and prepared for opportunities that might occur at any time.

By now we all know the benefits of carrying a camera with us at all times, and this includes everyday tasks such as when we are out walking with the dog. A good pet portrait is often the simplest one, such as a photograph of the dog observing its surroundings or the dog meeting a new friend in the park. Cats, being more independent, can be a little trickier to photograph. However, it is possible to catch them on the prowl, intently waiting to leap on their carefully chosen quarry. It is definitely easier to photograph cats when they are in a resting position.

If you are out walking with your pet, a zoom lens with a good small to medium telephoto ratio will be an ideal choice. This will let you get in close if

See also
▶ pp 26–27 Additional lenses
▶ pp 54–55 Aperture
▶ pp 62–63 Selecting a viewpoint
▶ pp 74–77 Wide-angle and telephoto lenses
▶ pp 112–113 Candid portraits

▶ **Being prepared**
You need to be quick when photographing pets. Here was a chance encounter between two dogs. As the one on the right stopped, the other walked towards it. I quickly got in position, as within seconds the moment had gone.

▶ **Studio portrait**
Using a black velvet background, I set two lights behind the dog pointing towards the camera. Reflectors each side of the camera reflected light back onto its face. The positioning needs care as light could flare into the lens.

▲ **Macro lens**
Even with compact cameras, stunning close-up shots can be made using the macro lens setting. These two pet rats are sharp in every detail and it's easy to follow their movements on the LCD screen.

▲ **High viewpoint**
I photographed this cat from a high viewpoint to make it look diminutive and innocent. I used a 35mm SLR camera fitted with a 120mm medium telephoto lens and an aperture of f2.8. Focusing with pin sharp accuracy on its eyes has drawn the viewer's attention to its face.

you are some distance from your pet and should be wide enough if they are relatively close to you. Set the ISO to 200 or use a film of a similar speed. Try to think of different angles when photographing pets. If you always take your shots from your own height, you will always be looking down on them. Try a few shots from low down so that you are much more on their level.

You might like to try a more formal approach by taking a portrait of your pet under studio conditions. This really will require patience, as no animal is going to sit still for any length of time. The great thing with this approach is that you have complete control over the lighting and its effect, and a fast shutter speed. The problem will simply be to get the animal to sit still long enough.

Flowers

Plants and flowers do not have to be the wild and exotic varieties to make good photographs. As with many photographic subjects, it can be the commonplace that is neglected when in fact these will provide the observant photographer with a wealth of photographic opportunities. If you are going to go in close to the flower, a macro lens or extension tubes or bellows will be essential accessories as would a tripod and reflector.

Wind can be a problem when taking close-ups of flowers so be patient, as there is usually a point when it subsides and the plant stays still. If you intend to do a lot of plant photography it may be worth constructing a box with four sides made out of clear perspex. This will enable you to surround small plants and eliminate the wind without obscuring the light. If the sun is very bright, look out for harsh shadows that could end up spoiling a great image. An overcast day may look grim to most people but to the photographer it can be a blessing by giving an even, shadowless light.

If you are going in really close it may be necessary to stop the lens right down to get as much depth of field as possible. This will mean a longer shutter speed, so use a tripod. Be careful when shooting close-ups that you do not cast your own shadow or that of the camera and tripod over your subject. Also remember, when going in very close, that unless you are using an SLR or digital camera with preview you must allow for parallax error. If not, you might find that the flower has been cropped out of your finished photograph. Although flowers are at their peak for a limited period – a day in some cases – try to plan when the best time of day will be to shoot them.

Choosing the composition

See also

▶ **pp 18–21** Film and DSLR cameras
▶ **pp 28–29** Accessories
▶ **pp 50–51** The viewfinder and auto-focus
▶ **pp 54–55** Aperture
▶ **pp 216–217** Close-ups

1 In the late afternoon light I saw these poppies growing in a field of grass. After a couple of shots, using a 35mm lens, I decided that I wasn't doing justice to either the colour or the light.
2 I decided get down lower, move in closer and change to a 70mm lens, but I was still unhappy with the overall composition.
3 I then changed lenses again for a 210mm

telephoto. This had the effect of isolating the poppies and, by using a wide aperture, minimizing the depth of field. However, the colours still merged into one another and I decided to move again.
4 By shifting my viewpoint just slightly and raising the camera a fraction, I was now getting the composition I preferred.

▶ **The final shot**
For the final picture I decreased the exposure by a stop on the shutter as I did not want to increase the depth of field. I now felt that I had isolated one poppy, which looked far more dramatic than my first attempt, and the viewpoint and angle of light were at their best.

Close-ups

Close-ups are fascinating. There is something captivating about seeing an object enlarged so its structure takes on a new dimension. Sometimes this enlargement can take an abstract form and create patterns that are worthy of being printed and displayed for their own beauty. In other cases, the magnification shows us the delicate detail not apparent to the naked eye.

The best method is to use a macro lens. This will enable you to get in as close as about 1–2 feet (30–50cm). Strictly speaking, a macro lens should allow you to shoot a subject lifesize. To get in closer than this means using extension tubes or bellows. If it is not possible to fit these to your camera, you could use a close-up lens. This fits on the front of your lens like a filter. However, these are not of the greatest optical quality and if your camera is not an SLR or digital you will have difficulty with accurate focusing and will have to make a greater allowance for parallax correction than the compensation marks in the viewfinder indicate.

Shooting this close, depth of field is minimal. If your subject is moving, such as an insect or small reptile, it would be best to shoot with a small aperture such as f16 or f22. This will give you as much depth of field as possible and the greatest scope for getting the essential detail sharp. You

See also
▶ **pp 26–27** Additional lenses
▶ **pp 28–29** Accessories
▶ **pp 46–47** Holding the camera
▶ **pp 156–157** Spring
▶ **pp 234–235** Extension tubes and bellows

▲ **Macro lenses**
These are essential for taking pictures of plants like this. They will enable you to get in really close and record great detail. When combined with extension tubes or bellows, a whole world of close-up photography becomes possible.

Choosing the right aperture

A common mistake when photographing close-ups is choosing the wrong aperture. If you stop down too far and use a small aperture such as f16 or f22, even at distances of 6 inches (150mm) or less unwanted background detail can come into focus.

Look at these two shots of a piece of rock, found on a beach in Egypt, showing interesting patterns of erosion. In the bottom picture a small aperture was used. Although not completely sharp, enough of the background has become sharp to become a distraction. When the lens was opened up to f4.5 the background became completely soft and forms a far more pleasing backdrop to the piece of rock, and all its detail appears to become sharper and clearer.

might find it easier to focus the lens to its full extent, then move the camera backwards and forwards until the subject is sharp and then take your shot (you can only do this if your camera has a manual focus option). There might be circumstances where you do not want any more in focus than just one point of detail. In this case use a wide aperture and preferably some type of camera support, such as a tripod, to keep the camera still so that the focus is sharp.

Whatever method of focusing or aperture you choose, take care the lens does not cast a shadow over the subject.

▶ **Keeping the camera steady**
A tripod is sometimes essential for close-up work, especially when using extension tubes and bellows, as the slightest movement backwards or forwards can result in the shot being unsharp.

Advanced Techniques

As well as the art of getting the right exposure and creating the best composition, there are further techniques that can help you to get more out of your photography and create eye-catching and distinctive effects. Many of these techniques go against the general rules of photography, but does this matter if the end result is a great shot? The important thing is to learn from what might be a mistake and turn it to your advantage. Another way to increase your range of techniques is to become conversant with the computer. In an increasingly digital age, this area of photography abounds with possibilities that only a few years ago would have been impossible.

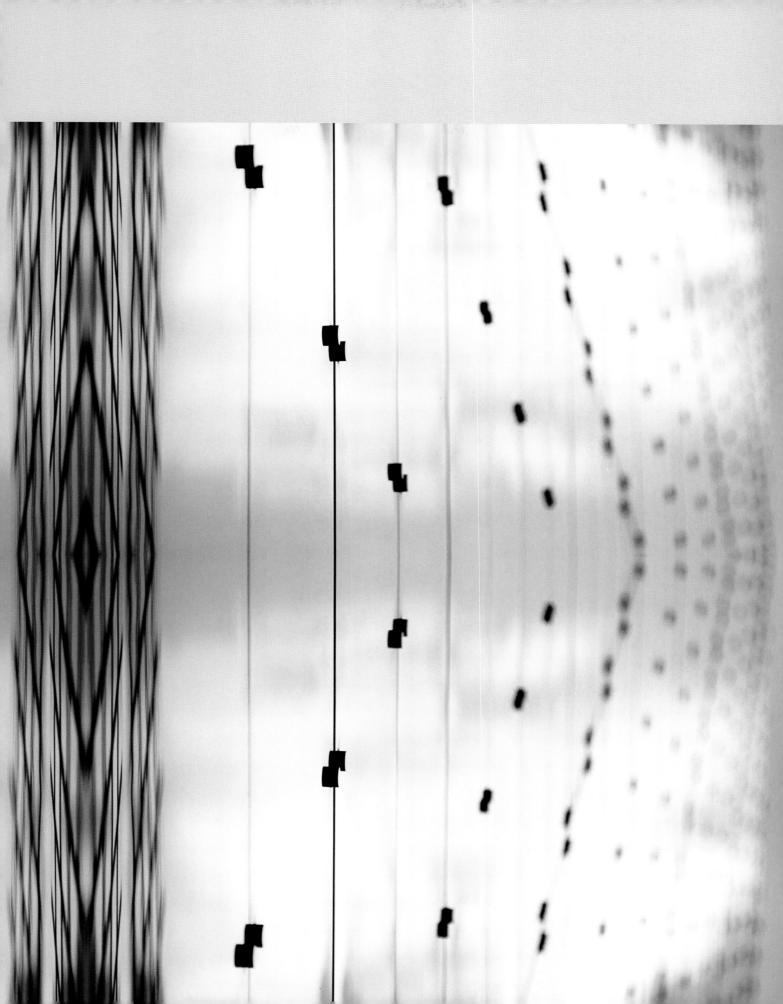

Action

Action photography can take many forms. At one end of the scale it could be sports such as motor racing, athletics or skiing, while at the other it could be capturing children running around or a bird in flight. Whatever it is, a camera that enables you to handle the shutter, will put you firmly in control. Why is having a variable shutter such an advantage? Because you will be able to convey a sense of movement, or action, that is not possible with a camera that has only limited shutter speeds that you cannot adjust manually.

Some cameras have shutter speeds as fast as 1/8000th second, but this doesn't mean they are the best for all forms of action photography. The trouble with such fast speeds is that they freeze the action. This is fine if you are looking at your subject coming towards you, such as a sprinter or hurdler at an athletics meeting or a shot of a skier in midair. But let's imagine photographing the sprinter or the car as it passes in front of us. If we use a speed of 1/1000th second or faster, the action will be frozen. The car and the background will be sharp and if a really fast shutter speed is used, the wheels will look static and the car could be mistaken for being stationary. The same is true with the sprinter, except that both his legs may be off the ground.

The technique to rectify this is called panning. Using a far slower shutter speed, follow the moving subject, taking the shot when the subject is directly in front of you. However, you still follow through with the camera in the same way that a golfer doesn't suddenly halt the swing of the club as soon as it has

▲ **Shutter priority**
With fast moving action there isn't time to alter the exposure continually. In this case I set the camera to shutter priority mode. This is where I set the shutter speed and the camera selects the aperture. The result is a perfectly sharp and exposed picture.

▶ **Lighting**
Most people think that sports photography can only be done on the track or field, but if the opportunity presents itself when you can take more time then great shots can be achieved. This gymnast was simply lit with a light either side of him. The tension of his body, as he hangs upside down, looks just as dynamic as any action shot.

Panning the camera

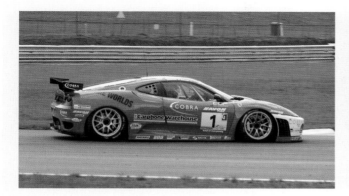

Often if we use a fast shutter speed to photograph a moving subject it freezes the movement so effectively that it can be difficult to tell whether the subject is moving at all. In many cases this is perfectly acceptable, but in sports photography it can be a drawback. Look at these two racing cars. In the picture above left, a shutter speed of 1/1000th second was used. It has not only stopped the car but the wheels as well. The car looks as though it has stopped.

In the picture above right, I chose a shutter speed of 1/100th second and panned the camera. This meant that I followed the car from left to right, keeping it in the centre of the frame. The slower shutter speed has recorded all the detail other than the car as blurred. Because the camera kept pace with the car it has recorded the car as sharp. This has given a real sense of speed and is much more effective at portraying action than using a fast shutter speed.

▲ Focusing

When photographing sports action it is surprising how quickly the moment can pass. This champion swimmer was coming towards the camera at lightning speed. You will need a camera that can focus on a subject moving towards the camera if you are to get a sharp shot.

made contact with the ball. It is the smoothness of the pan that will determine the sharpness of the moving subject in relation to the background.

When you have perfected this technique, you will have a sharp and well-defined subject and a completely blurred background. This will give the impression that the subject is moving at high speed and be more effective than using an ultra fast shutter speed.

Usually, if your camera has a variable shutter it will also have another function. This is called AI Servo on Canon cameras but different manufacturers use different terms. Once you have chosen this mode it will enable you to track a moving subject that is coming towards you and keep it perfectly sharp.

◄ **Positioning**
At most sports events it is relatively easy to judge where the best position for photography will be. In this case I laid low in the snow and a succession of snowboarders flew through the air right in front of me. I used a shutter speed of 1/1000th second to keep them sharp.

▶ **Wide-angle lens**
For this shot of beach volleyball I got right up to the net and used a 17mm wide-angle lens. It has given great perspective on the net and the sky in the background. A fast shutter speed has frozen the ball in midair.

Shutter burst

With digital cameras there can be a delay between pushing the shutter button and the camera taking the shot. This is known as shutter lag and is common with cheaper cameras. However, there is another problem with digital cameras and that is the number of shots you can take in a burst. Although your camera might be able to take six, seven or eight shots per second it can only do it for a limited time. This is because the on board processor cannot keep up with the information and stops you taking any more shots until it has caught up with itself. This is called buffering. When taking a sequence of pictures it is essential that your camera can keep up with the action, as we can see in these shots.

See also
▶ **pp 52–53** Shutter speed
▶ **pp 62–63** Selecting a viewpoint
▶ **pp 74–77** Wide-angle and telephoto lenses
▶ **pp 114–115** Black and white portraits

Multiple flash techniques

Although most cameras have a flash built-in, their use is very limited and they have very little power. If your camera has a hot shoe then you will be able to attach a separate flash gun. However, better still, you will be able to attach a radio transmitter to the hot shoe and use your flash off-camera. Not only that but you could combine several flash guns together to really lift your flash photography to a different level.

One such transmitter is the PocketWizard. The way these devices work is that you slide the transmitter into the camera's hot shoe and then slide your flash gun into the hot shoe on the transceiver. After turning on both units, you choose the channel on the transmitter and the same frequency on the transceiver. Now when you press the shutter release on your camera it will fire the flash even though it is not attached to the camera, and there aren't any leads or wires for you to trip over. This means that you can choose your viewpoint and camera angle and position the flash wherever you like. For example, it could be at the side of your subject so that you can get dramatic side lighting, or you could put the unit behind your subject to get backlighting. With two units you could have both at right angles to your subject for an even more dramatic effect. While these techniques could look good outdoors at nighttime, you might also want to use them in bright daylight as an advanced fill-in flash technique. Again, you could use more than one flash gun. Because the flash might be too far away from the camera for you to hold, you will need to have a stand to attach it to or enlist the help of a friend. Shooting digitally, you will be able to check each shot on the LCD so that you can get the perfect combination of flash output.

◀ Three flashes

It took three separate flashes to light this shot. One was to the left of the model and slightly behind her. This has given her hair a small amount of backlighting. The second was also to her left but more round to her face and can just be seen reflecting in her eye. The third was on the camera to act as a fill on her face and you can just detect it in the centre of her eyes.

See also

▶ **pp 28–29** Accessories

▶ **pp 62–63** Selecting a viewpoint

▶ **pp 92–93** Lighting for outdoor portraits

▶ **pp 134–135** Telephoto lenses in portraiture

▲ Colour balance

In this shot, one flash was mounted onto a lightweight stand to the left of the model. Another flash was mounted onto the camera's hot shoe and used as a fill-in on the front of her face. The exposure for both of these had to be balanced with the coloured lights on the wall.

◀ Shadow

This shot also required three separate flash units. The main one was positioned at right angles to the model, making a strong shadow on the wall. The second was further away, to give some light to the background, and the third was next to the camera to help fill in the shadow areas.

Shift and tilt lenses

Once it was only large format technical cameras that had the ability to shift and tilt the lens but now this facility is even available on some SLR cameras. Shift lenses, or PC (perspective control) lenses as they are sometimes called, allow the photographer to shift the axis of the lens in relation to the sensor or film plane.

The reason for wanting to make this movement, known as a shift, is to be able to get more of your subject into the frame without having to incline the camera either up or down. For instance, if you are photographing a tall building the only way you may be able to get it all in is to tilt the camera upwards. The result will be a problem known as converging verticals. This is where the building will appear to taper towards the top. Although this can sometimes be used to advantage in a shot, in other circumstances it might be essential to keep the sides of the building completely straight.

Another asset with this lens is the ability to keep you, your camera and tripod out of the picture. This might happen if you are photographing a mirror or another highly reflective surface, such as a car, a glass or a stainless steel building. By using the shift lens, you can stand to one side of your subject, to avoid being reflected in it, then use the shift mechanism to centre the subject in the frame.

If your lens has a tilt mechanism you will be able to control the area of sharp focus without the need to alter the aperture of the lens. This technique is known as the Scheimpflug rule (see above right).

The Scheimpflug rule

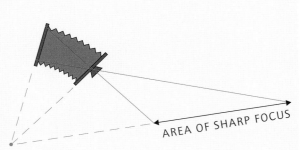

AREA OF SHARP FOCUS

When all the planes are parallel to each other (i.e. the subject plane, the lens plane and the film plane), then the image will be sharp all over. However, if you incline the lens plane, the area of overall sharpness will only be at the point where the two other planes meet at a common point with that of the lens plane.

In the photograph on the right, the lens was stopped down to its smallest aperture of f22 but the column nearest to the camera is still not sharp. In the shot below, by using the lens' tilt and swing function in its swing mode, we can get all the shot sharp even though the aperture finally used was f16 .

▶ **Shift lenses**

When photographing tall buildings it is often necessary to point the camera upwards (1), which means the buildings will taper towards the top. This is known as converging verticals. To keep the buildings vertical, the camera's film plane must be parallel to the subject, i.e. the buildings. However, this will mean that the tops of the buildings will be cut off (2). The only way to correct this is by using a shift lens. When the camera is level and the lens is parallel to the buildings, the tops of those buildings will still be cut off. However, when we use the shift function and move the axis of the lens upwards, the tops of the buildings come into view but their sides are still straight (3).

See also

1

2

3

Digital perspective

As we have seen, the way to get perfectly straight verticals in camera is to use a shift, or perspective control (PC), lens. However, these lenses are very expensive and unless you are going to do a lot of architectural photography they will not justify the expense. Another method is to correct your pictures in Photoshop after you have taken and downloaded them onto your computer.

You will need to make allowances when taking your picture and make sure to include plenty of detail either side of the frame. This is because much of it will be cropped out when you do your correction, so make sure you pull back sufficiently.

Once you have edited your shots and chosen the one that is to be corrected in Photoshop, you should use the Crop tool from the toolbar. When you make your crop, you will see on the menu bar at the top of the window a small icon on the right called Perspective. Highlight

1 Crop
To correct the leaning illusion, open the image in Photoshop and select Crop from the toolbar on the left. Click on the Perspective box (marked red) at the top. Now click on the top left hand point and drag it towards the centre until it is parallel with the leaning upright of the building.

2 Repeat the crop
Repeat the same process to the right hand side of the image. Click on Image in the menu at the top and then scroll down to Crop. Depending on how big the correction is, the image will be 'stretched' at the top.

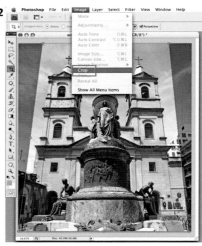

▲ **Converging verticals**
This shot typifies many architectural pictures, where the camera has had to be tilted upwards to get the whole of the building in. This has caused converging verticals and the church looks like it is leaning over.

◀ **Straightened up**
The building is now straight and no longer looks as though it is toppling backwards. However, notice how much of the image has been lost from the sides, so if you are taking a shot like this make sure you give yourself plenty of area around the building.

this icon and you will be able to move the crop in several directions other than just square. Once you have the picture to your liking, choose Crop and the verticals will now be straight.

The drawback with this method is that you are 'stretching' the pixels. As each pixel is stretched it loses tone and colour information and ends up with holes where there is no information present. Fortunately, Photoshop interpolates these discrepancies and fills in the holes by adding more pixels. It does this by collecting the information from the surrounding pixels and makes a judgement for tone and colour as to what the missing pixels should be. Stretching the pixels will affect the finished print and the larger it is the more visible the loss of quality will be.

Fisheye lenses

Fisheye lenses, as their name implies, have a very wide angle of view. Most brands give a full 180-degree view. Some produce a full frame image while others record the shot as a circular image on the sensor or film. Whatever the method, the one thing that they have in common is that the edges of the frame will be distorted and curve inwards at the top and bottom of the frame. This can be put to creative effect, but in everyday situations they are limited in their uses. On this basis, it is rare that you will find a photographer who actually owns such a lens. It is expensive and if you are only going to use it once in a while, the cost will never justify the financial outlay. On this basis it is worth considering hiring such a lens when the right situation for its use occurs.

Once you have decided on the shot you want to take with such a lens, it will probably be best to use a tripod. This is especially true if you are looking up to a ceiling. If the camera and lens are not completely level the balance of the shot might be impaired. To this end it is useful to carry a small spirit level in your camera bag to check that the camera is even in all directions. Even if you have spirit levels built into your tripod, they may not be accurate, especially if the camera is not mounted onto it completely evenly.

Another important point to bear in mind when using these lenses is that with such an extreme angle of view exposure can be problematic if, for example, one side of the shot is brightly lit and the other is in shadow. In this case you might have to use fill-in flash to balance the exposure.

See also
▶ pp 26–27 Additional lenses
▶ pp 62–63 Selecting a viewpoint
▶ pp 132–133 Wide-angle lenses in portraiture
▶ pp 188–189 Interiors
▶ pp 192–193 Architectural details

◀ **High viewpoint**
The atrium of this building had been temporarily converted for the evening to accommodate a dinner-dance reception. The evening light was dying and there was a lot of movement on the floor. By taking the picture from high up and using a fisheye lens I got the shot that portrayed the ambience of the surroundings.

▼ **Small space**
This spice shop was an Aladdin's cave. The only way to fit the whole of the shop's interior in was to use a fisheye lens. Although the walls curve noticeably, it adds to the general busyness of the shot.

▶ **Looking up**
Perhaps the most effective use of fisheye lenses is when they are used to photograph ceilings that have great architectural interest. In this case it was important that the camera was absolutely level otherwise the shot would look distorted.

Zoom lenses

Zoom lenses have a variable focal length. This might mean, for example, that such a lens has a variable focal range of 28–70mm or 70–200mm. The more you pay, the better quality the optics, and the speed of the lens will also be faster. This means that on a cheaper zoom lens the fastest aperture might vary with the focal length the lens is set on. For example, at a setting of 70mm the lens might be f3.5. However, if you zoom the lens to 200mm you find the biggest aperture available is f5.6. In itself this might not be a problem but in low light conditions the use of a slow shutter speed to compensate for the lack of a wider aperture may result in camera shake, or if the subject is moving, a blurred image. With more expensive lenses the aperture will be at least f2.8 and will remain the same whatever focal length the lens is set to.

The main reason for buying a zoom lens is that it cuts down on the amount of kit you have to carry around. For instance, instead of having wide-angle, normal and telephoto lenses, you can have just one. This can make a great difference if you are doing a lot of travelling, and the optics of the top lenses are so good they are on a par with prime lenses. As well as these advantages, zoom lenses have the ability to change focal length mid shot, or to zoom the lens. This can produce some astonishing effects and is a great way to create abstract images. There are no hard and fast rules about how to use this technique, as it requires a certain amount of practice, but once mastered it is another method to add to your photographic repertoire.

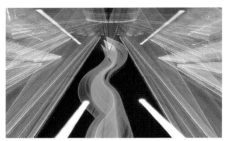

Neon lights
Here are examples of zooming the lens at night. Neon or illuminated signs are good subjects as their highlights streak well in the camera, making strong geometric patterns. In the examples above the camera was zoomed from its widest to its shortest, while in the shot on the left it was zoomed from its shortest to its widest.

See also

▶ **pp 26–27**
  Additional
  lenses
▶ **pp 28–29**
  Accessories
▶ **pp 52–53**
  Shutter speed
▶ **pp 74–77**
  Wide-angle
  and telephoto
  lenses

Zooming the lens

There are many ways to use a zoom lens effectively. As well as changing the focal length to frame a picture for a more pleasing composition, you can also zoom the lens, or change its focal length, while the picture is being taken. This will give the appearance of speed lines in the finished shot. Of course, the subject isn't moving at all and you aren't flying over it, but it will look like it. The most effective way of using this is to fix the camera on a tripod. This is necessary because you will need a slow shutter speed of 1/15th or 1/8th second to have time to zoom the lens so the camera needs to be steady. The results can be stunning, as seen here.

In picture 1, the lens was kept stable and no change of focal length took place when the photograph was taken. In picture 2, the camera's focal length was changed from 70mm to 210mm. By contrast, in picture 3 the lens was zoomed the other way, from 210mm to 70mm. The effect is altered considerably. Different lenses will give different results, as will different times of day. Perhaps the most important point to remember is that the more highlights, the greater the effect. However, it is only by experimenting with this technique in a variety of situations that you will discover how to get the best shot every time.

Extension tubes and bellows

Extension tubes and bellows allow the photographer to get very close to the subject. These accessories fit between the camera body and the lens. Extension tubes are available in various lengths and are usually sold in sets of two or three. The longer the extension tube, the closer you will be able to focus. You can also join the extension tubes together in various combinations for even greater magnification. However, whatever the combination you choose, the distance from lens to subject is fixed. Extension bellows, on the other hand, have the advantage of infinite magnification and allow for more precise framing of your subject at close distances.

When using either of these accessories you will need to make an allowance for exposure, as they increase the distance the light has to travel from the front of the lens to the film plane. If you are using TTL metering, this should not be a problem. If, however, you are using manual exposure metering, you will have to increase the exposure. If your equipment does not have a scale for doing this, then a certain amount of trial and error will be required. In any case, it would be advisable to bracket the exposures when taking your shots.

Depth of field with these pieces of equipment is minimal and becomes even less the closer you go. As it is likely you will be using slow exposures, it will be essential to have the camera mounted on a tripod or some other firm support. Focusing can be difficult, especially if the light is low. Care needs to be taken that you don't let the lens cast a shadow over your subject or, if you are working really close, that the lens hood impedes the degree of closeness you can get to your subject.

See also
▶ **pp 26–27** Additional lenses
▶ **pp 58–59** Exposure and auto-exposure
▶ **pp 152–153** Close-ups
▶ **pp 216–217** Close-ups
▶ **pp 248–251** Still life

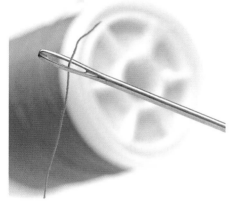

▲ **Close-ups**
When going in as close as this, you will need to be careful that you do not cast a shadow over the subject with the end of the lens or that the lens hood does not impede the lens from being focused correctly.

◀ **Backlighting**
To take this shot the camera was mounted with two extension tubes and a 140mm macro lens. The kiwi fruit were sliced thinly and placed on a sheet of perspex with a light behind. The magnification is larger than real life.

▲ **Fine detail**
When using extension tubes or bellows with your Digital SLR you will be
able to record the finest detail by getting in extremely close. This could
be just millimetres from the lens. The camera and lens will need a firm
support to eliminate camera shake.

Long exposures

Although most of the time we think it is only worth taking photographs in daylight, there are just as many opportunities at night. For instance, in most cities buildings are lit up, there are neon signs and street lighting. Also, there are events at night, such as firework displays, which make great shots.

The essential piece of equipment for night photography is a tripod. As most shots will be taken at very low speeds, in some cases several seconds, it will be impossible to hold the camera steady for this length of time.

Another consideration with nighttime photography is that long exposures can increase noise. If you are using film, 800 ISO might mean that you can take pictures with faster shutter speeds but it could be at the expense of grain. Again, this is where a tripod will be invaluable. 200 ISO with either digital or film should be adequate in most situations.

Many shots taken at night will look better in what is known as the twilight period. This is the time between sunset and complete darkness where the sky takes on that deep blue hue. Completely black skies at night can look very boring, especially if they take up most of the frame. However, this twilight period only lasts for about 20 minutes, so you will have to be quick to take advantage of it and a certain amount of forward planning might be necessary.

See also

▶ **pp 46–47** Holding the camera
▶ **pp 52–53** Shutter speed
▶ **pp 168–169** The changing day
▶ **pp 232–233** Zoom lenses
▶ **pp 264–265** Multiple images

▲ **Abstract lights**
For this abstract shot of different coloured lights I hand held the camera. I then selected a shutter speed of 5 seconds and as soon as the shutter was released I gradually panned the camera downwards, creating this eye-catching effect.

▶ **Fireworks**
To photograph fireworks effectively you will need to use a tripod. Ascertain where the fireworks explode in the sky. Try an aperture of f8 with an ISO of 100 and set the shutter to B and leave it open until there has been a burst of light. You might want to try a multi exposure. Do not use the flash on your camera.

Twilight

The best time to shoot at night is the twilight hour. This is the time between the sun setting and  the sky going black. Within this time there is a period when the sky appears as a very dark blue, which only lasts for a few minutes, as seen in these photographs of The London Eye. To be absolutely sure of the best exposure, bracket your shots.

Reciprocity failure

Although the quality of film manufacture has advanced significantly over the years, there is one problem that has not gone away. This problem is reciprocity failure. When shooting at ultra slow speeds, the ISO of a film loses its true value and becomes unstable. What this means is that when shooting at 1 second or less, it does not necessarily follow that, if your exposure meter, when set to the film manufacturer's ISO setting, say 100 ISO, indicates that you need to double the exposure to 2 seconds, the film will respond. It might need 3 seconds or more. The slower the shutter speed you use, the more this problem will grow. In other words, the ISO of the film will drop to 50 or perhaps 25 ISO or less. Only through getting to know your equipment and film through continual evaluation and experimentation will you be able to shoot at these slow speeds with some degree of confidence.

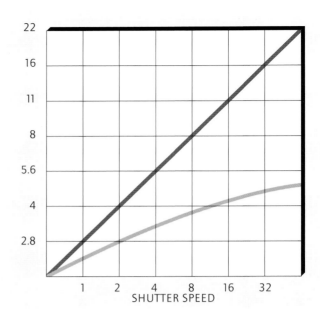

◀ **Stained glass windows**
On an overcast day I needed an exposure of 4 seconds to photograph these stained glass windows. The camera needed to be mounted on a tripod and I used a cable release for a smooth shutter operation.

One of the problems when shooting long exposures with a digital camera is an increase in noise, whereas when shooting film it is grain that is more pronounced. As with film, the higher the ISO, 3,200 for instance, the more pronounced will be the noise. One of the advantages of full frame DSLR cameras is that noise is less pronounced than cameras with smaller sensors. There are various plug-in filters that will help eradicate this, as well as a noise reduction filter in Photoshop.

Another problem when shooting long exposures digitally is the time that the camera's processor will take to process the shot. If your shutter is open for 30 minutes it could take as long as that again for the camera to process the image. Therefore, you will need to make sure that the camera battery is fully charged before you start. If your battery runs out while the camera is processing the shot, it will lose information and you will have to re-shoot.

◀ Palm trees
This shot of palm trees was lit using street lighting. The camera was mounted on a tripod and then pointed directly upwards to the sky. An exposure of 6 seconds was required at f8 and an ISO of 100 was selected.

▲ Church
This church interior was very dark and needed a 20 second exposure. The camera was on a tripod and then I used the 'mirror up' facility in the camera's menu to make the shutter release as shake-free as possible.

◀ Theatre
Many interiors can take a long time to expose, such as the interior of this theatre. Even though it was lit well, it still took a 10 second exposure. The difficulty was not to let the lights burn out so that they appeared as bright blobs of light.

Ring flash

Ring flash, as its name implies, is a 360-degree circular unit that fits around the lens it is mounted on. It synchronizes with the camera in the same way that conventional flash units do. There are many different models, ranging from small portable battery-powered units that are best suited to 35mm cameras and lenses, through to much larger, more cumbersome ones powered by studio flash units and more appropriate for use with medium format cameras. Ring flash can also be used in conjunction with other flash units, either as the main source or as a fill-in light.

The original use of ring flash was for medical photography, as you could get very close to your subject, using extension tubes or bellows, but still have a light source that would give you completely even illumination. However, ring flash soon became popular with commercial photographers, particularly those who specialized in fashion, as well as wildlife photographers.

Ring flash gives an almost shadowless light and very even illumination. If your subject is against a wall, for instance, there will be a soft halo-like shadow all around them. In colour photography, red eye can sometimes be a problem but this can easily be removed, either on the computer or retouched by hand later. Because of this shadowless lighting, ring flash is also great for intricate subjects that might have a lot of detail, such as the constituent parts of a car engine. If you were using conventional lighting in a situation like this you might have shadows on one side that would be difficult to soften, as it might not be possible to use a fill-in light or a reflector in such a space.

As with all equipment, using ring flash will require a degree of experimentation before you start to see how original this type of lighting can be.

See also
▶ **pp 28–29** Accessories
▶ **pp 60–61** Effective flash
▶ **pp 120–123** Further lighting techniques
▶ **pp 150–151** Using props
▶ **pp 248–251** Still life

▶ **Even lighting**
Using ring flash to photograph this girl kneeling on the floor has resulted in a very even spread of light. Although the shot was taken from an extremely low viewpoint, the floor is evenly exposed throughout.

◀ **Shadow**
Ring flash can be great for portraits, as it gives a very even light. At this distance it can cause red eye and I removed this in Photoshop. You can just make out the faint shadow all around the model.

Ring flash versus straight flash

Straight flash

Ring flash is great for mechanical and complicated subjects where it is difficult to get lights in. This shot (right) was taken with straight flash. Notice the harsh shadows and bright highlights where it has reflected off the shiny surfaces.

Even light

In this shot (far right), lit by ring flash, the lighting is much more even with few harsh shadows and greatly reduced flare on the shiny surfaces. Overall, it is a much more successful shot.

Specialist filters

Of all the accessories that will improve and enhance your photography, filters have to be the most effective for the minimum outlay. There are hundreds to choose from, ranging from colour balancing and colour correction filters through to special effects and light enhancement filters. While some of them are more applicable to film, some are equally relevant to digital.

Apart from the UV or skylight filters, which should be permanently attached to all your lenses to protect them, a polarising filter is a good one to start with. This filter serves two purposes. First, it can eliminate unwanted reflections and, second, it can enhance a blue sky and make the clouds stand out with greater clarity. All filters work best with SLR cameras, as you will be able to see the effect the filter is having as you look through the viewfinder or with live view on your DSLR. With extreme wide-angle lenses, polarizing filters can give an uneven effect, which can ruin landscape shots.

Another point to consider when using a polarizing filter is that it cuts down the amount of light passing through the lens. This can be as much as two stops or the difference between 1/125th second at f11, when not using the filter, and 1/125th at f5.6 when the filter is used. Nearly all filters, except for the UV variety, need an increase in exposure. This is known as a filter factor. When you buy a filter it will come with instructions that will tell you what this is. However, if your camera has TTL metering this should give you an accurate exposure reading regardless of the filter fitted to the lens.

▶ **Fluorescent light**
The trouble with taking shots in fluorescent light is that fluorescent tubes come in many different varieties. These could be warm light, daylight, cool light, and so on. Therefore, choosing the correct filter to remove the green cast (right) is rather a hit and miss affair unless you have a colour temperature meter. If using film, use a 40 magenta filter combined with a 10 blue, which works well in most circumstances (far right). With digital you will need to experiment with the white balance settings.

▼ ► Polarizing filters

Polarizing filters are excellent for enhancing skies and cutting down on haze. Compare these two photographs. The top one was shot without the polarizing filter whereas the bottom one was shot with it in place. You can also use these filters to cut down on reflections in glass and water. However, be careful when using them with ultra wide-angle lenses as the effect will be uneven on blue skies.

▼ ► Neutral density graduated filters

Often there is a disparity in exposure between sky and foreground. If you expose for the foreground (1), it can result in the sky being over-exposed and losing some detail. If you use a graduated neutral density filter (2), it will balance the two exposures, retaining detail in the sky while keeping the foreground correctly exposed.

1

2

Another filter worth buying is a neutral density graduated filter. This one, as its name implies, graduates from clear glass or plastic to a band of what looks like a grey coating. This grey coating comes in different strengths and cuts down the amount of exposure required without causing a colour cast. This is excellent for photographing landscapes, where the difference in exposure between the sky and the foreground would result in either the sky being burnt out or the foreground under-exposed. In other situations it is possible to use these filters where there is a strong line of contrast between highlighted areas and shadow. Practice will help you perfect this technique.

When shooting digitally you will be able to adjust the white balance, but if you are shooting in fluorescent or tungsten light with film you will need to use a filter that will take out the cast.

See also

► pp 28–29 Accessories
► pp 158–159 Summer
► pp 160–161 Autumn
► pp 166–167 Emphasizing the sky
► pp 168–169 The changing day

Underwater photography

There are very few places on the planet where if you put your head in the sea you won't see fish and other marine life. In warm waters the colours and shapes of such creatures can be truly magnificent and well worth making the effort to photograph.

The underwater equipment that you will require can range from a simple waterproof one-use camera through to a sophisticated camera housing that will take the most advanced SLR. The drawback with the one-use camera is that the optics are not very good and the results somewhat unreliable. However, it is possible to get some acceptable shots using these, so they should not be dismissed instantly.

The next step up is to get a waterproof housing for your digital compact camera. These are quite economical to buy and the results can be really stunning. Not all manufacturers make these but you can buy one for the Canon Ixus, for example. Shooting digitally means that you can check immediately on the camera's LCD. If you are a really experienced diver, a camera housing is probably the answer. With this you will be able to use a top-of-the-range camera and go down to greater depths.

Whatever the equipment, the one thing that they all have in common is that when you are under the water distances can be deceptive. For example, when you see a fish in front of you that looks only an arm's length away it will in fact be almost twice the distance away but will look twice as big. The other point to remember is that sea water can contain a lot of minute particles that cut down on visibility. With practice, you will be able to judge distance and size with a good deal of accuracy, so do not be put off if your first results are disappointing.

See also
▶ **pp 12–13** One-use and phone cameras
▶ **pp 32–33** Equipment care
▶ **pp 64–65** Filling the frame
▶ **pp 200–201** At the beach
▶ **pp 216–217** Close-ups

▶ **Jaws!**
This stunning photograph of a shark swimming around a coral wall is a real action picture. Obviously, this type of situation is only suitable for the most experienced divers and, as with all diving, you should always be accompanied by another diver.

◀ **Coral reef**
Besides fish, underwater plant life also makes stunning shots. The colour in this soft Fijian coral is particularly vivid and the overall shot is well composed and exposed. Notice how it fills more than half of the frame yet there is still a great sense of depth.

◀ **Scuba shot**
It is always good to get the human element into your underwater photographs and it shouldn't be too difficult as you should always be with another diver. Here, we see a diver examining a giant sponge in the sea off the coast in the Cayman Islands.

▲ **Tropical delight**
Exotic coloured fish make perfect underwater shots, as this close-up of an Angelfish illustrates. The depth of field is just soft enough to make the fish, which is pin sharp, stand out from the background.

Aerial photography

With more adventure sports becoming accessible to a greater number of people, many photographers want to shoot aerial photographs from gliders, hot air balloons, hang gliders, helicopters or regular aircraft.

Whatever the method, the one thing these shots have in common is that you will need to shoot at a relatively fast shutter speed. This is because most of these craft will generate a good deal of vibration, which at slow shutter speeds will result in blurred images even if your camera or lens has image stabilization. Therefore, use a reasonably fast film or choose a higher ISO if shooting digitally. If you are taking pictures through a window of an aircraft, helicopter or glider keep the lens pressed up against the glass to stop the lens reflecting in the window. It will probably be best to switch off auto-focus, as the window, which will be between the lens and the subject, might confuse the camera as to what it should be focusing on. The same is true with built-in flash. If this fires when you take your shot, it will flare over the glass and ruin what might otherwise be a great photograph.

If you are in an open-sided craft, don't lean out too far, not for the obvious reason of falling out but because the wind could take the camera out of your hands. If this happened in a helicopter, the consequences could be fatal.

See also
▶ **pp 18–21** Film and DSLR cameras
▶ **pp 34–35** Film
▶ **pp 40–41** Digital capture
▶ **pp 52–53** Shutter speed
▶ **pp 62–63** Selecting a viewpoint

Different perspectives

Although both of these pictures were taken from high up, only one of them was taken from the air. The shot of the buildings on the right was taken from a helicopter hovering high above the city of Los Angeles. However, it looks as though it could have been taken from another building. The shot of the swimming pool below was in fact taken from the roof of a hotel in Las Vegas. It looks much more like an aerial photograph than the real thing. Always be on the lookout for the unusual view.

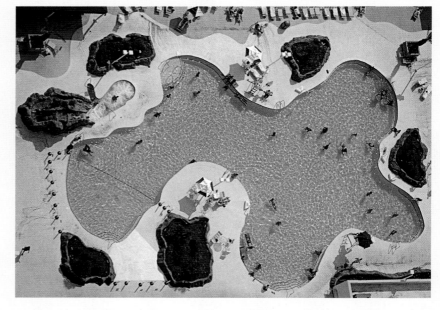

▲ Getting the right angle
One of the advantages that helicopters have over planes is their manoeuvrability and the ability to get them steady in the right position. I took this shot from a light aircraft with the door removed. It took several fly pasts to get it framed the way I wanted.

◀ Haze
This coastal picture is a good example of an aerial photograph. It is easy to see that it was taken from a high viewpoint by the curvature of the horizon. Fortunately, the day was clear, as haze would have ruined the shot.

▶ Fast shutter speed
This freeway makes a good subject for an aerial view. The different feeder roads make a strong pattern while the main highway stretches far into the distance. A fast shutter speed was required since the helicopter vibrated continuously.

Still life

The great advantage for the photographer when shooting in a studio is that you have complete control of the viewpoint and the lighting. There is no need to worry about changing light, time of day or weather. Studios do not have to be large rooms with high ceilings and a north light, nor do they have to be filled with expensive lighting and elaborate tables and supports. You don't even need a 10 x 8 or 5 x 4 camera. Indeed, many effective still lifes can be shot with just a single light source and a SLR camera, using the kitchen table.

When setting up a still life, give yourself as much flexibility as possible. Using a table means that you will have scope to shoot from above, straight on or looking up. Having these options is

▲ **Backlighting**
Still life photographs can be very simple arrangements, such as this flower display with a toy rabbit. This was photographed for an Easter card and was lit with natural backlighting and two reflectors placed either side of the camera to bounce light back.

▲ **Medium format**
This is another example of a simple still life and was shot with a medium format 6 x 7 camera fitted with a 140mm lens. The big focusing screen on this type of camera is a real advantage when it comes to composing your shot.

▶ **Wide-angle lens**
There are no hard and fast rules about what equipment or lenses you should use when photographing a still life. For this shot I used an extremely wide-angle lens (24mm) and focused in close on the table detail. It is the angle that makes this shot work.

important since the camera viewpoint can dramatically affect the overall appearance of the final photograph. The same is true when it comes to lighting. To be able to move your light source to the side, behind or above or below your subject will give an unparalleled degree of creative control. If you were to set up your subject on the floor or a wall shelf, you would restrict the movement of the camera and lighting, even if your final viewpoint is looking down.

If using an SLR camera, consider buying a close-up device. This could be extension tubes or bellows. These both fit between the camera body and lens and enable you to get closer to your subject. The great advantage of an SLR is that you see through the lens exactly what you will get on film. If you are using a DSLR you might have the benefit of live view, which is a great advantage. Used with a medium telephoto lens, they create space between your camera and subject while still achieving the illusion of being in close. This is important, as you may want to set up a reflector or flag between the camera and subject, which would be more awkward without some space between them. A medium telephoto lens will also give less depth of field, which might be advantageous if you want the background to fall out of focus or if you only want a small area of your subject to be sharp. A rigid tripod with adjustable legs and a pan tilt head will also be an asset.

Think about the lighting that will give the effect that you want to achieve. If you have only one light, consider the quality of that light. This does not mean the most expensive, but rather what type of light is being delivered. Whether it's flash or tungsten, the reflector or dish will determine the harshness and spread of the illumination. For example, a dish

Composition

Although simplicity can be the key to a good still life photograph, it doesn't mean to say that you cannot pay attention to detail. Look at these pictures here. I needed to shoot six wine glasses and to make the shot as clean but as interesting as possible. I began with the glasses on a white surface and placed a large soft box behind them, which was the background. I moved the glasses into various positions and tried different angles but the results all seemed quite ordinary.

I then had the idea to place them in a line, one behind the other. At first I was looking down on them, but decided that the surface they were standing on looked messy. Eventually I moved the camera until it was lower than the glasses and I was looking up at them. This made an interesting shape and a more pleasing composition. I made sure that each glass was absolutely straight and put black paper at the sides of the glasses, but out of view, to give a crisper edge.

with a white surface will deliver a light that is softer than one with a silver surface. A diffuser over the dish will have a similar effect. A honeycomb fixed over the front of the light will make it more directional and crisp. A large soft box will make the light softer still. Gels placed over the light will create different colour effects. Many of these attachments can be improvised from materials as simple as a piece of card and a bulldog clip. A spotlight will enable you to project light onto a small area and focus it. You will also be able to attach gobos that will allow you to create patterns of light.

Depending on how the spotlight is focused, a soft or harsh pattern will

be achieved. This could resemble the light coming in through a window or filtering through trees. The position of the light will have an effect as well. If the light is low, the shadows will be long. If it is high and near to the camera viewpoint, they will be smaller. Only by experimenting with angles and different light sources will you be able to see how the light changes.

See also
▶ pp 22–23 Medium format SLR cameras
▶ pp 26–27 Additional lenses
▶ pp 128–131 High key and low key
▶ pp 216–217 Close-ups
▶ pp 252–255 Photographing food

Photographing food

If there is one area of photography that seems insatiable in its appetite for new angles, concepts and themes, it has to be the art of food photography. It is on a par with fashion and beauty when it comes to the sheer number of magazines, newspaper articles and books that are dedicated to it. Every television chef, many of whom become household names, invariably produce a book to accompany their latest series. Everything from the humble potato to a national cuisine will have several books written and lavishly illustrated with photography dedicated to it. Even when certain foods go out of fashion, there are new ones to take their place and all need to be photographed to look as artistic and mouthwatering as possible.

◀ Depth of field
By using a large aperture, f2.8, I have reduced the depth of field. This has put the emphasis on the fruit in the foreground, making it stand out from the background.

Markets

As well as setting up food shots in the studio or on location, it is possible to get striking pictures in markets. Countries like France and Spain are noted for the freshness and variety of produce on sale in local markets. In the USA and UK farmers' markets are popular and provide a good source of photographic opportunities. Often the light will help in these situations by creating strong shadow detail. When a series of pictures have been taken, they can be displayed as a collage.

▲ Dappled light
This dish was photographed in a restaurant and I took full advantage of the sun filtering through the trees. It made a wonderful dappled pattern on the tablecloth and I needed to work quickly before the sun moved to another position.

Although the majority of food photography is done in the studio, it is by no means the only way it can be photographed. What is convenient about a food studio is that it has a kitchen dedicated to preparing food for photography. This doesn't necessarily mean that the food is treated in a strange and weird way, but that all the items required to make the food look good are on hand. This might be as simple as a cocktail stick and a pair of tweezers used to tweak and position various components of the dish, to various methods of making imitation ice cream that can be photographed without melting.

The people who prepare the food for the photographer to shoot are called home economists and they are extremely skilled in cooking food that looks fantastic in front of the camera.

Another person who is just as important as the home economist is the stylist. If you ever thought that the picture you saw in a magazine was photographed using a plate that just happened to be in the photographer's studio, or likewise with the tablecloth, cutlery and glassware, think again.

The stylist would have had a meeting with the photographer, the food editor of the magazine or book and the home economist to determine the 'look' that is required. Every aspect will be discussed, then the stylist will buy, borrow or hire all the props that are required to make each shot work. They may also be at the studio on the day of the shoot, helping the photographer to set up the shot by laying out all the props in individual groups for any particular shot.

With all this help you might wonder what is left for the photographer to do. For a start, the right lens needs to be chosen to get the desired effect. Today

▲ **Single light source**

To photograph this tart I used a single soft box at the back of the dish and pointed it down towards the camera. A mirror was placed on each side of the camera to bounce light back. Mirrors give a crisp light and in this case make the tomatoes glisten.

a lot of food is photographed with the minimum amount of focus. This is where just a small amount of the subject is sharp with the rest falling off, both in front and behind. A long lens with an extension tube might have to be used, enabling the photographer to get in close while maintaining a comfortable working area between camera and subject, and at the same time minimizing depth of field. This will also require a wide aperture to be used. In this case the photographer will have to position and adjust the lights not only to obtain the right exposure balance, but also to give the required ambience.

Many food photographers begin to light a shot with a single light source. This is invariably flash, as it is quick to work with and cool in operation. These are important considerations to bear in mind when purchasing equipment for this type of photography. From this one light they might employ various reflectors to bounce light back onto the food. These could be white card, foil or plain mirrors. All of these can be used to direct light to the position where it is required and if you practise with these you will be amazed at how effective and precise you can make the light. Once in the correct position, these reflectors can be held in place with a variety of clamps and supports. As with so much in photography, it is often the most simple set-up that succeeds.

▶ **Camera angle**
As with all photography, styles come and go. I was asked to photograph this breakfast egg in close with the emphasis on the yolk. I then angled the camera so that the dish was slanting to one side. This is a very popular style but it could easily go out of fashion.

See also
▶ **pp 52–53** Shutter speed
▶ **pp 124–127** In the workplace
▶ **pp 216–217** Close-ups
▶ **pp 234–235** Extension tubes and bellows
▶ **pp 248–251** Still life

◀ **Colour**
Sometimes it only takes a single ingredient to make an eye-catching food picture. These red chillies look vibrant in this sack and I went in close to fill the frame.

Mixed lighting

There are many situations, especially when shooting interiors, where the lighting comes from different sources. These could be daylight, tungsten, fluorescent or flash. When they are all present in your shot, the trick is to take the photograph so they all look natural and don't cause a colour cast. How this is achieved depends entirely on the mix of the different sources.

The simplest form of mixed lighting is where daylight needs balancing with flash. If you are photographing a room where you want to retain the detail that can be seen through the windows and doors, you will need to introduce flash. To balance the two, first ascertain what the flash exposure will be. Remember, it is the aperture that is important here. If this is going to be f11, you will need to take a reading of the ambient light coming in through the windows that matches this. When the meter shows the same reading of f11, you can then see what shutter speed is required for that aperture. If this is 1/15th second, your exposure will be 1/15th at f11.

If the room you are photographing is lit by fluorescent light, you will need to use a light balancing filter or adjust the white balance when shooting digitally to correct the green cast that would otherwise appear on your photographs. However, if the fluorescent light is insufficient, or if it would cause hot spots if used as the only light source, you will have to balance it with flash. To do this, cover the flash heads with a light balancing gel. This will turn the flashlight green, which will balance it with the fluorescent light. The filter will then correct the flash and the fluorescent light so that your finished picture does not have a green cast.

A similar procedure can be followed if you are balancing tungsten with flash. In this case you do not need a filter on the lens, but you will need to gel the flash to convert it to the same colour temperature as the tungsten light.

See also
▶ **pp 56–57** Light and colour
▶ **pp 60–61** Effective flash
▶ **pp 188–189** Interiors
▶ **pp 190–191** Lighting interiors
▶ **pp 242–243** Specialist filters

▲ **Fluorescent light and flash with film**
This room was lit predominantly by fluorescent light. However, it still required fill-in light and I chose flash. Because I was filtering the camera's lens to correct the fluorescent light for daylight film, I put green gels over the flash to make them the same colour balance as the room lights.

▶ **Flash, daylight and tungsten**
This enormous room required four separate 6,400 joule flash units, each firing 20 times and all on full power. I turned off the room lights after five flashes as I did not want them to burn out and become large white blobs. The time required for the daylight was calculated by the f stop used for the flash. The end result is an evenly lit picture that looks naturally lit.

◀ **Shop interior**
In this shot there are four different light sources: daylight coming through the windows, tungsten from the ceiling lights, fluorescent light from the refrigerated display unit and flash, which lit the fresh produce in the foreground. I decided to go with daylight, as that was balanced to the flash. The tungsten light required only a short exposure and I judged the level of fluorescent light to be acceptable for this photograph.

HDR

ometimes, especially when taking landscape photographs, it is impossible to expose correctly all the elements you want to include. In its simplest form it could be the disparity between the exposure required for the sky and that which is needed for the foreground. If you expose for the sky, the foreground could be under-exposed, and if you expose for the foreground, the sky will come out over-exposed. As we have already discussed, you could use a graduated neutral density filter, but what happens if some of the

foreground detail, such as a tree or a building, extends into the sky? If you use the filter in a case like this it will make the sky look correctly exposed, but it will be at the expense of the tree or building, which will look under-exposed. One way round this problem is to create an HDR picture. HDR stands for High Dynamic Range and its purpose is to prevent the highlights from suffering burnout and to stop clipping in the shadows.

So how does it work? Basically, an HDR image is made up of several shots. Each one is exposed for a particular area

and then they are merged together in your computer. Let's imagine a typical landscape shot where the sky is full of bright cloud detail and the foreground is much darker but full of interesting features and texture. We start by taking a series of bracketed shots – the same picture taken at different shutter speeds – so that some will be over-exposed while others will be under-exposed. Because each shot must be taken from exactly the same position, it is essential that you use a tripod. Once you have downloaded these pictures into the

▲ **Original pictures**
The three original pictures only have the correct exposure in certain areas, as we can see when they are opened in Photoshop. So we will be combining these to get the perfect image.

◄ **Layers**
Choose the image where the ground is the correct exposure and copy the other two images on top by holding down Shift and dragging the layer onto the middle of the image.

computer you can then select the best exposure for each part of the image. This could be as few as two but might include several. Having made your selection you then need to merge these pictures together. At first this image combination will look really flat and you will need to use the Shadow/Highlight tool to bring out the best in the shadow detail while darkening the highlight areas. Once you have got this to your liking you can then enhance the overall image in the normal way.

As with any Photoshop technique, a certain amount of practice will help you to perfect this rewarding technique.

▲ ▶ Eraser
On each layer, use the Eraser tool to erase everything apart from what you would like to see in the final image. Here we only want the sky and a little of the trees showing. It is also easier when you zoom in to erase around difficult images like trees.

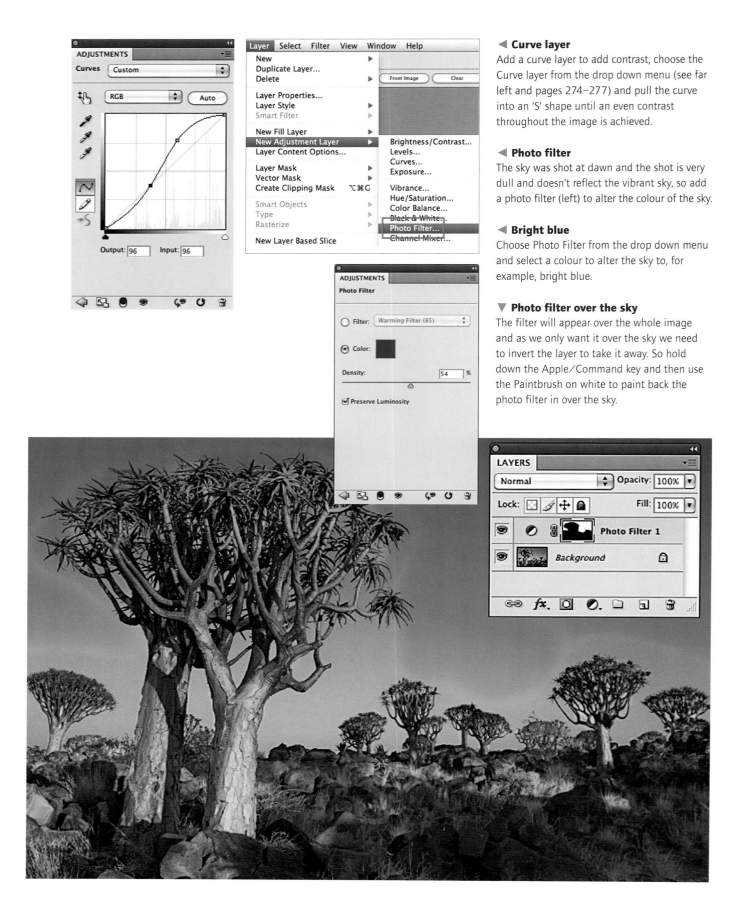

◄ Curve layer
Add a curve layer to add contrast, choose the Curve layer from the drop down menu (see far left and pages 274–277) and pull the curve into an 'S' shape until an even contrast throughout the image is achieved.

◄ Photo filter
The sky was shot at dawn and the shot is very dull and doesn't reflect the vibrant sky, so add a photo filter (left) to alter the colour of the sky.

◄ Bright blue
Choose Photo Filter from the drop down menu and select a colour to alter the sky to, for example, bright blue.

▼ Photo filter over the sky
The filter will appear over the whole image and as we only want it over the sky we need to invert the layer to take it away. So hold down the Apple/Command key and then use the Paintbrush on white to paint back the photo filter in over the sky.

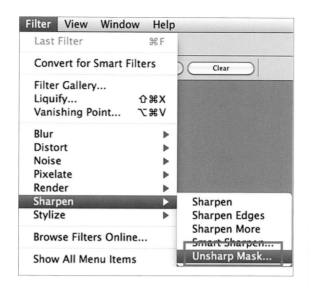

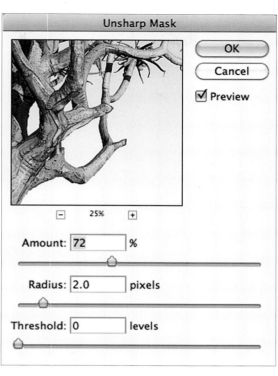

◄ Final adjustments
Every image needs a little sharpening (see pages 274–277). Select Unsharp Mask from the drop down menu, then make adjustments by moving the sliders to create the amount of sharpness required.

▼ Final image
Here you can see the Hyper Dynamic range; there is a deep vibrant sky, detail in the shadows and no areas of under- or over-exposure.

Effective use of grain

A s the supply of film diminishes, it is now almost impossible to find one that will give pronounced grain. Many older film brands, such as Kodak's Royal X Pan and 2475 recording film, have been withdrawn and replaced with what are thought to be superior versions. Even if you substantially up-rate film to 3,200 ISO it still won't give you the quality of grain as these old films. This is a pity because, although there is a place for fine grain, coarse grain can be used to great effect. However, if we have taken our shots, either on fine grain film or digitally, we can add grain once we have scanned or downloaded them onto the computer. We can do this by simply adding noise when using a program such as Photoshop, but a far better method is to use a plug-in filter such as Grain Surgery. This will allow you to add a much more realistic effect and have great control over it.

See also

▶ **pp 34–35** Film
▶ **pp 36–37** Processing film

▶ **Selective enlargement**
This image was taken from a shot that, if reproduced full size, would have measured 4 x 3ft (120 x 90cm) yet the grain is still fine. It is essential the shot is sharp to start with.

◀ **Adding noise**
This was taken on 400 ISO film rated at 800 ISO. It was push-processed, scanned into a computer and a degree of noise added. A small amount of toning was introduced. The same effect could be achieved in the darkroom by immersing the print in a sepia tone solution.

◀ **Grain and colour**
To take this shot in a dimly lit tunnel, I used 800 ISO film rated at 3200 ISO. It was then push-processed, which has increased the grain and the contrast. The result is a gritty image that reflects the sense of urban isolation.

▶ **Photoshop filters**
Another way of introducing grain is with Photoshop filters. The great advantage here, over film, is that you can be selective in just how much grain you add and the size of it. Another useful plug-in filter is called Grain Surgery. This picture of a leopard shows how grain can enhance an image.

◄ Original picture
The original is flat, dull and lacks contrast.

▼ Grain
From the drop down menu select Grain and you will see the default box appear.

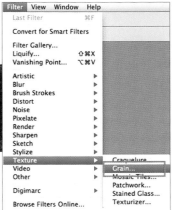

◄ Intensity and contrast
Use the sliders on the right to alter the Intensity and contrast until you achieve the desired effect.

▼ Finished image
The finished image creates drama and brings the photograph to life, adding texture, which complements the fur of the leopard.

Multiple images

Many cameras now have a facility that enables you to take multiple images. This technique can add to your creative repertoire and produce finished shots that are unusual and eye-catching.

When you take a multiple image photograph you need to plan it carefully and decide where you want each part to be. Some cameras have a feature that allows you to change the focusing screen. One of these is known as a grid screen and has vertical and horizontal lines running across it. These are a great asset when it comes to composing your shot, as you will know exactly where you put each previously shot image. Some digital cameras have grid lines as an option in the menu settings.

Other important areas to consider are background and exposure. If your background is predominantly light, then your multiple image photograph will look washed out and some of the exposures might be difficult to see.

The best backgrounds are black, or at least very dark. When you calculate the exposures for each image, try to keep them even. A multiple image photograph will fail if you have two images perfectly exposed but the others over- or under-exposed.

Another way of taking a multiple image photograph is to use multiple flash. In simple terms this would mean setting the camera's shutter to B. This will keep it open for as long as the shutter release button is depressed. If your model is placed against a black background and the flash fires, say, three times with your model moving after each flash, three separate images will be recorded on the film.

Portraits

These two photographs are both multiple image shots but taken with different techniques. In the one on the right, multiple flash was used. I placed the model against a black background and set the flash to fire three consecutive exposures. Each time the flash fired she moved her head and the flash recorded her in a different position. The shutter had to remain open for the duration of the flashes and all other lights in the room needed to be switched off.

For the shot below I exposed two different poses on the same piece of film. First I shot the model looking at the camera but placed her on the left side of the viewfinder. I had set the camera to multi-exposure so that when I wound on only the shutter was cocked and the film

Only a limited number of digital cameras allow you to take multiple image photographs, although you could take a multiple flash shot. However, you could combine separate shots together on the computer using Photoshop or other software.

was not advanced. I then panned the camera to the left and took another shot of her looking to the left. I now had two images on the same piece of film and wound on in the usual manner.

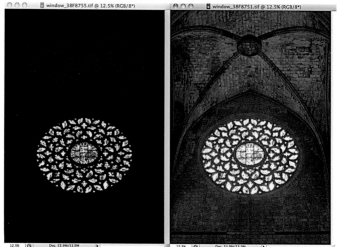

◀ **Original exposures**
Open the two original exposures
and you will see how one is over-
exposed and one is under-exposed.
But by combining both these
images we can achieve a full range
of detail from both the highlights
and shadows. In Photoshop,
combine both images by dragging
one layer on top of another (hold
down Shift and the images will
automatically line up exactly).

▶ **Eraser**
Use the Eraser tool,
to erase sections that
are over-exposed, to
reveal the correct
exposure on the
bottom layer. Make
sure you are on the
correct layer and
zoomed in for 100
per cent accuracy.

▲ ▶ **Final adjustments**
Here you can see the two images
edited together, yet it needs some
final adjustments to bring the
most out of the image (see pages
274–277). Crop to focus on the
best parts of the image.

▶ **Finished image**

Abstract images

As well as taking photographs of instantly recognizable subjects, correctly exposed, composed and printed, there are many other photographic possibilities that lend themselves to making fine images. These are called abstract images. Although some of these shots might be 'straight' photographs, the nature of the subject and the way it has been presented make them non-representational. Many of these pictures can have a painterly feel to them as they rely heavily on the use of strong areas of colour and a degree of draughtsmanship within their composition.

Such abstract pictures might be something as simple as a reflection in water or on a wet area of ground, or on the reflective side of a building or vehicle. When you focus on such a surface and use the auto-focus mechanism on your camera, it might have difficulty focusing on the reflection and instead focus on the surface. If this is the case, turn off the auto-focus mechanism and focus the image manually.

Another way to create an abstract image is to photograph it deliberately out of focus and with minimal depth of field. As before, you will need to turn off the auto-focus. This method will soften the edges of your shot and, depending on the degree of focus, will slightly blur the image, creating a watercolour effect.

An alternative technique is simply to photograph a small part of a much larger subject, or crop in tightly to an existing shot. This could be an area of a building, for example, that has strong geometric lines or a detail of tension cables and the bolt bosses that hold them in place.

The important aspect of this type of photography is to look at your potential subject from a different perspective. It helps, when looking through the camera, to zoom slowly in or out from the subject area. In this way you will see the frame get tighter or wider. By carefully looking at these nuances in the composition you will start to become discerning in seeing the potential of a shot that might not be apparent at first to the naked eye.

See also
▶ **pp 52–53** Shutter speed
▶ **pp 56–57** Light and colour
▶ **pp 62–63** Selecting a viewpoint
▶ **pp 64–65** Filling the frame

▶ **Slow shutter speed**
This is a photograph of scaffolding and red and white barriers to protect it. I deliberately used a slow shutter speed to get some movement and hand held the camera.

Reflections

Sometimes it is easy to make the same journey to and from work or visit what we think of as familiar environments and assume that there is nothing worth photographing or that we have already shot it. The truth is that there is always a new and refreshing way of seeing the familiar. As photographers, we should always try to observe things in a new light no matter how many times we have seen them before. This is a good exercise in visual awareness because until you start looking in a photographic way you will never see the potential in your environment. Often a view can be enhanced by cropping to make the final picture more abstract, such is the case here. It might be that viewed from a different way up transforms an ordinary picture into something more exciting.

▲ **Reflections**
One of the simplest ways to create abstract pictures is to photograph reflections. In this shot it is one building reflected into another. I then pushed the curves in Photoshop to make this graphic image.

▲ **Water patterns**
Abstract patterns can be found everywhere. I shot these water droplets on the sunroof of my car. Then I added a colour in Photoshop and turned the image upside down.

268 • Advanced Techniques

Slow sync flash

When using flash to photograph a subject that is moving, everything within its range of luminosity will be frozen if the camera's shutter is set to the manufacturer's recommended flash synchronization speed. This might be 1/60th or 1/125th second. However, if you were to deviate from this shutter speed and use one that was much slower, say 1/15th or 1/8th second, then you would produce photographs using a technique known as slow sync flash.

If you are using this technique in a situation where there is a certain amount of ambient light, then the moving subject will still record as mainly sharp but there will also be a soft edge to it that can look very effective. If the camera were to move too while taking the shot, then some eye-catching backgrounds can be obtained, especially if they are lit with either street lights or illuminated shop windows. In this case the subject will still be virtually frozen but the background lights will have streaked, creating interesting light patterns.

If you are using this technique outside, the best effects are obtained if you under-expose the daylight by about a stop. If your subject is then photographed against the sky, such as a skater or skate boarder jumping, for example, they will cast a shadow that will make it look as if the sky is directly behind them. The knack is getting the shutter set to a speed compatible with both the flash and the daylight. For instance, your exposure meter indicates that the daylight requires an exposure of 1/60th second at f8. However, for the slow sync flash technique to work, you require a shutter speed of 1/8th second. This means that for the daylight you need to set the camera at 1/8th at f22. Set the flash dial to this aperture or work out the flash to subject ratio that requires an aperture of f22.

Light trails

Because slow sync flash can be unpredictable, I always take a series of shots and then edit later. I selected the one above as I felt the light trails weren't too intrusive on the young girl's face while the lights made a great background.

◀ **Street scene**

By using a shutter speed of 1 second, I managed to get plenty of action into this street scene. There is a lot of movement in the cars to add to the slow sync effect.

See also

▶ **pp 52–53** Shutter speed
▶ **pp 60–61** Effective flash
▶ **pp 240–241** Ring flash
▶ **pp 266–267** Abstract images

Infrared

Along with mainstream films, infrared is also disappearing from the shelves. However, it is possible to take infrared pictures with certain digital cameras.

One of the advantages that digital infrared has over film, is that you will be able to see the results instantly on the camera's LCD. With film you would have to wait for it to be processed and then re-shoot if it was over- or under-exposed. Not all digital cameras are capable of taking infrared pictures. This is because most of them have a hot mirror filter over the sensor. This filter cuts out the wavelengths of the electromagnetic spectrum that are measured in nanometers and that are sensitive to infrared light. The light our eyes are capable of seeing falls between 400 and 700nm, but infrared light goes beyond this range. In my Canon cameras, such as the 1DS, the hot mirror filter is so efficient that it filters out the infrared wavelengths, but I discovered an older Fuji camera that is great for infrared photography.

This camera, the Fuji Finepix S2 Pro, gives consistently good results. It has a Nikon mount and I normally fit it with a Nikon AF-S 17–35mm f2.8. To get the infrared effect you will need to purchase a filter that transmits light above 730nms. This is a No 87 filter and appears completely black. Because of this and the extremely long exposures that are required, you will need to compose your picture with the camera on a tripod before you attach the filter. I choose from the camera's menu the black and white mode and start with an exposure of 10 seconds at f8. As I will see the

Digital infrared

I shot these pictures using a Fuji Finepix S2 Pro digital camera. The shot above was taken conventionally and the scene appears how one would expect it to, with the foliage of the trees recording green. For the shot at the top I chose the camera's black and white mode and placed a Kodak 88A filter over the lens. The captured scene looks much the same as if I had shot it on conventional black and white infrared film. At first it looks as though it is a negative, but the shadows of the trees are black and the sky is dark, while the clouds are white.

► **Slow shutter speed**
Because of the slow shutter speeds required for digital black and white, I had to pose the model here as if she was walking, but she is, in fact, standing still.

result on the LCD, I can then make adjustments to the exposure settings.

Digital infrared works best in bright sunlight and on heavy green foliage. Because of its unpredictability and the way infrared reacts in different light, you will have to carry out a series of shots on a trial and error basis, but with experience you should be able to get perfect results every time.

▶ **Foreboding sky**
In this picture the infrared effect has turned the sky almost black, adding a foreboding quality to the image, while the foliage has nearly all but turned white. Notice, however, the trees on the extreme right have hardly been affected at all.

See also

▶ **pp 34–35** Film
▶ **pp 92–93** Lighting for outdoor portraits
▶ **pp 98–99** Backgrounds
▶ **pp 184–185** Black and white rural landscapes

▶ **Movement**
This (opposite top) is one of my favourite digital infrared shots. The foliage is beautifully white and contrasts well with the dark sky. Because I was using a slow shutter speed, some movement in the foliage was unavoidable, but in this case adds to the surrealism of the picture.

▶ **Reflections**
Normally, trees would reflect into water as green, or dark tones if we had taken this shot as conventional black and white. However, here we can see that the infrared has not only turned the trees white but their reflection in the water has also appeared white.

▲ **Grain**
When producing large prints from digital infrared images, banding can sometimes be present, as was the case here. To soften and eliminate this, I add grain using a plug-in filter called Grain Surgery.

Using Curves and Levels

Of the many tools available to the photographer in Photoshop, Curves and Levels must be the ones most widely used. What confuses many people is what exactly is the difference between the two when they seem to be so similar. Basically Curves gives you far greater control than Levels over tones and brightness within an image. The curve is plotted on a grid; by default it is a straight line. The careful control of curves makes it possible to fine-tune an image by selecting Anchor along this line and then adjusting the curve without affecting the range outside those points. Usually you will be aiming for an S shape when adjusting the curve. As you push the curve up, the image becomes lighter; when you pull the curve down it gets darker. Levels gives you control of three key areas; these are the black point, white point and mid-tones. When you select Levels you will see a histogram in the dialogue box. A well-exposed image will appear with gentle peaks across the entire histogram. If the histogram shows that these peaks do not reach either end of the histogram, then you can use the slider to make adjustments. However, you should always leave an area at either end and not take the slider to the extremes. Although this is very useful, Curves will give you control over a greater range of points, so the adjustments that you can make are subtler. Often it is beneficial to use both Curves and Levels in combination.

There are other changes you can make by selecting Areas, Hue and Saturation and Sharpening.

Curves

▲ **Original image**
The original picture is flat, dull, slightly dark and lacks contrast.

▶ **Curves**
From the drop down menu select Curves and you will see the default as a straight line in the curves box. By clicking on this line and dragging it down the picture will darken, while pushing it out will lighten the picture.

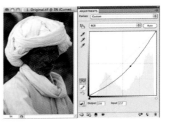

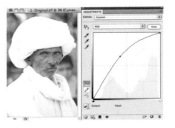

▶ **S shape**
What you should be looking for is a gentle S shape with the curve pushed out towards the top of the line – highlights – and the curve dragged down at the bottom of the line – shadows.

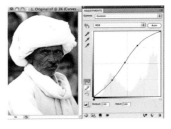

Levels

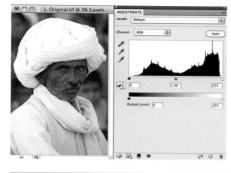

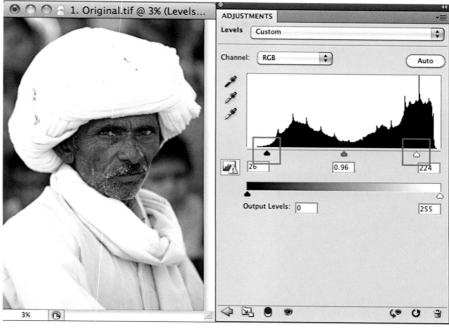

◀ ▲ Levels

From the drop down menu select Levels and you will see the default box showing a histogram. By clicking on the white arrow and dragging it towards the centre the image will lighten. By clicking on the black arrow and dragging it towards the centre it will darken the image. By moving both arrows you can adjust the picture to your liking. Many people find the histogram in Levels easier to use than Curves; however, once you have gained experience with Curves you will achieve greater accuracy.

Selective areas

▶ Eye surgery

Sometimes it is necessary to adjust a small area of the image, in this case the person's eyes. To do this, choose the Lasso tool from the tool bar and circle the area to be lightened. You will need to feather the edge, otherwise adjustment will be visible, as can be seen here.

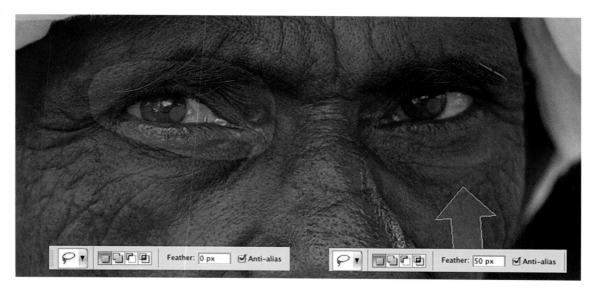

Hue and saturation

▼ Colour controls

From the drop down menu choose Hue/Saturation. To saturate all colours, select Master and then drag the middle slider towards the right; to desaturate an image simply reverse this process, by sliding the slider to the left. If an image has a coloured cast or tone to it, you can reduce this by dragging the Hue slider until the cast has been removed.

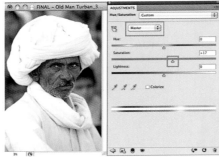

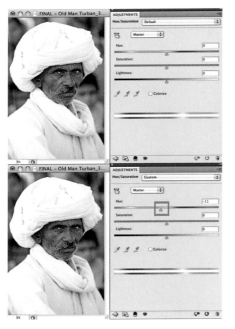

▼ ▶ Lasso tool

To select only a certain part of the image to alter, choose the Lasso tool from the tool palette and feather this by around 50 pixels to give it a soft edge. Then draw around the area you would like to alter. Once the area has been selected, you can choose Hue/Saturation from the drop down menu and drag the saturation to the left. You will be able to see that the yellow has been removed from the white in the image.

Sharpening

▼ Unsharp Mask

When you have made all your adjustments, you can sharpen the image by choosing Filter from the drop down menu and selecting Sharpen and then Unsharp Mask. When the window opens, make your adjustments to Amount and Radius. An average would be 1.5 for Radius and 50 for Amount.

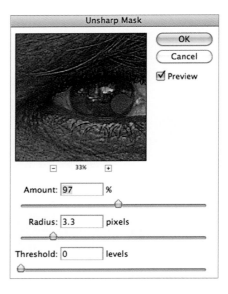

▶ **Final image**
The finished result is brighter and has no yellowing of the whites. It is sharper, has more contrast and greater detail in all areas.

Digital panoramas

Sometimes when taking a shot it is not possible to get in as much detail as we would like for the finished photograph, perhaps because the lens does not have a wide enough angle of view. On the other hand, it might be the case that if we used an extremely wide-angle lens, the detail of the landscape might be pushed so far to the back that what attracted us to the view in the first place becomes lost in a mass of sky and foreground. Now it is possible to take several images of a landscape and 'stitch' them together on the computer.

Most cameras come with a panorama building program that can even produce 360-degree virtual panorama. Under ideal conditions these programs give excellent results but blurring can often be seen where textures overlap, or exposure differences are noticeable due to vignetting by inferior quality lenses. For the best results and with a little perseverance, use your image editing program to create superior panoramas.

It is best, when taking your shots that you will use for the panorama, to use a tripod with a pan tilt head. The tripod must be exactly level. The best way to do this is to place a spirit level on the tripod before you attach the pan tilt head. Adjust the legs so that the tripod is level in all directions. Place the pan tilt head on the tripod and, using the spirit level, make sure that the pan tilt head is also level in all directions. Attach your camera and you are now ready to shoot.

▼ **Original exposures**

▲ Creating a new file

Create a new file big enough to line up all eight images; one way to do this is by adding the widths of the eight photographs together. Drag each image onto the new file in the correct order.

See also

▶ **pp 66–67** Perspective

▶ **pp 184–185** Black and white rural landscapes

▶ **pp 202–203** At the landmarks

▶ **pp 288–289** Producing digital composites

◀ ▼ Layers

In the Layers palette you can lower the opacity of a layer to match it up with the image below. Do this for all eight exposures, then trim off any unwanted edges.

◀ **Eraser**
Use the Eraser tool to erase the visible joins between images.

▼ **Removing major joins**
Here you can see all major joins have gone. However, the sky to the right of the image remains a different exposure.

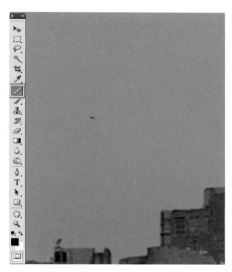

▲ Healing and cloning
Use the Healing tool or Clone tool to clean up
the image (see pages 282–283).

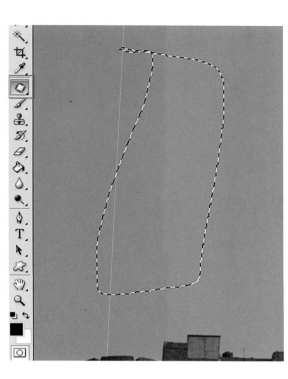

◄ ▲ Patching
Use the Patch tool to even up
the sky. To use the Patch tool,
draw around an area of clean sky
and drag it over the area of the
sky that you would like to replace.

▼ Further changes
The finished image is dark and
not truly representing the dawn
light when it was originally
captured. So I added a Curve layer
and Hue/Saturation layer to it.

▼ Finished scene

Photoshop beauty retouching

For many photographers, the digital age is one of manipulated images where there is little left of the original image. They see people's body shapes being altered and enhanced, their hair colour and eyes changed and the lines of age or fast living being eradicated by the click of a mouse. All this, they assume, is to make the final photograph more appealing to a wider or targeted audience, so a product will sell more or a celebrity will look more attractive.

What these purists overlook is that photographs have been altered ever since photography began. Look at the work of the esteemed Hollywood studio photographers such as George Hurrell or the great British photographer Cecil Beaton. A critical inspection of these photographers' negatives and prints will show a multitude of retouching. This was an art in itself and on no account should it be dismissed as mere trickery. After all, even the great painters used poetic licence when painting a commissioned portrait.

When you retouch a portrait, aim to enhance the image overall, not try to create a completely different image. Handled sensitively, the computer should be seen as a tool to aid creativity and to educate the photographer into different ways of seeing.

See also
▶ **pp 40–41** Digital capture
▶ **pp 116–117** Hair and make-up
▶ **pp 140–143** Tone, texture and form
▶ **pp 286–287** Digital archival retouching
▶ **pp 288–289** Producing digital composites

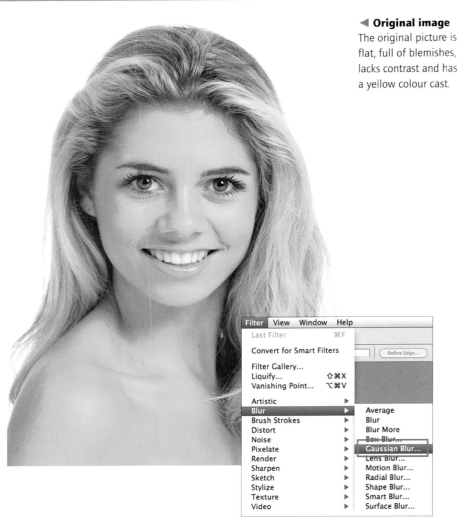

◀ **Original image**
The original picture is flat, full of blemishes, lacks contrast and has a yellow colour cast.

▲ **Gaussian blur**
The skin needs softening so that the pores and fine lines aren't so visible. Choose Gaussian Blur from the drop down menu.

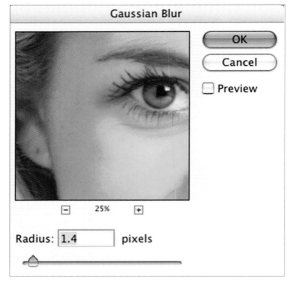

◀ **Amount of blur**
Select the amount of blur by moving the slider across (do not blur too much as we still want the detail to remain).

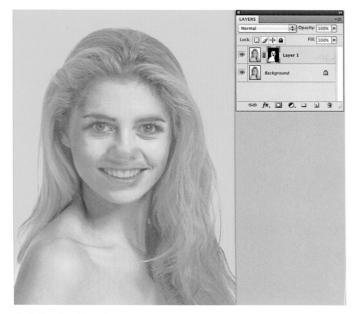

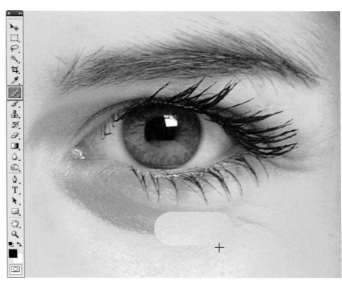

▲ Selective blurring

The Gaussian Blur will cover the whole image and we only want it on certain parts of the skin to be treated. Hold down the Apple/Command key and press the i key to invert the layer. Then we want to paint the layer back in onto the skin: press the \ key (this will turn the image red but will make it easier to see where you are painting the blur). Use the Paintbrush tool on white and 100 per cent opacity and paint over the skin. Once finished, press the \ key to remove the red mask.

▲ Healing tool

Create a new layer (file, new, layer). Cleaning up the image. Use the healing tool to remove unwanted blemishes and fine lines or in this case, darkening under the eyes. Press the alt key and click to copy the area and then draw over the line to replace it with clear skin.

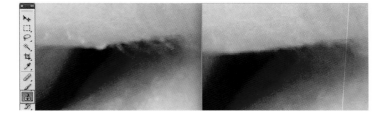

◄ Clone tool

When there is a very contrasty edge that you need to neaten up, use the Clone tool (which works very similarly to the Healing tool) as the Healing tool can't cope with dramatic colours. So press the alt key and click on an area you would like to copy and then replace the edge with clear skin.

◄ Even up image

When editing an image you should leave moles and other natural features since these give people character. However, if something unbalances the image or distracts the eye, remove it using the Healing tool.

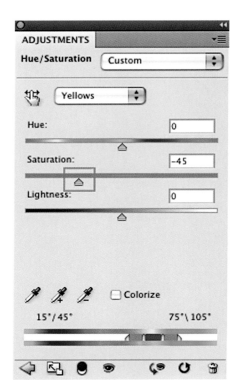

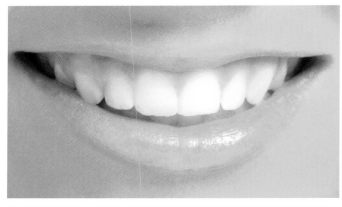

◄ Teeth whitening
Most people's teeth aren't perfectly white, so to create a subtle enhancement, first make a new saturation layer and click the drop down menu for yellow and drag the slider on Saturation to the left (see page 276). Invert the layer (press Apple/Command i) then paint over the teeth with a white paintbrush. In this image I have done the right-hand side.

▲ Skin
Remove any uneven skin tone throughout the image using the Clone tool.

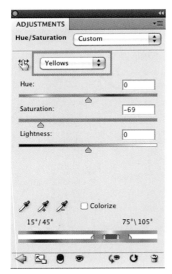

▲ Yellow cast

▲ Cast removed

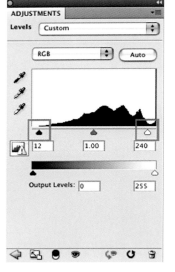

▲ Tone
Check the image for colour casts. This image is very yellow (it doesn't help that the model has blonde hair and a tan). To remove the cast, make a new saturation layer (like before) and select the yellow and pull the slider on Saturation to the left to counterbalance this.

▲ Levels
To even up the contrast within the image, create a new Levels layer. Do not use a Curves layer (if as in this image, you do not want to increase the saturation). Drag the sliders until you get the desired contrast.

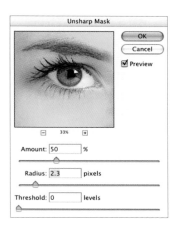

◄ ▲ **Crop**

Crop to focus on the best parts of the image. Flatten the image to avoid a big file size.

▲ ► **Sharpen image**

Choose Unsharp Mask from drop down menu. Adjust the sliders to control the amount of sharpening.

► **Extra sharpening**

Portraits often focus on the eyes, so extra sharpening is sometimes required. Use the Lasso tool and draw around the area, then select the Unsharp Mask (like before) but this time it will only sharpen the highlighted areas.

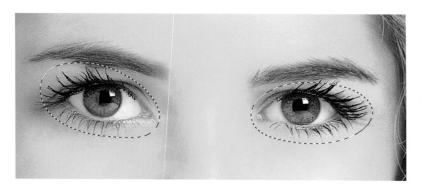

▼ **Image fully retouched**

Some portraits look better in black and white and this is one, because of the strong colour cast.

Digital archival retouching

All of us have pictures that have been in the family for some considerable time. Some of these could now date back a hundred years or more. In the passage of time many of these may have faded, become torn and creased or stained. Of course, it is highly unlikely that the negatives will still exist and so the only option is to revive the existing print. Not long ago this would have meant re-photographing the print and

producing further copies from it. However, without spending many hours hand retouching the new print (which would then need to be re-photographed again, thereby reducing the quality), you would still be left with

a new version of a damaged image. With the computer and a good quality scan it is now possible to reproduce an archival image to its original quality or, in some cases, enhance it by different printing methods.

See also
▶ **pp 90–91** Group portraits
▶ **pp 282–285** Photoshop beauty retouching
▶ **pp 288–289** Producing digital composites
▶ **pp 292–295** Digital toning and lith

◀ Scanning the image
If the picture to be retouched is a print, most modern desktop scanners will produce excellent results. If it is a transparency or lantern slide, it will be best to have this scanned by a professional bureau who can supply you with a high quality image.

▲ Tonal adjustments
It is important to retain as much detail as possible in the scan. It is better to scan the picture soft and grey, as you can add contrast but you cannot restore detail that has been lost. The contrast should be added in your image editing program using the Levels or Curves function.

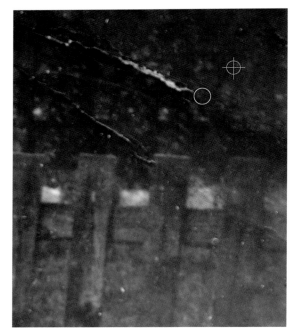

▲ Repairing the damage
This print has sustained surface damage that appears as cracks due to poor storage. By borrowing from undamaged surrounding areas you can use the Clone tool to cover the damaged parts. It takes practice to get a seamless repair.

▲ **Image building**
Where parts of the picture have become lost forever, you will need to rebuild them. If there is an area of similar tone, you can copy and paste large areas to form a convincing montage. If there is no useful texture left, you might have to borrow from another photograph.

▲ **Equalizing fogged areas**
Fogging on part of the image can be corrected by selecting the fogged area and applying maximum feathering to the selection. Levels and Curves can again be utilized to restore balance and contrast to the image. You can build this up over several adjustments.

◄ **The image restored**
As can now be seen, the image has an acceptable tonal range and all cracks, tears and fogging have been removed or those areas enhanced. You might want to consider other treatments such as toning or printing on a fine art paper.

Producing digital composites

One of the great assets of digital photography is the range of adjustments that the photographer can make to an existing image. How often is it that we have photographed a stunning landscape, only for the shot to be ruined by the weather?

Here, we can see the potential of an attractive image but the featureless sky lets down the finished shot. However, with the aid of the computer we are able to take the sky from another picture and composite the two images together. As can be seen, this opens up a world of possibilities. Once you have mastered this technique it could mean that instead of not taking a potential shot because of the weather, you will begin thinking of an existing shot or look out for one that can be amalgamated in this way. With practice you will soon learn which two images can be used together, as it will not look particularly effective if you use images from different tonal ranges.

▶ **The final image**
The image has now been transformed from a pleasant but dull landscape photograph to one that is more vibrant and pictorially pleasing. This has been achieved in a matter of a few steps and is a good illustration of how you can bring life to many of your previously discarded photographs.

See also
▶ **pp 56–57** Light and colour
▶ **pp 68–69** Foreground composition
▶ **pp 166–167** Emphasizing the sky
▶ **pp 278–281** Digital panoramas

◀ **Original picture**
The original image was taken on a grey and dull day with minimal sunshine. The composition is good but the sky in particular lacks definition. It is a perfect image for a digital composite.

▲ Selecting the elements

Having found the two pictures with similar tonal ranges, remove all blemishes (see pages 260–261). Tonal and colour adjustments can be made once the composite is complete. Roughly erase the sky from the main image and replace it with the alternative sky.

▲ Importing the sky

Having transferred the new sky, you can enlarge or reduce certain parts of it so that it looks convincing and fits perfectly. Some parts of the new sky might have to be cloned or rebuilt. It can help to make the main image semi-transparent to aid accurate positioning.

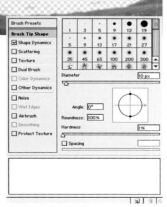

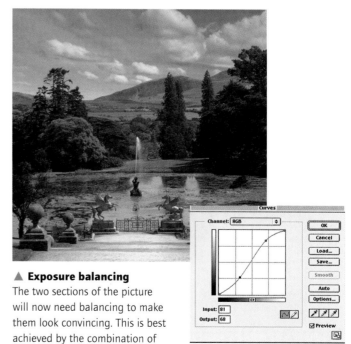

▲ Magic Wand

By using the Magic Wand tool, which makes a selection based on colour, the more intricate parts of the sky, such as around branches of trees, can be removed easily. Some areas might need removing with the Eraser tool. With experience this can be done relatively quickly.

▲ Exposure balancing

The two sections of the picture will now need balancing to make them look convincing. This is best achieved by the combination of Levels, Curves and Hue/Saturation dialogue boxes. It is only through trial and error that you will find the combination that looks the most realistic.

Black and white from colour

Many digital cameras do not have a black and white mode and will only let you shoot in colour. In itself this is not a problem and it is always good to have both versions, because if you shoot in black and white you will not be able to turn it into a colour photograph later on, whereas if you shoot in colour you can convert it to black and white as we will discover here.

There are three methods for converting colour to black and white using Photoshop. The simplest is Desaturation and Greyscale. The former is quite a crude method and your image will end up looking flat, especially in the highlights and shadows. I generally use this method only to give me a quick idea of what my colour photograph might look like in black and white. The Greyscale method also has its limitations and it is 'destructive' in the sense that it changes the image file permanently.

The next method is the Hue/Saturation method. By converting a colour image to black and white using this method and then adjusting the Hue, Saturation and Lightness can produce a wide range of effects. However, my favourite method for converting colour to black and white is to use the Channel Mixer. Adjusting the values of the red, blue and green channels can produce fantastic clarity and be very similar to using colour filters on the camera with black and white film.

Whatever method you use, your results will only be as good as your original, so it is essential that you start with a well exposed shot with a good range of tones. If, for instance, you choose a shot where the sky is burnt out, very little will be possible to get detail back into it.

See also
▶ **pp 56–57** Light and colour
▶ **pp 170–171** Seas and oceans
▶ **pp 184–185** Black and white rural landscapes
▶ **pp 274–277** Using curves and levels

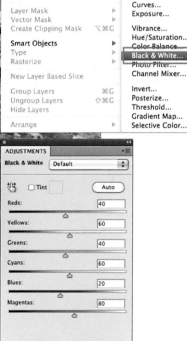

▲ **Starting point**
The original picture is flat, dull and lacks contrast.

▲ ▶ **Black and white**
From the drop down menu select Black & White and you will see the default box appear. Use the sliders to alter the different colour channels until you achieve the effect you want.

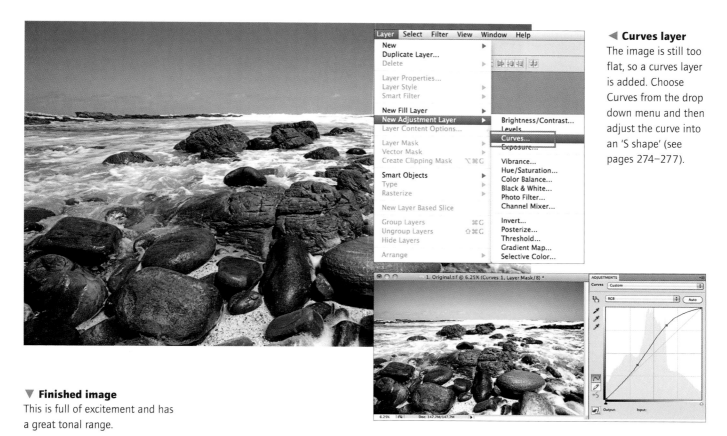

◀ Curves layer
The image is still too flat, so a curves layer is added. Choose Curves from the drop down menu and then adjust the curve into an 'S shape' (see pages 274–277).

▼ Finished image
This is full of excitement and has a great tonal range.

Digital toning and lith

Besides converting your colour images to traditional black and white images, there are other methods where we can create prints that are generally associated with the wet darkroom. This could be something as simple as a sepia toning effect or a little more complicated like creating a lith print.

One of the advantages that digital has over the wet darkroom is that there are no harmful chemicals to pour down the sink. Of course, there are some people who are traditionalists and argue that producing images on a computer is merely manipulation needing the minimum of skill. But ever since the first print was sepia, toned photography has been about

manipulation and as such is no different than any other art form.

In simple terms, to tone a black and white print I use Curves and boost the Red channel and then select the Blue channel to add warmth. To create a lith print I start with a black and white image and then use the same method as above. Then I fine-tune by going to Hue/Saturation and adjusting the intensity of the colour with the Saturation slider. To give the image a more characteristic lith look, I add grain from the plug-in filter Grain Surgery.

With experience, a full range of traditional tones can be created using these methods and the chances are that in time you will probably find yourself developing new ones.

See also

▶ **pp 184–185** Black and white rural landscapes

▶ **pp 186–187** Black and white urban landscapes

▶ **pp 286–287** Digital archival retouching

▲ **Original image**
It is not necessary to start with black and white film when producing monochrome images on a computer. A colour digital image or print can be converted. It is important to choose an image that will convert well to black and white. It should have good contrast and plenty of detail throughout, right from the highlight through to the shadows, such as the landscape shot above. Before you start the toning, perform the basic adjustments and remove any blemishes. You can either turn the image to a greyscale or desaturate and keep it in RGB colour mode.

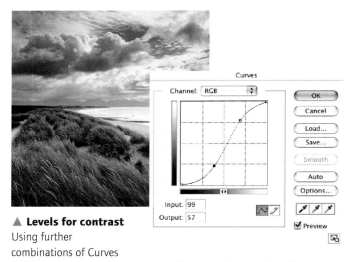

▲ **Levels for contrast**
Using further combinations of Curves and Levels, we can inject more mood into the picture. This is the equivalent of making a hand print on black and white paper in the darkroom. As in the darkroom, parts of the image can be selected to be lightened or darkened and the edges burnt in to hold the composition. The print could be considered finished at this stage and printed onto a fine art rag paper.

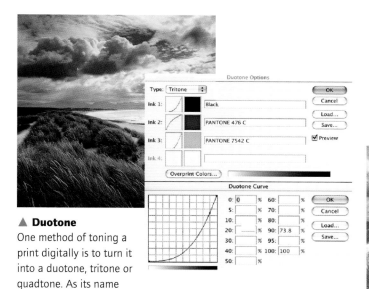

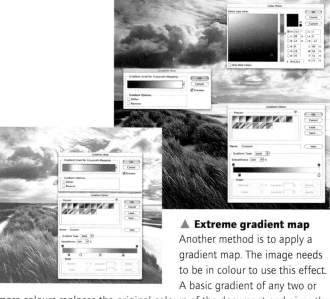

▲ Duotone
One method of toning a
print digitally is to turn it
into a duotone, tritone or
quadtone. As its name
suggests, there are two or more colours involved but one colour is
usually black. The other colour(s) are selected and specified and a Curve
box is used to control how the colours run through the image. If your
image editing package does not support duotones, a similar effect can
be created by colouring the image using the colour balance or
Hue/Saturation commands.

▲ Extreme gradient map
Another method is to apply a
gradient map. The image needs
to be in colour to use this effect.
A basic gradient of any two or
more colours replaces the original colours of the document and gives the
effect of a toned print in the colours of your choice. The gradient can
contain as many colours as you like, with wild results from gradients
containing contrasting and clashing colours. As with all things creative,
experimentation is the key.

▶ Finished image
The final result is a monochromatic
image with a full range of tones
that originally started as a colour
transparency. This image was
particularly suitable for this process
since it was full of detail. The digital
darkroom can realize the hidden
potential in many photographs
already in your archive.

◄ **Contrast**
The image has been converted to black and white but looks very flat because it lacks contrast. You can increase the contrast by clicking and dragging the Curves tool until the desired effect has been achieved.

▲ Curves

It is not necessary to start with a black and white picture when producing monochrome images on a computer. Although this is a perfectly acceptable shot, I felt a lot more could be achieved if it were converted to black and white. I used Photoshop Curves to adjust the tones and colour. The curve is plotted on a grid; by default it is a straight line. The bottom left point represents the brightest part of the image and is known as the D-min, or the point of minimum density. The top right point is the darkest part of the image, or D-max. Any point between these can be clicked on and dragged with the mouse. The image becomes brighter if pulled down and darker if pushed up. By default the Curves dialog box opens with all the colours (RGB) selected; this means that you alter all the colours together, and only the brightness is adjusted.

► Curves or Unsharp Mask

I added contrast using the Curves command. You can also use the Unsharp Mask tool to do this by applying a low amount with a high radius.

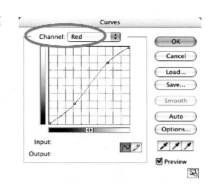

◀ Further changes

I used curves in the red channel to obtain a lith effect and then introduced red in the highlights and lith in the shadows. Lith prints are quite grainy, so I added noise to create grain.

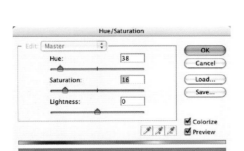

▶ Hue/ Saturation

To introduce a sepia tone, I used the Hue/Saturation control. The Hue slider selects the colour (or chroma), and the Saturation controls the intensity of the colour. For a toned print it is best to keep the saturation low.

Presentation

Having taken your pictures and edited the ones that you really want, you can now turn your attention to presentation. Not many years ago this would have meant getting a print done and putting it into an album or frame. If you had shot colour transparencies you might have put together a slide show. Anything more than this, a properly bound book for example, would just seem out of the question. Today there are so many options it is difficult to choose the one that would be best.

Let's start with the most traditional, a print. This can be put into a frame as a single image or you could create a montage of images and output them as a single print for framing. You might want to make a folio of a particular series of prints, portraits for instance, that you can show to prospective models or to generate commissions. These can look very impressive and you can personalize them by having your name embossed on the front. They can also be bought with a slipcase for a truly professional finish.

Having a properly bound book of your photographs couldn't be easier. For example, if you work on an Apple Mac computer you can go to iPhoto and at the bottom of the window click on the icon that says Book. From here you can choose the style of book, the size, whether you want hard or soft cover, and so on. You can then design the book by simply dragging the pictures to the page and sizing them up. In fact, if you want, it will lay out your pictures automatically. You can then add captions and text. Once all this is done and you have paid for the service, your pictures are uploaded and a week later a beautifully bound book comes through the post. It couldn't be easier. You can also produce cards and calendars in a similar way.

Printing your photographs on t-shirts or other clothing can be a good way of promoting your work while bringing information to the public's attention. This might be for a charity or school event.

Another way of presenting your images is with a digital picture frame. These can look like traditional frames but can store many hundreds of images. They can be displayed individually or as a slide. Some may have built-in speakers so you could add a sound track, and most will have a timer to switch it on and off. There are even some that support wi-fi. This means that once you have set it up you can send a shot over the internet to the frame from anywhere in the world.

You might want to consider making a slide show with either a commentary or a sound track. You can then show this on your computer, burn it onto a DVD and project it through a digital projector, or email it to friends and family. Along with still images, you could put it up on a web page so that anyone could see it. Of course, you could restrict access by creating a password for use only by those who you want to see it. Naturally, you could also play the slide show back through your television.

Another way of showing or sharing your pictures with a wide audience is to put them on a photo sharing site such as Flickr or a social networking site such as Facebook.

Finally, you might just want to print a passport-sized photo that you can keep in your wallet or purse.

◄ Printed folios
Printed folios are still an effective way to display your work. If you use an Apple Mac computer there is a facility in iPhoto for creating books and you can also include text.

▲ Wall presentation

Often it is difficult to beat a favourite shot printed, framed and hung on the wall. An alternative to a paper print is to have your images reproduced on canvas. It is important when displaying pictures in this way that they are well lit.

▲ Digital frame

The great benefit of a digital frame is that you can create a slide show. You can vary the time the image is displayed in the frame from a few seconds to several minutes. On some frames your pictures can be accompanied by a commentary or music.

◄ Website

Websites are a great way to present your work. These can range from a simple site where you can display pictures for family and friends to a more commercial site that you could sell your work from.

► Projectors

Digital projectors have taken over from traditional projectors that showed slides/ transparencies. You can make up a slide show on DVD, memory stick, or direct from the computer and have it running automatically or manually, together with other elements such as maps and a commentary.

Glossary

AI Servo
Continuous autofocus, particularly good for subjects moving towards the camera.

Alpha Channel
Extra 8 bit grayscale channel is used for creating masks to isolate part of the image.

Analogue
Continuously variable.

Aperture
A variable opening in the lens determining how much light can pass through the lens onto the film.

Aperture Priority
A camera metering mode that allows you to select the aperture, while the camera automatically selects the shutter speed.

Apo lens
Apochromatic. Reduces flare and gives greater accuracy in colour rendition.

APS
Advanced photo system.

ASA
American Standards Association; a series of numbers that denotes the speed of the film. Now superseded by the ISO number, which is identical.

Auto-focus
Lenses that focus on the chosen subject automatically.

AWB
Auto white balance. The camera assesses the correct white balance.

B or Bulb
Setting on shutter speed dial that keeps the shutter open for as long as the shutter release is pressed.

B Setting
Setting on the camera's shutter speed dial setting that will allow the shutter to remain open for as long as the shutter release is depressed.

Back Light
Light that is behind your subject and falling onto the front of the camera.

Barn Doors
Moveable pieces of metal that can be attached to the front of a studio light to flag unwanted light.

Between The Lens Shutter
A shutter built into the lens to allow flash synchronization at all shutter speeds.

Bit
A binary digit, either 1 or 0.

Blooming
Halos or streaks visible around bright reflections or light sources in digital pictures.

BMP
File format for bitmapped files used in Windows.

Boom
An attachment for a studio light that allows the light to be suspended at a variable distance from the studio stand.

Bracketing
Method of exposing one or more frames either side of the predicted exposure and at slightly different exposures.

Buffer Ram
Fast memory chip on a digital camera.

Byte
Computer file size measurement.
1024 bits = 1 byte
1024 bytes = 1 kilobyte
1024 kilobytes = 1 megabyte
1024 megabytes = 1 gigabyte

Cable Release
An attachment that allows for the smooth operation of the camera's shutter.

Calibration
Means of adjusting screen, scanner, etc, for accurate colour output.

CC Filter
Colour correction filter.

CCD
Charged coupled device. The light sensor found in most digital cameras.

CDR
Recordable CD.

CDS
Cadmium sulphide cell used in electronic exposure meters.

Centre-weighted
TTL measuring system which is biased towards the centre of the frame.

CMYK
Cyan, magenta, yellow and black colour printing method used in inkjet printers.

Colour Bit Depth
Number of bits used to represent each pixel in an image.

Colour Temperature
A scale for measuring the colour temperature of light in degrees Kelvin.

Compact Flash Card
Removable storage media used in digital cameras.

Compression
Various methods used to reduce file size. Often achieved by removing colour data (see JPEG).

Contrast
Range of tones in an image.

Cyan
Blue-green light whose complementary colour is red.

Data
Information used in computing.

Dedicated Flash
Method by which the camera assesses the amount of light required and adjusts flash output accordingly.

Default
Standard setting for a command or software tool.

Depth of Field
The distance in front of the point of focus and the distance beyond that is acceptably sharp.

Dialog Box
Window in a computer application where the user can change settings.

Diaphragm
Adjustable blades in the lens determining the aperture size.

Diffuser
Material such as tracing paper placed over the light source to soften the light.

Digital Zoom
Digital camera feature that enlarges central part of the image at the expense of quality.

DIN
Deutsche Industrie Norm.
German method of
numbering film speed, now
superseded by ISO number.

Download
Transfer of information from
one piece of computer
equipment to another.

DPI
Dots per inch. Describes
resolution of printed image.

DPOF
Digital print order format.

Driver
Software that operates an
external device or peripheral
device.

Duotone
A black and white print that
has another colour added at
the printing stage.

EV
Exposure value.

EVF
Electronic viewfinder found
in top quality digital cameras.

Exposure Meter
Instrument that measures the
amount of light falling on the
subject.

Extension Bellows
Attachment that enables the
lens to focus at a closer
distance than normal.

Extension Tubes
Attachments that fit between
the camera and the lens that
allow close-up photography.

F Numbers
Also known as stops. They
refer to the aperture setting
of the lens.

File Format
Method of storing
information in a computer file
such as JPEG, TIFF, etc.

Filter
A device fitted over or behind
the camera lens to correct or
enhance the final photograph.

Filter Factor
The exposure increase
required to compensate for a
particular filter.

Firewire™
High speed data transfer
device up to 800mbps (mega
bits per second), also known
as IEEE 1394.

Fisheye Lens
A lens that has an angle view
of 180 degrees.

Fixed Focus
A lens whose focusing cannot
be adjusted.

Flag
A piece of material used to
stop light spill.

Flare
Effect of light entering the lens
and ruining the photograph.

Flash Memory
Fast memory chip that retains
all its data, even when the
power supply is switched off.

Focal Plane Shutter
Shutter system that used
blinds close to the focal
plane.

Fresnal Lens
Condenser lens which aids
focusing.

Fringe
Unwanted border of extra
pixels around a selection
caused by the lack of a hard
edge.

Gel
Coloured material that can be
placed over lights either for
an effect or to colour correct
or balance.

Gif
Graphic file format.

Gigabyte
A billion bytes.

Gobo
Used in a spotlight to create
different patterns of light.

Greyscale
Image that comprises 256
shades of grey.

Hard Drive
Computer's internal
permanent storage system.

High Key
Photographs where most of
the tones are taken from the
light end of the scale.

Histogram
Diagram in which columns
represent frequencies of
various ranges of values of a
quantity.

HMI
Continuous flicker-free light
source balanced to daylight.

Hot Shoe
Device usually mounted on
the top of the camera for
attaching accessories such as
flash.

Image stabilization
Canon's method for reducing
camera shake especially when
using telephoto lenses.

Incident Light Reading
Method of reading the
exposure required by
measuring the light falling on
the subject.

Internal Storage
Built-in memory found on
some digital cameras.

Interpolation
Increasing the number of
pixels in an image.

Invercone
Attachment placed over the
exposure meter for taking
incident light readings.

ISO
International Standards
Organisation. Rating used for
film speed.

Jaggies
Imags where individual pixels
are visible due to low
resolution.

JPEG
A file format for storing
digital photographs where the
original image is compressed
to a fraction of its original
size.

Kelvin
Unit of measurement of
colour temperature.

LCD
Liquid crystal display screen.

Lossless
File compression that doesn't
lose any data or quality.

Lossy
File compression that does
suffer from data loss or
reduced quality.

Low Key
Photographs where most of
the tones are taken from the
dark end of the scale.

Macro Lens
A lens that enables you to
take close-up photographs.

Magenta
Complementary colour to
green, formed by a mixture of
red and blue light.

Megabyte
A million bytes.

Megapixel
A million pixels.

Mirror Lock
A device available on some
SLR cameras that allows you
to lock the mirror in the up
position before taking your
shot in order to minimize
vibration.

Moiré
An interference pattern similar to the clouded appearance of watered silk.

Monobloc
Flash unit with the power pack built into the head.

Montage
Image formed from a number of different photographs

Morphing
Special effect where one image changes into another.

Network
Group of computers linked by cable or wireless system so they can share files. The most common form is ethernet. The web is a huge network.

Neutral Density
A filter that can be placed over the lens or light source to reduce the limited exposure.

Noise
In digital photography, an effect that occurs in low light that looks light grain.

Pan Tilt Head
Accessory placed on the top of a tripod that allows smooth camera movements in a variety of directions.

Panning
Method of moving the camera in line with a fast moving subject to create the feeling of speed.

Parallax Correction
Movement necessary to eliminate the difference between what the viewfinder and the camera lens see.

PC Card
Removable cards that have been superseded by flash cards.

PC Lens
Perspective control or shift lens.

Photoshop
Image manipulation package that is the industry standard.

Pixel
The element that a digitized image is made up from.

Polarising Filter
A filter that darkens blue skies and cuts out unwanted reflections.

PPI
Pixels per inch.

Predictive Focus
Method of auto-focus that tracks a chosen subject, keeping it continuously sharp.

Prime lens
A lens with a fixed focal length, unlike a zoom lens, which is variable.

Prop
An item included in a photograph that enhances the final composition.

RAM
Random access memory.

Rangefinder camera
A camera that uses a system that allows sharp focusing of a subject by aligning two images in the camera's viewfinder.

Reciprocity Failure
The condition where, at slow shutter speeds, the given ISO does not relate to the increase in shutter speed.

Resolution
The measure of the amount of pixels in an image.

RGB
Red, green and blue, which digital cameras use to represent the colour spectrum.

Ring Flash
A flash unit where the tube fits around the camera lens, giving almost shadowless lighting.

ROM
Read only memory.

Shift and Tilt Lens
Lens that allows you to shift its axis to control perspective and tilt to control the pane of sharp focus.

Shutter
Means of controlling the amount of time that light is allowed to pass through the lens onto the film.

Shutter Lag
Delay in pressing the shutter release and the picture being taken.

Shutter Priority
Metering system in the camera that allows the photographer to set the shutter speed while the camera sets the aperture automatically.

Slave Unit
Device for synchronizing one flash unit to another.

SLR
Single lens reflex camera.

Smart Media
Type of digital camera removable media used by some camera manufacturers.

Snoot
Lighting attachment that enables a beam of light to be concentrated in a small circle.

Spill
Lighting attachment for controlling the spread of light.

Spot Meter
Method of exposure meter reading over a very small area.

Step Wedge
A greyscale that ranges from white to black with various shades of grey inbetween.

Stop
Aperture setting on a lens.

Tele Converter
Device that fits between the camera and lens that extends the lens' focal length.

TIFF
Tagged inventory file format. The standard way to store digital images.

TTL
Through the lens exposure metering system.

TWAIN
Industry standard for image acquisition devices.

USB
Universal Serial Bus. Industry standard connector for attaching peripherals with data transfer rates up to 450mbps (mega bits per second).

Vignetting
A darkening of the corners of the frame if a device such as a lens hood or filter is used that is too small for the angle of view of the lens.

VR
Nikon's method for reducing camera shake, especially when using telephoto lenses.

White Balance
Method used in digital cameras for accurately recording the correct colours in different light sources.

ZIP
An external storage device that accepts cartridges between 100 and 750 megabytes.

Zoom Lens
Lens of variable focal length.

Index

AUTHOR'S ACKNOWLEDGEMENTS

This book would not have been possible without the help of many people. In particular, I would like to thank Alex Dow, without whom there would be no book! His dedication to the project and technical expertise, especially in the area of digital photography, cannot be spoken of highly enough. All my other assistants, especially Gemma Andrews for her outstanding work on this revision. Roger Bristow, who first approached me with the idea and Gillian Haslam, my editor who kept the whole project going and made it happen on time; and Chris Stone likewise with this revision. My assistants, Sam Coleman and Nicole Johnson, Phil Ringrow and Brenda Lally for organizing the loan and purchase of equipment from Calumet Photographic, and Teresea Neenan for faultless travel arrangements. Stuart Russell and Paul Prigg at Barclays Bank Plc. Bettina Graham for hair and make-up.

I would also like to thank Joshua Ayshford, Nick and Booj Beak, Steve Benbow, Rich Benner, Peter Brooke-Ball, Natalie Chamberlain, Christian, Tino Clarke, William Cook, Michele Cooper, Daz Crawford, Ken-E, Jeune and Sophia Ephson, Bill and Antoinette Erickson, John Fawdry, Debbie Frankham, Allegra, Katie and Luke Freeman, Gaia and Thibaud Friedman, Sandrine Galbert, Manolo, Maite and Nekane Garcia, Bel, Brittany and Georgia Gibbs, Kelly Grant, Greenford Celtic Football Club, Griff, Steve Hooper, Roz Houchin, Marcela Christina Jaques, Sarah Jobling, Lydia and Rosie Johnson, Alex Jones, Patricia Jones, Lily Kachere, Rachel Kelsey, Adela Lana, Katie Lawrie, Mee Lenh, Nathan Long, Rob Lowe, Charlee Lyn, Jane Mahida, Elsa Marainelli, Robert Marsh, Philip, Mia, Holly and Jack Matthews, Kate Miller,

Natalie Miller, Helen Moody, Lisa Moore, Holly Newberry, Amma Nkrumah, Tamara Noon, Martha and Oscar North, Abigail, Tiphaine and Thomas Popesco, Salina Reid, Pieter and Victoria Richter, Fifi Russo, Djakoly Sangare, Michael Scroop, Eloise Shepherd, Otis Lindblom Smith, Allana Thomas, Abigail Toyne, Jody Trew, Armani Utepbayez, Amzie Villadot, Lynsey Watt, Maurice Wilhelm, Charlotte Wiseman, Caroline Wooton, Jennifer Young, Tomasz and Zosia Zaleska, and a special thank you to Vanessa Freeman for being there when it mattered most.

All photographs were taken by John Freeman except those on pages 244–245 which were taken by Deborah Coles, Diman Oshchepkov, Ian Scott, John Anderson at www.dreamstime.com.

The author and publisher would like to thank Calumet Photographic for the loan and supply of photographic equipment.
www.calumetphoto.com

Canon (UK) Ltd for the supply and use of illustrations.
www.canon.co.uk

Intro 2020 Ltd for the supply of equipment and illustrations.
www.intro2020.co.uk

Nikon UK Ltd for the supply of illustrations.
www.europe-nikon.com/en_GB/

Sigma Imaging (UK) Ltd for the supply of equipment and illustrations.
www.sigma-imaging-uk.com.